Egerton Ryerson Young

Winter Adventures in the Great Lone Land

Egerton Ryerson Young

Winter Adventures in the Great Lone Land

ISBN/EAN: 9783337258504

Printed in Europe, USA, Canada, Australia, Japan

Cover: Foto ©Andreas Hilbeck / pixelio.de

More available books at **www.hansebooks.com**

WINTER ADVENTURES

OF

THREE BOYS

IN

THE GREAT LONE LAND.

WINTER ADVENTURES

OF

THREE BOYS

IN

THE GREAT LONE LAND

BY

EGERTON R. YOUNG

AUTHOR OF "BY CANOE AND DOG-TRAIN," "THREE BOYS IN THE
WILD NORTH LAND," ETC.

> "The visions of memory are the dreams of youth;
> And fancy weaves garlands of flowers of truth."
>
> E. R. Y. JR.

LONDON:
CHARLES H. KELLY, 2, CASTLE ST., CITY RD., E.C.;
AND 26, PATERNOSTER ROW, E.C.

1899.

HARMER & HARLEY, LTD.,
PRINTERS,
40 TO 44, COWPER STREET, FINSBURY, E.C.

EXPLANATORY.

THIS book of Winter Adventures of Three Boys in the Great Lone Land follows the one entitled Three Boys in the Wild North Land. In the previous volume the stories were those of the Summer and Fall. In this book they are of the Winter and Spring. Each volume is complete in itself.

In sending out this volume the author is profoundly thankful to the indulgent reviewers who had so many kind words to say about the first book. In about the only adverse criticism that we saw, and which was kindly written, the reviewer seemed to think it strange that boys could have such a jolly time with a lot of Christian Indians as we had described. He rightly stated that boys' ideas of Indians were associated with the tomahawk and the scalping knife, and that they had the impression that the only good time they could have among them was when the blood-curdling war-whoops were heard and the redskins were being shot down by adventurous lads led on by cowboys. There has been altogether too many of these false and erroneous ideas

EXPLANATORY

about the Indians circulated. Such things are now impossibilities.

In these volumes we have given the correct idea of the Indian as he is to-day in regions where for years we lived. The Gospel has transformed his once cruel nature, but has not marred his cleverness and skill as a hunter or a guide. The brief glimpses into his religious life are absolutely true, and the insertion of them will, we trust, not weaken, but rather strengthen the book.

CONTENTS

CHAPTER I.
Sagasta-weekee—A Happy Home in the Great Lone Land—Three Boys there Welcomed—The Sudden Coming of Winter—Various Sports Discussed—Hurrah for the Dogs!—Useful Animals—Dog-whips—Kinesasis, the Dog-keeper. . . 13

CHAPTER II.
Bringing Home the Dogs—The Thin Ice—Method of Crossing Dangerous Places—The Dogs' Summer Home—The Return Trip—The Unexpected Goose Hunt—The Saucy Fox—Kinesasis's Question—"Why do the Geese go to the South Land?". 24

CHAPTER III.
Selecting Their Dogs—Various Methods of Breaking Them In—Frank's Success by Kindness with Monarch—Sam's Troubles with Spitfire—Conquered at Last—Training and Capturing Dogs with Dogs—Alec's Train of Part Staghounds. 37

CHAPTER IV.
Numerous Dogs—Useful Animals—Food Supply—Frozen Fish—Bringing Them Home—Vigorous Work for Boys and Dogs—Frank's Tumble—Sam's Ducking—Skating Parties—Alec's Thrilling Adventure—The Race for Life—Northern Gray Wolves—Their Cunning—Their Various Stratagems—Mr. Ross Fears—The Search Party—Alec Rescued—The Wolves Shot. 52

CHAPTER V.
The Invitation to the Indian School Examination and Sports—Trapping Experiences—The Cunning Cross Fox—Frank Seeking Aid from Memotas—Method of Successful Trap-setting—Joyous Trip to the Mission—An Abiding Christian

Contents

Civilization for the Indians—Sam's and a Young Indian's Novel Hunting Methods—Wild-cats Captured—The Queer Battle Between a Fox and a Wild Cat. 71

CHAPTER VI.

The Winter Birds of the Great Lone Land—The Whisky Jack—The Ptarmigan—Their Beds in the Snow—Mission Visits—Cupid's Darts—The Wood Supply—Primitive Way of Capturing Partridges—Great Snowy Owls—Methods of Capture—Sam's Experience—The Fearful Grip of the Owl's Claw. 88

CHAPTER VII.

Wounds from Claws versus Teeth Discussed—Mr. Ross's Story of the Battle with the Eagles—Their Mountain Eyrie—Their Hunting Skill—Their Voracity—The Eaglets—The Conflict—The Result—The Painful Wounds. . . . 101

CHAPTER VIII.

Sundays in the Great Lone Land—Services at the Mission—By Skiff or Canoe in Summer—By Dog-train in Winter—Napoleon, the Tame Bear, and His Load—Services at Sagastaweekee—Missionary Journeys—Native Ministers—The Queer Sermon—Happy Christmas Times—New Year's, the Great Day—Oo-che-me-ke-se-gou, the Kissing Day—Varied Experiences—The Great Feast—Happy Indians—Thanksgiving. 110

CHAPTER IX.

The Indian School Examinations—The Prizes—Noble Indian Boys—The Skates to Kepastick—The Various Sports—Foot Races—The Skating Race—Tricky Clerk Outwitted—Frank and Kepastick Tie as Winners—Football—Hockey. 127

CHAPTER X.

The Great Race with the Dog-trains—Careful Preparations by Alec—The Different Breathing Places—The Treacherous Half-breeds—Their Signal Failure—Alec's Triumph. 138

CHAPTER XI.

Pasche Disappears—The Search—Big Tom and Mustagan—The Whisky Jacks—Pasche Found in a Hollow Tree—Chased

Contents

by an Angry Moose Bull—Pasche Rescued—His Quaint Account of His Adventures. 148

CHAPTER XII.

Kinesasis's Wonderful Story—How He Wooed Shakoona—Their Youthful Days—Miskoodell Rescued from the Bear—Oosahmekoo with His Gold—Kinesasis's Successful Hunt—His Furs Stolen—Marries Shakoona—Conflict with the Old Warrior. 161

CHAPTER XIII.

Comments on Kinesasis's Wonderful Story—The Pack of Furs Recovered—Honesty of Indians—Their Different Hunting Grounds—The Golden Rule—The Dishonest Foreign Indian—His Sudden Death. 177

CHAPTER XIV.

Home Amusements and Studies—Happy Days at Sagasta-weekee—Stories of the Early Hunters—Methods of Hunting Before the Introduction of Firearms—Wolves More Dreaded Then—Story of Two of Kinesasis's Children—Killed by Wolves—Shakoona's Sorrow—Saved by the Caresses of Little Children. 185

CHAPTER XV.

The Beavers, and Something About Them—Two Hunters at Sagasta-weekee—A General Invitation to a Beaver Hunt Accepted—The Preparations—The Trip—Dog-traveling in the Woods—Saucy Wild Animals—The Wolf's Cove—The Boys' Plunge in the Snowdrift—The Rescue. 194

CHAPTER XVI.

Still on the Way to the Beaver House—The Winter Camp in the Woods—Work for All—Feeding the Dogs—Our Boys Guarding Their Own Train—The Evening Meal—Bitter Cold—Milk in Lumps of Ice—Evening Prayers—The Wintry Camp Bed—Tucked In—Mysterious Sounds in the Forest—Smothering Sensations—Sam's Nightmare—Breakfast—Tricky Dogs—Methods of Capture—Carioles and Sleds Reloaded—Trains Harnessed—Journey Resumed. 210

Contents

CHAPTER XVII.

Still on the Way to the Beavers—The Blizzard in the Camp—Sleeping and Eating under Difficulties—Vicious Little Beaver Dogs—The Beaver House—Preparations for Their Capture—The Beavers' Kitchen—Discovered by the Little Dogs—How Destroyed—The Method of Capture—Man's Experience versus Animal Instinct—The Rich Harvest of Beavers. 228

CHAPTER XVIII.

Wise Economy of Indian Hunters—Game Never All Killed—Beavers' Tails—The Boys Interested in Them—Preparations for the Return Trip—Loads Packed—Wolverines—Their Cunning Theft of Five Beavers—Dogs and Men on Their Trail—Surviving Beavers Already at Work—The Return of the Hunters—Captured Wolverines—Journey Resumed—The Camp—The Cry of "Wolves!" 245

CHAPTER XIX.

The Coming Battle with the Wolves—Thorough Preparations—The Cry of the Wolves for Reinforcements—The First Attack and Repulse—Wounded Wolves Devoured—Memotas's Comments—The Second Attack—The Powder Explosions—Final Victory—Dogs Reluctant to Attack Wolves—Explanations—Mr. Ross's Story of the Bears Stealing His Pigs—Dogs More Confident in Attacking Bears. . . . 259

CHAPTER XX.

A Bear Hunt in Winter—Mustagan a Famous Indian Guide—Bears' Den—How Discovered—Boys' Perplexity—The Journey to the Den—A Cold Morning—The Telltale Column of Steam—The Attempt to Dig Down to the Bears—Total Failure—Successful Tunneling Operations—Exciting Fight in the Icy Cavern—The Battles Between the Men and Dogs and the Escaping Bears. 275

CHAPTER XXI.

The First Signs of Spring—The Eagle Moon—Expressive Indian Names for Some of the Months—Chats Among the Boys About the Phenomena of the North Land—Power of the Frost—Cunning of Animals—Cleverness of the Guides—Invi-

Contents

tation to a Muskrat Hunt—Gladly Accepted—Habits of These Little Animals—Methods of Capture—Their Many Foes—The Queer Battle Between Wild Cats and Wolverines. . . 297

CHAPTER XXII.

Niskepesim, the Goose Moon—Excitement Among the Indians—The First Goose—Their Northern Migrations—Feeding Grounds—Methods of Hunting Them—Nests—Decoys—Our Boys Off with the Indians—The Shooting Grounds—Their Camp—Great Success—Frank's Queer Accident—Hit by a Dead Goose—Sam's Comments—Laden with Spoils. . 312

CHAPTER XXIII.

Sudden Transition from Winter to Spring—Interesting Phenomena—Sam's Last Great Run with His Dogs—His Unique Adventure—The Open Water—His Novel Raft—Sucessful Crossing—Frank's and Alec's Duck-shooting Trip—The Mighty Nelson—A Hunter's Paradise—Returning Under Difficulties—One More Shot at the Wild Geese—Frank and Alec Both Through the Rotten Ice—The Rescue—Alarming Rumors—The Fair Visitors at Sagasta-weekee. . . 327

CHAPTER XXIV.

The Arrival of the Spring Packet—Welcome Letters—Arrangements for the Home-flitting—Sam's Raillery—Rachel and Winnie at Sagasta-weekee—Happy Hours—Canoeing Excursions—The Cyclone—Young Excursionists Exposed to Its Awful Power—The Narrow Escape—The Refuge of the Rock—Napoleon, the Tame Bear, in Possession—Gun Signals—The Happy Rescue. 341

CHAPTER XXV.

Homeward Bound—Farewell to Sagasta-weekee—Old Norway House—Sam's Clever Surmisings—A Glad Surprise for Frank and Alec—Sam's Well-deserved Ducking—A Glorious Evening—The Early Call—Just One More Sweet "Good-bye"—"All Aboard!"—On Great Lake Winnipeg—Sam's Successful Shot at a Bear—Red River—First Glimpse of the Prairies—Fort Garry—The Bells of St. Boniface—The Long Trip Across the Plains—The Exciting Buffalo Hunt—Saint Paul's—Still On by Lakes and Rivers—Montreal—On Board Ship—The Ocean Voyage—Liverpool—Home at Last. . . . 361

ILLUSTRATIONS

	FACING PAGE
THE BATTLE WITH THE EAGLE	*Frontispiece*
ALEC'S RACE WITH THE WOLVES	52
DOG-TRAVELING UNDER AURORAL LIGHTS	71
VERY GLORIOUS WAS THE SCENERY	101
SUMMER SUNDAY TRIPS TO CHURCH	110
CHURCHGOING IN WINTER	118
NORWAY HOUSE, THE HUDSON BAY COMPANY'S TRADING POST	127
ALEC, VICTOR IN THE DOG RACE	138
PASCHE TREED BY A MOOSE	148
THE MEETING OF KINESASIS AND SHAKOONA	161
A WINTER SCENE IN THE GREAT LONE LAND	185
THE CAPTURE OF THE BEAVERS	228
THE LAST OF THE BUFFALO	245
EXPLOSIONS MINGLED WITH YELLS OF PAIN AND TERROR	259
THE BEAR STILL HOLDING ON TO HIS PIG	272
SAM WITH HIS DOGS ON THE ICE RAFT	327
RACHEL AND WINNIE	341
THE VILLAGE OF THOSE NOTED WARRIORS OF THE PLAINS	361

THE BATTLE WITH THE EAGLE.

Frontispiece, see page 109.

ALEC'S RACE WITH THE WOLVES.

VERY GLORIOUS WAS THE SCENERY.

SUMMER SUNDAY TRIPS TO CHURCH.

CHURCH-GOING IN WINTER.

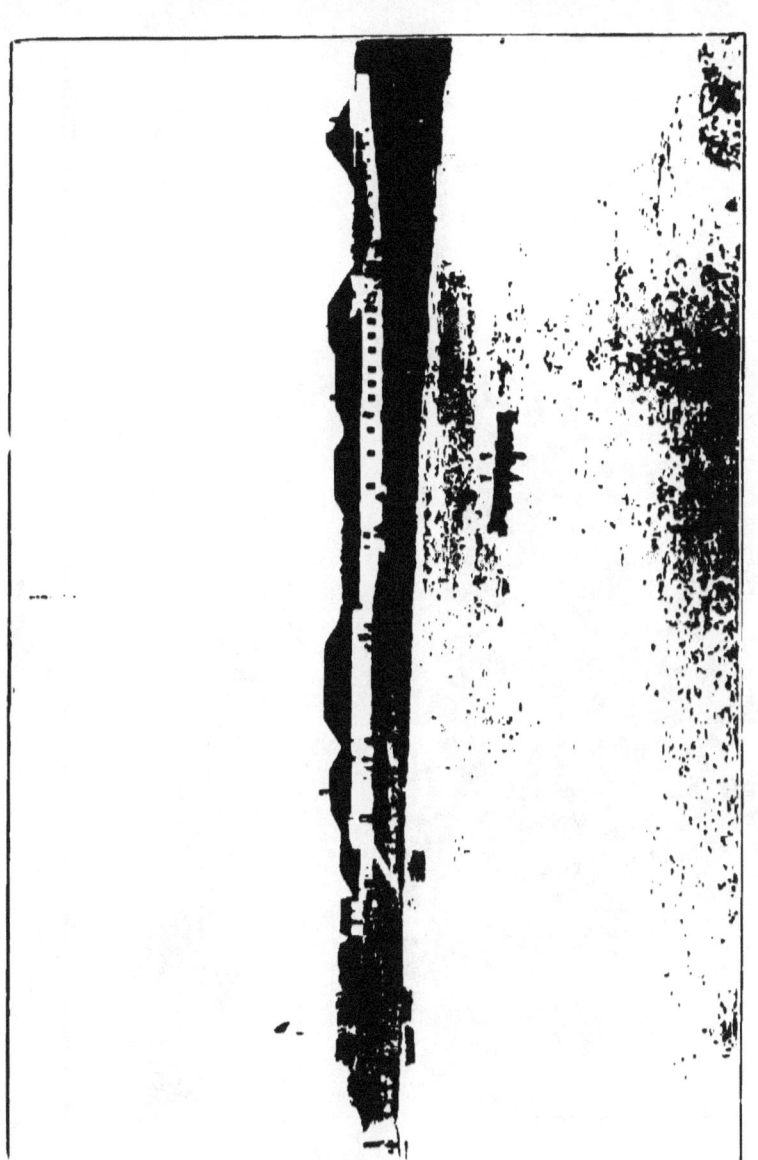

NORWAY HOUSE, THE HUDSON BAY COMPANY'S TRADING POST.

ALEC VICTOR IN THE DOG RACE.

PASCHE TREED BY A MOOSE.

THE BEAR STILL HOLDING ON TO HIS PIG.

A WINTER SCENE IN THE GREAT LONE LAND.

THE CAPTURE OF THE BEAVERS.

THE LAST OF THE BUFFALO.

SAM WITH HIS DOGS ON THE ICE RAFT.

RACHEL AND WINNIE.

THE VILLAGE OF THOSE NOTED WARRIORS OF THE PLAINS.

DOG-TRAVELING UNDER AURORAL LIGHTS.

EXPLOSIONS MINGLED WITH YELLS OF PAIN AND TERROR.

WINTER ADVENTURES OF THREE BOYS
IN THE
GREAT LONE LAND

CHAPTER I.

Sagasta-weekee—A Happy Home in the Great Lone Land—Three Boys There Welcomed—The Sudden Coming of Winter—Various Sports Discussed—Hurrah for the Dogs—Useful Animals—Dog-whips—Kinesasis, the Dog-keeper.

WHILE a wintry storm was raging outside, in the month of November, three happy, excited boys were gathered around the breakfast table in a cozy home in a far North Land.

To those who have not read of the previous doings of these young lads we would say that our heroes were three noble boys from across the sea. They had come out the previous summer from Great Britain by the Hudson Bay Company's ship and had had several months of most delightful and exciting adventures in the wild North Land. They were the guests of Mr. Ross, a retired official in the Hudson Bay Company, who, when his long term of active service in the fur trade had ended, had preferred remaining in the country rather than returning to any other land. During the many years he had traded with the Indians he had ever been on the most friendly terms with them. He had observed so many noble traits and characteristics in them that he and his family preferred spending the greater portion of each year surrounded by them. Then the quiet charm of such a life had more attraction and a greater fascination for them than the rush and worry and demands of our so-called highest civilization.

Mrs. Ross was a native Indian woman, but, like many other wives of Hudson Bay officials, was a highly educated woman. The years spent in foreign lands at the best of schools had not spoiled her. She was beloved and honored by all who knew her, and she was indeed a benediction and a blessing among the poor of her own people.

The musical and expressive Indian names of Minnehaha and Wenonah had been given to the two bright, winsome little girls in the household, while the wee brother was called by the old Scottish name of Roderick.

Cordially had Mrs. Ross, with her husband, welcomed the three boys, who at their special request had come out to be their guests, or rather, more correctly, to be loved members of their own household, for at least twelve months in that land. Sagastaweekee, the house full of sunshine, was the beautiful Indian name given to the cozy, comfortable house which Mr. Ross had built for himself and household. It was a delightful home, well furnished with everything essential to the enjoyment and comfort of all its inmates.

We need not here repeat all that has been previously mentioned about the three heroes of our story. Suffice it to say that Frank, the eldest, was the son of an English banker; Alec was a genuine Scottish lad, while Sam was a jolly Irish boy. They had a splendid trip across the ocean, and had met with varied adventures while on the long journey up the rivers and across the portages between York Factory, on the Hudson Bay, where they had landed, and Norway House, where they had been welcomed by Mr. Ross.

The summer and autumn months had been full of wonderful and exciting trips and adventures. Their last excursion, which had so recently ended, had been one of great pleasure and intense excitement. It had been made in canoes to a distant part of the country where reindeer and other large game abounded. The boys would have been delighted to have there remained longer, but the experienced guide and canoemen had been quick to notice the significant actions of the wild beasts, as well as the frightened cries and incessant flights of the wild geese and ducks to the South Land.

Spurred on by the signs of coming winter, they had pushed on toward home with unremitting toil and but little rest, and had fortunately managed to land the boys safely at Sagasta-weekee the day before the wintry gale broke upon them.

Great indeed was the amazement of our three boys at the transformation wrought by this sudden incoming of winter.

People living in more southern latitudes, where the transition from one season to another is so slow and almost imperceptible, can hardly realize the suddenness with which the Frost King can set up his throne and begin his despotic reign. There are no long premonitions of his coming. No noisy heralds for weeks warn of his approach. The birds and beasts seem to have some mysterious intimations that he draweth near, and act accordingly. But man knoweth not of his approach; he heareth not his stealthy steps.

Yesterday may have been balmy and reposeful, with only a few breezes from the summer South Land. To-day the wild north winds may howl and shriek, while full of frost and pinching cold is the icy, biting air. Yesterday the waves may have been merrily rippling in the sunshine on the beautiful lakes. To-day, after a night of storm and boreal tempest, the ice is rapidly forming, and is binding down in strongest fetters the highest billows.

Mr. and Mrs. Ross were much pleased and amused at the genuine excitement of the lads as they realized the wondrous transformation wrought by this first wintry storm, and the possibilities it opened up to them for other kinds of sport than those in which, for some time past, they had been so deeply interested. Eager and excited as they were, they had as yet no definite plan of action for their winter amusement. So sudden had been the transition, there had been no time to think. However, with boyish candor and joyous anticipation, they were all ready with their suggestions.

"Skates!" shouted Alec, as he caught a glimpse of an icy expanse that glittered in the distance as a ray of sunshine shot out through the parting clouds and for a moment rested upon it.

"Toboggans!" cried Sam, as he saw a steep hillside one mass of beautiful snow.

"Let us make an ice boat," said Frank. Although he had never seen one, yet he had eagerly read much about them, and at the sight of the frozen lake was wild to set about the manufacture of one of these dainty craft, that he might enjoy the exhilarating sport he had so long anticipated.

"Capital suggestions are all of these," said Mr. Ross. "Still, as the ice is not yet twenty-four hours old, and therefore not very safe for skating, and the snow has not yet fallen in sufficient quantity upon the hills to make them smooth enough for tobogganing, and the carpenter will require some time to make an ice boat, and we will have six good months of winter in which to enjoy these and other sports, my suggestion is that we get ready to-day to start, as soon as the ice will be safe, for the island fisheries and bring home the dogs."

"The dogs! the dogs! yes, hurrah for the dogs!" cried all the boys in unison.

So everything was for the moment forgotten, or postponed, in their eager anticipation to become intimately acquainted with the dogs, about which they had heard so much. During the summer months the dogs were sent away to a distant island, where they were cared for by Kinesasis, a careful old Indian, who with a few nets easily caught all the fish they required for food. This island was quite out of the route of travel, and so our young friends had seen but little of Mr. Ross's dogs, about which many interesting stories had been told them. Now at the prospect of soon seeing them they were greatly delighted.

Although so much can be done with dogs in winter in those high latitudes, there is practically no use for them in summer. It is true that some enterprising missionaries had used them for plowing up their little potato fields and gardens, and yet it was slow work and not long continued. But through the long winter the dog is practically the only draft animal that can be utilized by the inhabitants of those regions. From the far-off forest the wood for fuel is dragged home by the dogs. The frozen fish, which are caught and piled up on stages beyond the reach of wolves or other wild beasts, are drawn home to the villages from the distant fisheries by the well-trained dogs.

When a Christian decides to exchange his old wigwam for a house, all the squared timber and logs required in its construction are dragged, if not floated by water in the summer time, it may be several miles, by the dogs. Christian hunters use them to drag home the moose and reindeer or other heavy game they may shoot. Formerly their wives and mothers had to do this heavy work, but now Christianity has relegated this and many other heavy duties to the dogs.

However, the greatest and most arduous work to which the dogs are put is that of drawing the carioles and dog-sleds of travelers and tourists or fur traders for long distances through various parts of that great northern land. Without the dogs, traveling in that country would be practically impossible in the winter months. So full of lakes and rivers is the country that it is possible to go almost anywhere in a birch canoe in summer by making occasional portages. But when the severe cold freezes up those water stretches and the snow lies thick, and there is not the least vestige of a road or trail, then the value and sagacity of the dogs are seen and the power and endurance of the guides and drivers are put to the severest test.

Mr. Ross still prided himself on his splendid dogs. In his younger days he had the reputation of being one of the most active and energetic of the young officers in the service of the Hudson Bay Company. His father, who was for many years one of the chief factors in the Company's service, was proud of his son's endurance and skill, as well as of his tact and ability in managing strange Indians and thus opening up new trading posts among them. So constantly employed had he been in thus advancing the interests of this fur-trading corporation that some winters he traveled thousands of miles with his own dog-train and guides. In his wanderings he had met with some strange adventures, and had passed through some trying ordeals. Later on we may hear from his own lips the recital of some of these stirring events.

Now, however, that he had retired from active service he had left these long and dangerous journeys to be taken by younger men. Still, the love for the dogs was so ingrained within him, and he had so much work for them to do, that he was the possessor of some very valuable trains, which every winter did his work and gave him as much pleasure as ever a man derived from the possession of a fine carriage and a splendid span of horses.

Knowing well the habits of the old Indian who had charge of his dogs, Mr. Ross said to the boys:

"It is very likely that Kinesasis will come in to-day with some of the dogs. If he does we will harness them up to-morrow, and if the ice is strong enough to be safe we will return with them for the others. I understand he has a number of fine young dogs; doubtless there will be enough to make a good train for each of you, after they are broken in. So there will be plenty of work for all to-day, to get ready for the first day's outing with dog-trains."

Soon everybody was at work. Indian women, under Mrs. Ross's direction, were busily employed in making large mooseskin moccasins and mittens. Beautiful white blanket overcoats, with warm capotes or hoods, had already been made for each of the boys. They were to be worn over the deerskin suits when they stopped to rest in the heavy trail, and also while the boys were riding over the long stretches of icy roads where it was possible for the dogs to easily draw them.

While the Indian women were thus busily engaged in fitting out the warm apparel necessary for traveling in such a cold land the boys were making themselves useful, under Mr. Ross's guidance, in overhauling carioles, dog sleds, harness, robes, snowshoes, and other things essential for the trip on the morrow. While almost everything was novel and strange to them, they were most interested in the heavy dog-whips, and, boylike, must try their hands in wielding them. These whips differed very much from anything they had ever seen in civilization. While the handles were only eighteen inches in length, the lashes, which were loaded with shot, were over fifteen feet long. To skillfully handle one requires much care and practice. An inexperienced person is apt to get into trouble when he first attempts to use one.

Sam was the first of the boys to attempt to display his skill, but he soon found that a heavily loaded dog-whip was a different weapon from an Irish shillalah. He had admired the skill and dexterity with which Mr. Ross, at the boy's request, had used one, and, foolishly thinking that he could successfully imitate him, had with any amount of assurance made the attempt. To his surprise and chagrin the cracker of the whip, instead of exploding with a pistol-shotlike report at a spot about fifteen feet away, as it had done for Mr. Ross, had by some remarkable movement, entirely unexpected, squarely landed with stinging effect upon his nose!

Alec was the next to try his skill. He was a little more successful than Sam, in that he escaped inflicting any injury upon himself, but he succeeded in striking Frank upon his ear, although he stood fully six feet away from the spot at which Alec had aimed. Frank, with his ear hot and stinging from the effects of the blow so unexpected and so unintentionally given, wisely decided that he would postpone his first attempt with a weapon that seemed to be as uncertain as a boomerang.

To the great delight of the boys, as Mr. Ross had predicted, toward evening in came Kinesasis with about a dozen dogs at his heels. The splendid animals were delighted to get home again after their long summer's outing, and joyously they greeted Mr. Ross and the other inmates of the household. To our three boys, who had arrived since their departure, they were somewhat distant and unsociable. It is a well-known fact that the native dogs are much more hostile to white people than to the natives. This offishness and even hostility on the part of the dogs did not much disturb the boys. They, boylike, had all confidence in themselves that by tact and kindness they would soon become warm friends, and in this they were not disappointed. After Kinesasis had seen the dogs well fed and put into their kennels he was taken into the kitchen and given a hearty meal. A pipe of tobacco was then put in his hands, and shortly after he had begun to smoke he made his report of his summer's doings to Mr. Ross.

To the great delight of Frank, Alec, and Sam, Mr. Ross was able to inform them that the number of young dogs of the right age to break into work was so large that he would be able to furnish each of them with a capital train, which they should have charge of and call their own as long as they remained in the country.

The few short hours of sunshine of that November day sped away all too soon for the completion of the work to be done, and so by lamplight willing hands toiled on until everything was ready for the journey. So rapidly did the temperature fall, and so intense became the cold, that Mr. Ross decided that with careful, experienced Kinesasis as their guide the ice would be quite strong enough to bear them on the morrow, and so if the storm was not too severe they would be off as soon as there was sufficient light, as it was too risky to travel in the dark over such thin ice.

Cozy were the beds and warm were the blankets into which three happy, excited boys tumbled that night, and if in their pleasant dreams there were sounds of cracking whips and jingling, musical dog-bells—well, we will not envy them, still we wish we were there.

CHAPTER II.

Bringing Home the Dogs—The Thin Ice—Method of Crossing Dangerous Places—The Dogs' Summer Home—The Return Trip—The Unexpected Goose Hunt—The Saucy Fox—Kinesasis's Question, "Why Do the Geese Go to the South Land?"

LONG before daylight the next morning the lamps were brightly burning in Sagasta-weekee. As it was fully twenty miles to the island where Kinesasis had kept the dogs, and Mr. Ross was anxious that they should return home that night, it was absolutely necessary that every hour of the daylight should be utilized. Thus it was that all were stirring long before daybreak. A good warm breakfast was eaten and all final preparations made.

As Kinesasis had brought back with him twelve dogs, they were thus able to rig out three trains for the trip. Extra sleds and harness were taken along, as well as food and blankets, in case any serious accident or delay should happen to them. In such a land it is always best to be prepared for any emergency.

The boys were very proud and happy in their new mooseskin costumes and snow-white blankets, only relieved by the black stripes on the sleeves and skirts. Kinesasis, who had been on the lookout, at length reported the morning star, just visible as the harbinger of dawn. This was good news, and so the start was soon made.

Mr. Ross up to a late hour the previous evening

had not thought of going, but now, at the sight of the dogs and the preparations for the journey, he seemed to catch the enthusiasm of the boys, as well as the fire of earlier days, and resolved to accompany them. Three Indian dog-drivers had been secured, while Kinesasis, old as he was, was proud to act the part of guide for the whole party.

Sam shared a large cariole with Mr. Ross, while Frank and Alec occupied another. To each cariole was assigned a careful driver. The third Indian made up his load of several dog-sleds piled on each other. All were well loaded with supplies. Kinesasis armed himself with a stout pole about ten feet long, which he carried as an Alpine climber would his alpenstock, although it weighed as much as a dozen of them. The boys were surprised at seeing him thus encumber himself with a pole so heavy. They were also perplexed, when it grew lighter, to see a similar one tied on to the sled of the third driver. However, before the journey was finished they saw the wisdom of his forethought.

At first some of the dogs seemed to resent the restraint of the harness, and acted as though they would still have preferred the liberty which had been theirs all through the summer months. Others, however, seemed to be delighted to hear the music of the little open bells with which the collars of their harness were decorated, and joyously barked and jumped about as though, in glad sport, they were dancing to the music they themselves were making.

The trail selected at once led them out along Jack River, and then southwest into Playgreen Lake.

Kinesasis's alert eye was on the ice continually. Now he was glancing at the long stretches before him, and then quickly deciding the best route to follow. When this was selected he seemed to critically examine every yard of the ice over which, on his moccasined feet, he so lightly and yet so rapidly glided. His constant alertness was absolutely necessary; for while the ice was apparently strong enough to be safe, yet when ice freezes up thus rapidly air holes frequently abound, which may be so thinly coated over that none but an experienced eye can detect them. They are very treacherous, as the ice, which to any ordinary observer may appear safe, may not be a quarter of an inch in thickness, and so the unfortunate person stepping on one may suddenly drop out of sight.

The rate at which Kinesasis led the party was about five miles an hour. To do this he kept up a swinging jog trot, and was ever on the alert for danger. Mr. Ross, whose cariole immediately followed the guide, well knowing that there was a certain spice of danger associated with a trip like this so soon after the ice had formed, also kept constantly on the alert, as his long years in such kind of traveling made him almost equal to an Indian in this respect. After traveling for ten miles they reached a spot where one of the great currents of the mighty Nelson River, from Lake Winnipeg, had kept the ice from forming as solidly as where the water was not so rapid in motion. By its ominous bending and cracking under him Kinesasis saw the danger and suddenly brought the whole party to a halt. As the weakness in the ice apparently extended a long way in each direction, it was evident that the party must get across in some way or else return home. The latter idea was not for a moment to be entertained, and so arrangements were at once made for crossing the dangerous place. This novel plan was witnessed by the boys with a great deal of interest. At first they wished to jump from the warm fur robes in their carioles, but this Mr. Ross would not hear of. They could be of no service and would only get thoroughly chilled.

The crossing over the dangerous place was accomplished in the following manner: Kinesasis first untied the other heavy pole from the dog-sled, and then, advancing to the place where the weak ice began, he carefully laid one of the poles on the poor ice, and using the other as a ropewalker would his balancing pole, he carefully walked out on the one on the ice. Then carefully placing the one in his hand down on the ice, in a straight line before him, he stepped on it and cautiously lifted up the one over which he had just walked. Using this as he had handled the other one, as a balancing pole, he thus went on and on, using his poles alternately, until he reached the strong ice on the other side. Then he returned in the same way and reported to Mr. Ross his opinion, which was that by doubling the under surface of the carioles they could pass over in safety.

This was quickly done by taking the sleds, which the third Indian driver had in charge, and securely lashing them to the sides of the carioles, in such a way that the area of surface on the ice would be doubled, and thus the pressure would be only half. As an extra precaution a long rope was tied to the rear of each cariole. Then Kinesasis once more crossed over with his poles to the firm ice. The dogs were put to the gallop, and being urged by those behind, as well as by Kinesasis's well-known voice in front, the dangerous place was passed in safety.

"Now I see," said Alec, "the solution of what was bothering me. I wondered how Kinesasis was able to get along over the weak places in the ice yesterday, but with those poles to help him it is now plain enough."

"It must require a great deal of practice to do it safely," said Frank. And so in after days he found it out when he made the attempt himself, and in trying to transfer himself from one to the other ignominiously fell off, with such force that he broke through the thin ice. Fortunately he had presence of mind enough to seize hold of one of the poles, which was in such a position that each end rested on the unbroken ice. His frightened shouts soon brought help, and he was quickly rescued.

Nothing else occurred to cause delay on the route, and so before noon the dogs, excited by the near approach to the spot where they had spent their happy summer, sprang into a gallop and fairly flew over the good ice that was found for the last few miles. Kinesasis and the Indian drivers had all they could do to keep up with them.

With great delight did the boys spring out of their carioles, and then and there declared that dog traveling was the most exhilarating of sports and the very poetry of motion. Some time later they changed their views. Immediately on their landing they were surrounded by a crowd of dogs of all ages, and doglike they acted. The old fellows that had done good work in other years and were now only kept for drawing wood for the fires, or hay from the distant beaver meadows for the cattle, were dignified and sedate, and yet manifested the greatest affection for their old master, who was kind and gentle to all the animals in his possession. This kindness was well repaid by the intelligent obedience they all gave him. Eagerly the boys scanned the young dogs, for from among them were to be selected the promised trains which they were to call their own.

While the boys were discussing the dogs and indicating their preferences old Kinesasis had rekindled the fire in the large wigwam in which he had passed the summer, and, aided by the other Indians of the party, busied himself in preparing the dinner out of the supplies which had been brought along. Never did a dinner seem to taste better than did that one in that leather tent to those boys, who had so enjoyed the exhilarating twenty-mile trip.

After Mr. Ross, Frank, Sam, and Alec had dined, Kinesasis and the Indian dog-drivers soon had a hearty dinner, and then, after the inevitable pipes, the work of preparation for the return trip speedily began. It was the desire of all to reach home before dark. To accomplish this would be no easy matter, as there were so many untrained dogs. At first it was decided to harness up a number of these, as harness had been brought for the purpose, but after some consultation with Kinesasis about the thin ice Mr. Ross decided against it, thus leaving the young dogs to follow. Only the old dogs were harnessed. This added a couple more trains to the party. The sleds of these were loaded down with the tent, nets, and other things which had made up Kinesasis's outfit during the summer.

At length everything was loaded up, and the return trip began. There was some trouble in getting a number of the younger dogs to take to the ice and keep up with the trains; numbers would persist in turning round and hurrying back.

"We cannot blame them," Sam said afterward, and his Irish oratory burst forth as he described what had been their happy condition. "Just think," he said, "on that beautiful island in the pleasant springtime they were born. There they have had a happy, careless puppyhood life. There they have spent the pleasant summer time with plenty to eat and nothing to do. On the sandy beaches and over the smooth rocks they have gamboled together, and in the warm, rippling waters they have splashed and battled. Now the cold weather has suddenly come and the snow has covered their favorite romping grounds, and even their great bathing places are hard with slippery ice."

There was, however, but little sentiment in the minds of Mr. Ross and the Indians. On the contrary, they were very much annoyed at the delay the refractory young dogs were causing, and so had to adopt prompt measures, or they well knew that the night would be upon them ere home was reached. The younger puppies were packed in the carioles around our travelers, and some of the more obstinate older ones were led by ropes fastened to their collars and tied to the sleds, while the great majority, coaxed by little pieces of meat occasionally dropped on the ice, kept well up to the trains. Thus on they pushed until they reached the rapid current in the lake where the thin ice had given them so much trouble in the morning. Fortunately the additional hours of bitter cold had so strengthened it that no serious difficulty was anticipated in crossing over, even if the loads were much heavier.

But another event occurred, quite unexpected, indeed, and which, while it did much to impede their progress, created a good deal of excitement and interest. The first intimation of its coming was the sudden cry of wild geese not very far away. Their "Honk! honk!" was very distinct, and not only excited the boys, but also the dogs. The loose dogs, in spite of all the calls of the Indians, at once dashed off in the direction from which the loud calls were coming, while the sleigh dogs were almost unmanageable. Prompt and quick were the men to act. The excited dog-trains were bunched and tied together and left in charge of a couple of Indians, while Mr. Ross and the boys and a couple of Indians went forward to investigate.

To the right, a couple of hundred yards away, was a rocky island, on one side of which was a reedy marsh. From among the reeds and rushes the loud calls of the geese were coming. Into these plunged the dogs, while the men and boys climbed up on the rocks where they could overlook the whole spot, which was only of a few acres in extent. The experienced eyes of the Indians took in the whole situation at a glance. The young geese had not been strong enough to fly away to the sunny South Land when the call to go had come, and so the old geese had left them behind to perish. And so now here they were, over twenty of them. A novel goose hunt was organized, and, while the boys looked on, the Indians, with the dogs' help, soon secured quite a number. Some of them were easily killed, as they were securely frozen to the icy reeds. Others rushed about in a vain attempt to escape, but they were so chilled by the cold that they were easily captured. The sleds were piled up with this additional load of geese, and the journey was resumed.

Later on in the evening the boys heard from Kinesasis more about those young geese and why they were there. They also learned some truths from nature that abode with them for many a day.

Without much difficulty the dangerous places in Playgreen Lake were passed, and the return run down Jack River was begun. The loose young dogs were pretty well wearied by the long trip and required some coaxing, and even the occasional crack of the whip was necessary to urge them to keep up. It is amazing what a latent amount of strength and speed there is in a tired dog. Here was a striking example of it. While the trains were jogging along, and the young dogs with tongues out and tails down were wearily following after and looking as though they were deeply bemoaning their lot, suddenly a splendid cross-fox sprang out from the dense forest on one side of the river and deliberately dashed across before the dogs on the frozen ice toward the other shore. All evidence of weariness at once disappeared. With a hue and cry that would have done credit to a first-class pack of hounds they were all off, sleigh dogs as well as loose ones.

The ice was so slippery that it required quite an effort on the part of the drivers of the carioles to control their dogs and get them in line. If the truth must be told, the boys richly enjoyed the short burst of speed and the exciting chase, which ended almost as soon as it began, for Reynard was too much for the young dogs and soon reached the shelter of the wooded shore.

The beautiful evening stars were shining in the western sky ere the welcome lights in the windows of Sagasta-weekee were seen. A hearty welcome was given to the returning party by Mrs. Ross and the children. All were anxious to hear about the first day's winter outing, and each boy had to give his own version of the day's excitements and pleasures.

The commodious kennels were soon taken possession of by the tired dogs. Indian servants had abundance of fish ready for them, and a watchful oversight was kept upon them that the stronger ones should not rob the weaker or younger ones, a trick, we are sorry to say, of which some dogs are guilty.

After the hearty supper and prayers were over in

the dining room, and the younger children had retired to rest, Mr. and Mrs. Ross and the boys went out into the capacious kitchen to hear old Kinesasis give his version of the goose hunt. To please the old man, Mr. Ross filled a beautiful calumet and presented it to him as a gift, in addition to his wages, for his thoughtful care of the dogs while under his charge at the island. For some minutes he smoked his new pipe in silence. Indians are the least demonstrative people in the world, and Kinesasis was one of them. He was never known to say "Thank you" in his life, and yet none could be more grateful or pleased than he to have his faithful services thus recognized. Mr. Ross thoroughly understood him, and the grateful look in his expressive eyes as he received the pipe from Mr. Ross's hand was all that was expected or that would be received. Without one word of reference to the pipe, Kinesasis began about the wild geese. Here is his story, which was a sort of monologue. He said:

"I have been much thinking about it, and I feel that it is my fault that the young geese could not go south with the old ones when the call came in the voice of the North Wind that it was time to go. I well remember that last spring, when in the big boat I carried the dogs out to the island, we saw some geese flying around that island where we caught the young ones to-day. We could not get a shot at the old geese then, they were so wary, but we pulled ashore, and there among the rushes we found some nests full of eggs. Of course, we took the eggs and ate them. No doubt those old geese when they returned, after we had gone, were very angry at our taking the eggs, but they were not discouraged, and so they went to work and filled up their nests with another setting of eggs and hatched them out. But they had lost a full month of time, and there was not enough warm weather left for these broods of young geese to grow strong to rise up in the air when the call came to fly away to the South Land."

For a few minutes he puffed away vigorously at his calumet, and then continuing his story said: "Wild geese are strange things. I have hid myself from them and watched them years ago, when they were more plentiful and hatched their young at many places around our lakes and rivers here. Then we had only bows and arrows, and so did not kill as many as we do now. Their greatest enemies were the foxes, but no fox would dare attack a goose on her nest or a brood of young ones if the old gander were around. One blow of his powerful wing would kill any fox. I have found dead foxes that have thus been killed."

Then, looking up, the old Indian said, in a voice that showed he was deeply impressed by what he was uttering: "There was always some strange mystery about their call to go south and their leaving. To-day they would be acting as though they would be intending to stay with us all the time. They were all very quiet and only busy in getting their food, while the old ones were alert against their enemies, and would even risk their lives to defend their young ones. Then to-morrow would come, and there was such a change in them. They were all so excited and noisy; their cries filled the air. The old ones would stretch their wings and circle round and round in the air about their young ones and encourage them to follow. Soon all of them would rise up and up, and, starting away for the South Land, we would see them no more that year. And yet not all, for sometimes there were late broods, like the one we found to-day. They came too late to be strong enough to fly. They could not go, and here is the mystery to me. Why was it that the parent geese, that yesterday would risk their lives in fighting against wild animals to save their young, would to-day, when the call came to go, leave their young broods behind them to perish? They all did it. Never was an old goose known to stay behind when the call came. That voice was louder and stronger than was even the love for their offspring. Can any of you tell old Kinesasis why it is so?"

CHAPTER III.

Selecting Their Dogs—Various Methods of Breaking Them In—Frank's Success by Kindness with Monarch—Sam's Troubles with Spitfire—Conquered at Last—Training and Capturing Dogs with Dogs—Alec's Train of Part Staghounds.

WITH this question of the old Indian ringing in their ears the party in the kitchen broke up, and as the day had been a long one they all soon retired to rest.

The boys were more than delighted with the day's experience, and were full of joyful anticipation for the morrow, for then it was that they were to select the dogs that were to constitute their own trains and at once to begin the work of breaking them in. So long and soundly did they sleep the next morning that the second breakfast bell was ringing when they awoke, and so they had but little time in which to dress ere breakfast was served. However, to their joy they found that others had also overslept themselves. Even Mr. Ross himself, who was one of these, declared that the capital outing of the previous day had done him a great deal of good, as he had not slept so well for a long time.

The events of yesterday and the anticipations of the present day were discussed with great animation. The boys were questioned as to the style and disposition of the dogs they each desired and the methods they intended to pursue in their training. Frank wanted his to be strong and powerful, able to carry him over any difficult place and able to draw any reasonable load assigned him. Alec's ambition was for a swift train, that he might have all the fun and excitement of rapid traveling.

"All right," said Sam, "but give me the darlings with any amount of mischief and tricks in them. Those are the dogs for me!"

A hearty laugh from all greeted Sam's queer wish.

"I think, as regards the tricks, we can easily satisfy you," said Mr. Ross. "And it will be amusing to see how a young Irish gentleman can circumvent them; for you will find out, before you get through with them, that tricky dogs are not only very clever, but very provoking, in some of their deeds."

Mr. Ross had been very careful for years in the selection and breeding of his dogs. There is as much difference between good and bad dogs as there is between high-spirited horses and miserably lazy ones. The hardy Eskimo was still the prevailing element in his dogs. There were, however, many crosses with some of the finest breeds of civilization, such as the English mastiff, the Newfoundland, and the large Scottish staghound. Dogs are considered old enough to be broken to harness when they have reached their ninth month. They should not, however, be expected, no matter how willing, to draw very heavy loads until they are considerably older. They are much more easily trained when young, and are not so apt to be sullen and ugly as are dogs which are only broken in after they have reached the age of two or three years.

Soon after breakfast and prayers an early visit was made to the kennels. The boys were desirous of having the pleasure that morning of giving the dogs their breakfast. They were very much surprised, however, when informed that the dogs were only fed once a day, and that that one meal was given to them in the evening, when their day's work was done. This information at first aroused their sympathies for the dogs, but after some experience they found out that they could not only do much better work on one good meal a day, but were always in much better health.

Some dogs submit readily to the harness and never give any trouble; others are very obstinate and will take any amount of whipping before they will surrender. Some that seem docile and affectionate before being harnessed, when they find themselves collared and strapped, develop the ferocity of wolves and make the most desperate efforts, not only to get loose, but to attack their own masters. Mr. Ross had, after some discussion with the boys, promised them the privilege to do the breaking in of their own dogs, provided the animals did not develop too obstinate dispositions, which would require a good deal of punishment ere they would submit. Generally this work was done by the Indian servants, as many kind-hearted masters cannot bear to inflict the punishment themselves, which seems to be necessary for some dogs to receive ere their wills are conquered.

Several methods are used in breaking in young dogs. Some trainers securely harness them up and fasten them to a sled, then vigorously, by voice and whip, keep at them until they yield and do what is demanded of them. They must at the first harnessing be so securely fastened that they cannot possibly in any way squeeze or pull themselves out from the harness. Nearly all dogs at first make desperate efforts to escape. If they once succeed in doing so, during the process of training, they are never absolutely reliable afterward. They will occasionally try to repeat the experiment of squeezing themselves loose, and may do it at a critical place on a long journey, and thus cause annoyance and delay.

One of Mr. Ross's methods, which he now suggested to the boys, was to have an old train of four steady dogs harnessed up in tandem style and one of the young dogs, which was to be broken in, harnessed in between the third and fourth dog of the train. Frank was given the first selection. He chose a large, powerful dog that seemed to be part mastiff and part Newfoundland. He had a fine head and kindly eyes. Frank, who was a great lover of dogs, and knowing much about them, had taken the precaution to make a visit to the kitchen, and now, with his outer pockets supplied with broken bits of meat and buns, he began the work of making friends with this big, burly young dog, which was his first choice. The fact that only in the evening were they supposed to be fed was quietly ignored by Frank just now.

Kinesasis called him Ookemou. This Frank translated into Monarch, and by this name he was always called. Frank began his approaches by a liberal use of the contents of his pockets, and who ever knew a young dog proof against such an argument? Growing dogs are always hungry, and will take kindly to anyone who will stuff them. The

Indian servants speedily had a train of old dogs ready, with a vacant harness placed as we have described. Into it Monarch willingly allowed himself to be harnessed by Frank. The whole train was then fastened to a dog-sled, and the word "Marche!" was shouted by the driver. The well-trained dogs at once responded and started off, and as long as Frank ran by the side of Monarch the young dog did very well, but when he dropped behind and sprang on the sled with the Indian driver Monarch also made an effort to do likewise. This, however, he found to be an impossible feat, as the three strong dogs before him kept him on the move, and so he was obliged to proceed, which he did very unwillingly. Frank shouted to him to go on. This, however, was a great mistake, as the dog, at once recognizing his voice, and not knowing as yet the meaning of "Go on," would much rather have come back to the one who had so thoroughly won his friendship. Seeing him beginning to act ugly and obstinate, the Indian driver drew his heavy dog-whip and was about to strike him. This Frank hotly resented, and so the Indian quickly recoiled his whip and quietly waited to see what the young white master wanted to do. Frank's quick intellect was at work. He was a wide-awake, kindly lad, with a love for as well as a knowledge of dogs, and so when he saw this young dog so resolutely pull back at the sound of his voice, thus showing that he would rather come toward him than run from him, he instantly made up his mind that he could be broken in by kindness and persuasion. Quickly he resolved upon his own plan of action. Ordering the Indian driver to stop the train, Frank speedily ran to Mr. Ross with an urgent request for another train of old dogs. Mr. Ross, who was at once interested by the intense earnestness of the lad, speedily granted him his request, although as yet he could not understand the reason why two trains were desired, where one was generally considered sufficient.

Very quickly did willing hands harness up a train of old dogs and attach them to a dog-sled.

"Now," said Frank to the driver of them, "you drive on ahead of that other train and let me ride with you."

Orders having been given to the driver of the train in which Monarch was harnessed to follow after, Frank, who was now on ahead and in plain sight, began calling to his dog to follow. To this call he at once responded, and as the train in which he was harnessed was allowed to come alongside of the first Monarch was rewarded by receiving from his master's hands some dainty bits of meat. There was no trouble with him after this. No matter how fast the first train was now driven, with head and tail up, on came Monarch, with as much vim and dash as the best of the old dogs with which he was harnessed. When it was thought that he had had enough exercise for that day, and as they were about two miles from home, they rested for a few moments, during which Frank spoke kindly to his dog and fed him with the remaining pieces of meat. Before leaving he gave orders to the driver of the train in which Monarch was harnessed to wait until he and the other train would have time to reach home. Monarch, as he saw the other train leaving, became very much excited and was eager to follow. He was, however, restrained by the driver, as were the other dogs. All sleigh dogs of any spirit hate to be thus left behind, and so when the word "Marche!" was uttered they sprang forward with a will, Monarch being as eager as any of them.

In the meantime, when Frank with the one train of old dogs returned to Sagasta-weekee, he was met with laughter and quizzing remarks from both Alec and Sam. Coming as he did without his young dog, they could only imagine that he had met with complete failure and had given up the business in disgust. Mr. Ross, however, older and more experienced, after one searching glance in Frank's triumphant, satisfied face, surmised something better, and so was prepared for the lad's triumph, which soon came.

Frank very good-naturedly took the guying of his comrades, but his eyes were along the trail made by the sled from which he had just alighted. Keen was his vision then, and alert his eye, and so when the coming train was still far away he knew by their rapid pace that he had triumphed. Turning to Mr. Ross, he triumphantly exclaimed:

"There they come, and Monarch as eager as any of them, and no whip has ever touched his back, or ever will."

It did not take the rapidly advancing train long to reach the now interested group of spectators.

Frank's triumph was complete. None could have

imagined that the finest-looking dog in that train, that bore himself so proudly, had that day for the first time ever had a collar on his neck. Yet such was the case, and as Frank petted and unharnessed him warm and sincere were Mr. Ross's congratulations.

From that day forward Monarch was a model sleigh dog, and never failed to respond to the voice of his new master, whose kindly tact had saved him from the lash.

There was still time before lunch for another experiment or two, and so Alec suggested that Sam, who wanted dogs full of fun and tricks, should make the next choice.

Sam, nothing loath, selected a handsomely built dog with the queerest combination of colors. He had a bright, mischievous-looking eye, and it was evident that he had a good opinion of himself. His small, erect, pointed ears, his foxlike muzzle, and his curly, bushy tail told that there was a good deal of the Eskimo in him, and therefore until better acquainted with the paleface he would not have much love for him. Sam soon found this out. At Mr. Ross's request Kinesasis skillfully threw a lasso over him and brought him out of the kennels. This undignified procedure considerably ruffled his temper, and so when Sam, in sweet simplicity, took up a harness and endeavored to put it on him the dog viciously sprang at him and buried his teeth in the heavy moose-skin mitten of the hand which Sam was fortunately able to quickly throw up, thus saving his face from injury. Mr. Ross and others sprang forward to help the lad, but Sam's Irish was up, and as the lasso was still upon the dog's neck, and his teeth had only cut through the tough leather without injuring his hand, he cried:

"Please let me have the satisfaction of conquering him alone."

Suddenly throwing himself forward, Sam seized hold of the lasso, and, tightening it about the dog's neck, he quickly tangled him up in the loose coils and managed to throw him on the snowy ground. Seizing the harness, he dropped down upon the excited, half-choked animal, and, guarding his hands against his snappy teeth, he managed to get the collar over his head. But the work was not yet completed, and Mr. Ross, seeing the danger the boy was in of being badly bitten by the now furious animal, ordered a couple of Indian men to his assistance. He highly complimented Sam, and said that in getting the collar on such a dog he had succeeded well. The Indians cautiously but quickly muzzled the dog, and then, letting him get up, they finished Sam's work of harnessing him. The next thing was to get him into the train with the other dogs, and this proved to be no easy matter.

"Give him a name," said Alec.

"Spitfire!" shouted out Sam, and by this name he was ever after known.

He seemed to have an idea that his personal liberty was being interfered with, and so he resisted everything done by Sam or the dog-drivers. When by main force he was placed in position and the traces were fastened he made most violent attempts to escape. He struggled first to one side and then to the other in his frantic efforts. Then he tried to crawl under and then over the dog in front of him. Failing in this, he suddenly sprang forward with such force that he managed to seize hold of the short, stumpy tail of the dog in front of him. This was an unfortunate move on his part, as the dogs that are accustomed to work together will readily fight for each other when one is in trouble. So before Sam or the Indians could interfere, if they had been so disposed, the dogs ahead of Spitfire, hearing the cry of pain from their comrade, quickly turned upon him and gave him a thorough shaking. When the Indians thought he had had enough they interfered, and once more straightened out the dogs.

Spitfire was most decidedly a sadder, if not a wiser, dog as the result of his rashness. But, poor fellow, his troubles were not yet over, for the old sleigh dog behind him was also indignant at the attack upon the tail of his old comrade, and so he was also resolved to mete out some punishment to the rash young offender. This was just what the Indians wanted, and so, telling Sam to jump on the sled with them, they shouted, "Marche!" to the head dogs, while the old fellow behind sprang at Spitfire.

At first the young fellow, seeing that he could not get away, had resolved to balk, but when the big dog with fierce growls made his desperate efforts to seize hold of him he was glad to spring as far away as his traces would permit. The result was that before he knew what he was about he was rapidly galloping in unison with the rest of the train. Sam kept him at it until he was so tired that all the venom and fight were worked out of him. If for an instant he tried to act ugly or break loose, all Sam had to do was to call on the sleigh dog to attack him. This was quite sufficient and Spitfire surrendered to the inevitable, and in less than three hours had well learned his first lesson.

To conquer the dog's repugnance to Sam, and to make them fast friends, Mr. Ross had him, when taken out of the harness, fastened up in a dark root cellar without any supper. The next day Sam went in to bring him out, but was met only with savage growls.

"All right," said Mr. Ross, "it seems hard on you for the present, but it will be better for you in the end;" and so the heavy door was shut, and Spitfire had another twenty-four hours in solitude and quiet to ponder over his ways. The next day, as directed by Mr. Ross, in whom he had all confidence, Sam suddenly threw open the door, and, while the dog was still blinking in the sudden sunshine that poured in, Sam without any hesitancy or fear strode in and, unchaining him, led him out and up to an abundant supply of food and drink.

Spitfire was conquered, and from that day he and Sam were the best of friends. A few more lessons in the harness, with a growling, cross sleigh dog behind him, made him one of the best and fleetest of the train.

Sam, who was quick to utilize a good thing when he observed it, saw in this dislike of this old sleigh dog to having fresh young dogs ahead of him just the assistance he needed; and so, although he selected three other dogs, that at first were about as ugly and intractable as Spitfire had been, he was able in this way to subdue them all with firmness and patience, and he not only made them his affectionate friends, but he became the master of one of the most spirited trains in the country. They were obedient and quick to respond to Sam's calls upon them, but woe to anyone else who tried to drive them when the spirit of mischief or contrariness which was in them showed itself.

Alec had stated that he wanted a swift train for the fun and excitement of fast traveling. It was fortunate for him that Mr. Ross had some young dogs with a large strain of the Scottish staghound in them. The pure staghounds are unable to stand the severe cold of the long winters, but the mixed breeds at Sagasta-weekee, while retaining much of the speed of the staghound, had a rich, warm coating of fur-like hair. Still, they enjoyed a warm blanket when the weather was very severe. The young, untrained ones were very wild, and when Kinesasis attempted to bring out from the kennels a beautiful one that he had lassoed, and which Alec had fancied, the frightened, agile creature jerked the lasso out of his hands, scaled the walls, and dashed away over the snowy fields. To have followed him would have been absurd, as the frightened dog if pursued would have continued his flight until he had reached the distant island where he had spent the summer. Kinesasis knew a better plan than that, and so he quickly let loose about a half dozen sagacious old dogs, trained by him for such work, and quietly told them to go out and bring that young wanderer back. The frightened dog, after running several hundred yards, when he saw that he was not being followed, slackened his pace and more leisurely continued his journey. He would, however, frequently stop and look about him, and especially back toward the place he had so abruptly left.

Soon he saw the dogs that Kinesasis had sent out, and that were now gamboling and playing with each other. He was attracted by the sight, and stopped his flight to watch them. They were apparently not noticing him in their sporting with each other, but they were nevertheless drawing nearer to him. At first he was inclined to be suspicious of them, but this soon left him, and he seemed to become pleased to greet them, as doubtless he had already begun to feel lonesome, for the dog is indeed a social animal. When once he was thrown off his guard it was not long ere the trailing lasso was seized by the teeth of a couple of the most sagacious dogs, who immediately started on the return trip. The rest of the dogs followed growling in the rear of the runaway. When necessary they used their teeth upon him, and so they soon brought him, cowed and submissive, to the hands of Kinesasis.

Tame elephants take great delight in helping to capture and subdue wild ones, but not greater is their satisfaction at their successful work than is that of old dogs who are trained to it when they have a share in the capturing or breaking in of obstinate, refractory dogs.

The boys enthusiastically expressed their surprise as well as admiration at this wonderful cleverness on the part of these trained dogs in capturing the runaway. They were also amused at their evident delight at the success of their efforts.

"Yes," said Mr. Ross, "and if that young dog had been able to elude them, either by keeping out of their reach, in the first place, or by slipping the lasso over his head and thus escaping from them, and they had had to return without him, they would have been thoroughly ashamed of themselves, and would have skulked off to their kennels."

"I have read," said Frank, "that that is the way the St. Bernard dogs in the Alps act if they are unsuccessful in bringing any belated or lost traveler back to the monastery, when they are sent out by the monks to search for any in distress. They are very proud if they succeed, but if they fail to find anyone they skulk back ashamed of themselves and sulk in their kennels for a couple of days, or even longer."

Alec, taking advantage of the methods adopted by both Frank and Sam, and other plans suggested by Mr. Ross, at length succeeded in breaking in his four dogs. He had the misfortune to have one of them, on account of his small head, squeeze himself out of his harness and escape. Great difficulty was experienced in capturing him, and then even when conquered he at times gave endless trouble by slipping his collar and skulking in the rear.

Another of his dogs, when being broken in, made the most desperate efforts to cut himself loose with his teeth. He ruined in this way some valuable harness, and several times cut the traces of the dogs in front of him. Having exhausted the patience of Alec, he received a first-class whipping ere he stopped trying these tricks.

In about a month the dogs were thoroughly trained and seasoned to their work. Frank clung to Monarch as his favorite, while Sam and Spitfire were almost inseparable. Alec, true to the romantic love of his country, made the runaway his favorite and called him Bruce. His other three he named Wallace, Gelert, and Lorne.

CHAPTER IV.

Numerous Dogs—Useful Animals—Food Supply—Frozen Fish—Bringing Them Home—Vigorous Work for Boys and Dogs—Frank's Tumble—Sam's Ducking—Skating Parties—Alec's Thrilling Adventure—The Race for Life—Northern Gray Wolves—Their Cunning—Their Various Stratagems—Mr. Ross's Fears—The Search Party—Alec Rescued—The Wolves Shot.

It may seem strange to some of our readers that such numbers of dogs were kept by Mr. Ross. It must be remembered that they were, in those regions, the only animals in those days that were of any use to man.

So abundant were the fish that the dogs were kept with little expense. The lakes and rivers so swarmed with them that a few gill nets and an Indian could easily take care of a large number of dogs during the summer months. For the winter supply an immense number of whitefish were caught just as the winter was setting in. These fish were hung up on high stagings beyond the reach of wolves and stray, prowling dogs. So intense and steady was the frost that the fish, which immediately froze solid after being hung up, remained in that condition until well on into the next April. Such a thing as the temperature rising high enough to even soften the fish was almost unknown. The result was the fish were kept by this great preservative, the intense frost, in prime condition for both the people and the dogs. On account of their abundance, and the ease with which they could be obtained, they were for many years the principal article of food.

The Indians take but little care of their dogs in the summer time; they literally have to fish for themselves, and very clever are some of them at it. So abundant are the fish, and so clever are the dogs in capturing several varieties that haunt the marshes and shallows along the shores, that the dogs easily secure sufficient numbers to sustain life and even grow fat upon. On these fishing excursions the Indian dogs often wander over a hundred miles away from the wigwams of their masters, and are gone for months together.

While quantities of fish were being caught during every month of the year—for even in the coldest parts of the winter they could be caught through holes in the ice—yet the actual fall fishery season only lasted a few weeks. On this fishery everybody depended for their principal winter supply. It generally began a short time before the ice set, and continued about as long after. The fish, which were principally whitefish, were all caught in gill nets. When brought ashore they were stabbed through the flesh near the tail. Through this incision a sharp-pointed stick was inserted. Ten were always thus hung up on each stick, with their heads hanging down. While still warm a single slash of a sharp knife was given to each fish between the gills. This caused what little blood there was in them to drip out, and thus materially added to the quality of the fish, and also helped in its preservation.

The work of bringing these thousands of fish

home was done by the dog-trains. It is heavy work, as each train of four dogs was expected to draw twenty sticks of fish at each load. However, the track was generally all ice, and so it was much easier than traveling in a forest trail in the deep snow. Six hundred pounds are considered a good load for four dogs on ordinary trails.

As Mr. Ross's fishermen had hung up about fifty thousand fish, besides packing a large number of the finest ones in ice or snow, there was considerable work for the trains in dragging them home. The work is so steady that it is considered capital training for young dogs. Of course, they are not at first given as heavy loads as are the old trains. The boys were allowed to go with their trains about three times a week. This was quite sufficient for them, for, although they rode on the empty sleds, wrapped in a buffalo skin, on the outward trip to the fishery camp, yet they felt in honor bound to imitate the Indian drivers of the older trains, and walk, or rather trot, as much as they could on the return with their heavy loads.

The kind-hearted Indians, while admiring the pluck of the boys when, on the first trip, they urged for heavier loads, wisely and firmly insisted that they should take light ones to begin with.

"This is only fun," said Alec, "just running on the ice. I have walked all day in the Highlands, and was all right the next day. I want a full load, for I intend to run the whole distance on the home stretch."

"Twenty miles on ice, with some slipping and

falling and managing a lively dog-train, will seem a long journey ere it is ended," said Mustagan, a grand old Indian who that year had charge of the work of bringing home the fish.

Frank thought that with his strong dogs he could take more than Sam or Alec, but even to this Mustagan objected.

"Yes," he said, "fine big dogs, but very young, bones still soft. Big loads by and by, but not now."

"I wish we had brought our skates," said Sam, "and then we would have had no trouble in making the twenty miles." This, it was unanimously agreed, was a capital suggestion, and one that would be carried out on future trips.

So in the meantime they decided to carry out Mustagan's request and only take light loads. The wisdom of this was seen before they had gone many miles. The gait at which the old, experienced dogs struck out, and which was kept up by the drivers, as well as by the dog-trains of the boys, was altogether too rapid for them.

Very gamely they kept up the pace for four or five miles, when Mustagan called a halt for the first pipe. His observant eyes had been on the boys, and while he was pleased with their pluck, he was too wise to allow them to injure themselves; so, taking the matter into his own hands, he so arranged the sticks of fish on their sleds that, with the aid of the buffalo skins, he made for each a comfortable seat. It is not surprising that the boys were willing to accept of the situation, and, while on the remainder of the trip they rode a good deal, they often sprang off and, by the vigorous exercises of keeping up with the Indians on their famous jog trot, kept themselves warm, and also put in a good deal of training to fit them for longer journeys.

On future trips to the fisheries, as long as the ice kept free of snow, they carried with them their skates, and not only on the home trip with loaded sleds, but even on the outward journey, did they have some capital sport. Alec especially was a splendid skater. Coming from Scotland, where they had so much more ice than there was in England or Ireland, he had had greater opportunities for becoming an adept in this exhilarating sport. He was very much amused at the temper and annoyance of his dogs when, on a fine stretch of smooth ice, he would dash away from them at a rate which it was impossible for them to keep up. They would make the most desperate efforts to travel as fast as he did. When they realized the impossibility of doing this, hampered as they were by their heavy load, they would at times set up a most dismal cry that was a cross between a bark and a howl. At other times some of the dogs would think that one of the train was shirking his work, and then they would unmercifully pile on him and give him a sound thrashing.

Well was it for Alec that he had these splendid skating trips; unconsciously was he preparing for a race for his life.

On one of these home trips Frank, while sitting on his load, wrapped up in his buffalo robe, went to sleep. He was all right while the sled was going along in a straight trail, but at one place the road turned at a sharp angle, and here he had a sudden awakening. The ice was firm and the dogs were going at a good speed. When they reached the sharp turn the sled slid around at a great rate, and poor Frank, who like the other boys had when awake securely hung on to the straps on other trips, was now so fast asleep that when the sled flew around he was sent in the air at a tangent, and then went sprawling on the ice quite a number of yards away. He was well shaken up and badly bruised. After that he took good care to take his naps on the sleds in less dangerous places.

Sam had a worse adventure than that. One day, while running behind and driving his train and cheerily talking to his dogs, he had the misfortune to step through the thin ice into an air hole. He fortunately had presence of mind enough to throw out his arms, and so, as the hole was a small one, he only went in up to his armpits. That, however, was quite enough, as the temperature was many degrees below zero. He was speedily pulled out and cared for by the Indian drivers. They quickly threw all the fish from Alec's sled, and, taking the three buffalo robes which the boys were accustomed to use on the outward trips, carefully wrapped Sam in them, and securely tied him on it. Then they said:

"Now, Master Alec, here is your chance to show the speed of your dogs. Hang on securely yourself, and see how quickly you can make the ten-mile trip from here to Sagasta-weekee."

Alec needed no other incentive than the desire to

get his beloved Sam home as quickly as possible. The boys all dearly loved each other, and a serious accident to one gave sorrow to the other two. The cold was intense, and it was necessary that Sam should be taken home as speedily as possible. The weight of the two boys was but little to the active-spirited dogs, and so when the sharp cracks of the whip sounded around them, but not on them, and the urgent cries of "Marche! Marche!" with unusual emphasis kept ringing out from the lips of their master, they seemed at once to realize that something unusual was the matter; and as it was also on the home stretch, away they flew at a rate that soon left the heavily loaded sleds far behind.

In less than an hour's time the distance was covered. Sam was soon in the hands of loving, experienced friends who knew just what to do, and so in a day or two he was out again, none the worse for his adventure.

The skating was simply perfect. Just fancy miles and miles of ice, smooth as glass and stretching out over lake and river in every direction; no pent-up little pond or skating rink where in a few hours the ice is ruined by the crowd or melted by the rising temperature. Here were great lakes and rivers of it that lasted for months. Lakes full of beautiful islands, whose shores not long ago were lapped by the murmuring, laughing waves, are now gripped, as in fetters of steel, by the Frost King. In and out among them glide the merry skaters. Everybody in that land big enough skated, and skated well.

Jolly parties from the fur-trading posts and mission home joined with others in making merry groups, who for hours at a time engaged in this joyous and exhilarating sport. Sometimes several young gentlemen in the service of the Hudson Bay Company would come over from the fort and join them in their moonlight excursions. So glorious were the surroundings, and so exhilarating the sport, that the nights would be far spent ere they thought of returning home.

There seemed a strange fascination in seeking out new places and exploring untried branches of the great rivers, which seemed like streams of molten silver in the bright moonlight as they stretched away into primitive forests, where the trees on the shores hung heavy with icicles, or were so bent under the weight of snow that, at times, they looked like ghostly visitants from dreamland.

As the days passed on these skating excursions were much more extended, and as the skaters began to get familiar with the different routes the vigilance which was at first kept up, that none might go astray, was much relaxed. When there were any indications of a storm or blizzard it was well understood that no skater was to go out alone. and even then not beyond some well-defined landmarks. However, when the weather seemed settled, and the sun shone brightly by day and the moonlight was clear and beautiful at night, no positive restraint was upon anyone. Thus, day after day, they merrily skated in little groups or in pairs as they desired. Sometimes one would dash off alone, and for hours amidst the weird, picturesque surroundings, such as a skater alone can find in such a land, would, in the very intoxication of his bliss, push on and on, without any idea of the progress of time or of the distance he was traveling.

To Alec, the Scottish lad, there came one beautiful moonlight night an experience which nearly had a tragic ending. The night was one of rarest beauty, but it was very cold, so cold that Mr. Ross remarked that the moon looked more like burnished steel than silver. As the merry party started out he warned them to keep their furs well around them or severe frostbites would be theirs, in spite of the vigorous exercise of rapid skating.

The company of half a dozen or so kept together for a time, and then, in joyous rivalry, shot out and in along the icy stretches between the granite, fir-clad islands that on that lake were so numerous. As further they advanced they became more and more separated, until Alec found himself alone with a young clerk from the trading post, who prided himself on his skill and speed as a skater. He had been considered the champion the previous winter, and naturally wished to retain his laurels. Finding himself alone with Alec, whom he thought but a novice compared to himself, he endeavored to show off his speed, but was very much annoyed and chagrined to find that, skate as rapidly as he would, the Scottish lad kept alongside and merrily laughed and chatted as on they sped. Ruffled and angry at being so easily matched by Alec, the clerk abruptly turned around and skated back. Alec was at first a little hurt by this discourteous action, but this feeling quickly wore off as on and on he skated, fairly entranced by the beauty of his surroundings and the excitement of his sport. After a time he noticed that the lake was abruptly ending. Just as he was about to circle around and begin the return journey he saw the mouth of a beautiful little ice-covered river which ran up into the forest. The ice looked so smooth and was so transparent, as there it lay in the beautiful moonlight, and he was so fascinated by the sight, that he could not resist the impulse to dash in upon it. On and on he glided, on what seemed to him the most perfect ice that skater ever tried. He did not appear to observe that this glassy, winding river, on which he was so joyously skating, was gradually narrowing, until he observed the great branches of some high trees meeting together and cutting off the bright moonlight. Skating under these great shadowy branches, with the glinting moonlight here and there in great patches of white upon the ice, alternating with the shadows, was a new experience, and very much did he revel in it, when——

What sound was that?

It must have been only the falling of some drift of snow from an overloaded branch, or a broken branch itself, and so, although Alec was startled at hearing any sound amidst these almost noiseless solitudes, he soon recovered his spirits and dashed on along the narrowing, crooked stream; but—there it is again! And now as Alec quickly turns his head and looks he sees what blanches his face for an instant and shows him the peril of his position. Four great northern gray wolves are skulking through the snow on the shore, and already their eyes are gleaming in triumph, and their mouths are watering for their prey. Quick as a flash he turns, and so do they. Well is it now that the sturdy lad, on his native lochs in Scottish winters, had practiced every movement, and had become an adept in twisting and rapid turning on his skates. He will need it all to-night, as well as the hardened muscles of his vigorous sports since he came to this wild North Land; for the wolves will not easily be balked in their efforts to capture and then devour. The very fact of there being four of them seemed at first in his favor, as the instant they turned they appeared to get in each other's way. In the brief delay thus caused Alec was away and was increasing his speed every instant. But he is not to be let off so easily. Looking behind, he sees that two are coming on in their long, galloping, speedy way. Where are the other two? Soon enough will he know.

As we have stated, this little river was very crooked. The cunning wolves well knew this, and so a couple of them made a short cut through the woods, to intercept their prey at a spot **ahead of him.** As an inspiration, the quick-witted lad took in the situation. He had heard much already about the cunning of these gray wolves in hunting in relays the moose and other species of deer, and by having some of their numbers sent on ahead or stationed in narrow defiles to intercept their prey. So, suspecting the trap being laid for him, he made up his mind, if possible, to reach that danger point before those wolves. It was a long sweep around, like a horseshoe, and he had to make the whole distance round, while they had but to cross the tongue of land. He had to traverse at least twice the distance that the wolves had to go, but then he had the advantage in being on the ice, while they had to loup through the snow. Still, there were no risks to be taken For an instant the thoughts came, as he heard the faint thud, thud on the ice of the fleet wolves behind him: What if anything should happen to my skates? Or if I should get in a crack in the ice? But he quickly banished these thoughts as unworthy. He had all confidence in the splendid skates on his feet, and saw with delight that he was emerging from the last place where the trees entirely hid the bright moonlight. Every crack and dangerous place could now be easily seen and guarded against.

On and on he fairly flew. The wolves, in spite of their desperate efforts to keep up, were being left further and further behind. At this Alec rejoiced; but his heart fairly jumped, and fear for an instant again seized him, as there suddenly burst upon his ears the blood-curdling howlings of many wolves. It was begun by those in the rear. It was answered by others that seemed ahead of him. It was re-echoed back by others that appeared to be further off Looking back, he observed that the two that had been following him, when they had finished their howlings, suddenly disappeared in the forest, evidently bent upon some new plan of attack.

No wonder that the plucky lad felt that this was a crisis in his life, and that if ever he had his wits about him they were needed now. As the result of his early teachings, and the memory of his godly mother, there sprang from his heart and lips a whispered prayer: "God of my mother, remember her boy to-night;" and he felt that he was not forgotten.

Like as with fresh soldiers on the battle field, so now, that the first terror had come and gone, a strange spirit of exhilaration came to him, and seemed to nerve him for the race. He had no weapon with him, not even a stick in his hand. His wits, his skates, and his powers of endurance must be his reliance in this unique encounter. As well as he could he endeavored to recall the different windings in the river, and the places where he was likely to be attacked later on, if he escaped the spot where he felt sure the next effort would be made by his cunning foes.

Rapidly as he was skating, his quick eye caught sight of two of his foes. They were crouching together on a snow-covered rock that almost overhung the edge of the stream where it was narrowest. To endeavor to escape by such fierce brutes, now so aroused by having once missed him, would have been madness. To have retreated would have been certain death. Quick as a flash came the ruse to Alec. Dashing up, with a shout that was a challenge, he made as though he were going to fly by, but the instant before he reached the spot where his quick eye saw they would spring upon him he whirled upon the heels of his skates. That instant they sprang upon the spot where their instinct told them he ought to have been. He was not there, however, but a few yards in the rear; so they missed him, and with the momentum of their spring went sprawling out on the smooth ice. Another turn on the skates, as quick as the first, and Alec was by them ere they could recover themselves. Thoroughly baffled and furious, they were speedily in pursuit, and it required all of Alec's effort to much increase the distance between them and himself. Several times they cut across short necks of the little river, and once so near did they get that the snappings of their terrible teeth were distinctly heard. One long stretch more, then a double twist, like the letter S in the river, and he would reach the lake.

Alec was heated now; his clothes were wet with perspiration, in spite of the bitter cold. That some wolves were ahead of him he was certain. Home was far away. The other skaters had long since returned from their outings. Around the great blazing fireplace Mr. Ross had more than once said:

"I am sorry that Alec has remained out so late."

Unknown to the rest of the family, some hunters had reported to him that already tracks of wolves had been seen in the hunting grounds not many miles away. These brutes are always very vicious in the beginning of winter. Their summer supplies of food are cut off, and the deer have not yet begun to run and thus leave their tracks in the woods. When another hour had passed on Mr. Ross could stand it no longer, and earnestly exclaimed:

"Who saw Alec last?"

The young clerk who had been last seen with him, and who had not as yet returned to his trading post, said:

"I left him near the other side of the lake."

Mr. Ross was indignant, but there was now no time for anything but action. Short and stern were his orders. Alec must be sought after at once. Hastily rousing up three trusty Indian servants, he and they were soon out on the lake. All were on skates and armed with guns. A few dogs were allowed to accompany them, among them being Alec's train. Mr. Ross wisely judged that if they once struck his tracks, such was the love they had for him, they would soon find him, even if he had become bewildered and lost his bearings. So, while Alec was still in danger, help was coming.

Fortunately for him, the river was wider now, and his eyes were so alert that he could detect his foes, even when quite a distance from them. He was thus able to see through the disguise of a couple of them that lay crouching out on the ice, trying to look like the little piles of snow that the eddying winds had gathered. Still, although he saw them, and by another clever ruse flew by them, yet so close were they to him, when they sprang at him, that some of the froth from the mouth of one of them fell upon him.

To his surprise, these two did not long follow him, but sprang into the gloom of the forest and disappeared. In the last half of the S-like river Alec was now speeding. He felt confident that if he could once reach the lake he would be able by speed, and perhaps some quick dodging, to elude them; but this last portion of the crooked river troubled him, and made him doubly cautious.

There is need for it all, for look! There are now not less than a dozen of them, and they are so arranged on the ice and on the shore that there is apparently no escape. Those strange howlings, so blood-curdling and so weird, which the first pair of wolves uttered were understood by others, and here they are, ready and eager to join in the attack and to divide the prey.

They seem so confident now, and so loudly do they howl that the great high rocks echo back the doleful music. To Alec it was now the martial music that only sharpened his faculties and made him more cautious and more brave. Boldly skating up to them, he suddenly turned, when almost in their clutches, and instantly started back up the river as rapidly as he could skate. On and on he fairly flew, until, owing to the bend in the river, he was completely out of their sight. Then skating near to one of the shores he pushed on a couple of hundred yards or so. Crossing over to the other side, he quickly turned to a spot where, sheltered by a large tree, he was securely hid in the deep shadow, which was in sharp contrast to the bright moonlight near him. In this retreat he had not long to wait ere he saw the wolves, evidently disconcerted, but coming on his trail. They were stretched out quite apart from each other, and covered such a distance that he saw that those in front would be doubling back on him ere all had passed. However, he was confident that so suddenly could he dash out that, by skillful dodging on the glassy ice, where the wolves would not have much of a foothold, he could elude them.

It was a trying moment for the boy, as on the opposite side of the tree, which rose up directly out of the ice, he heard the measured steps and even the heavy breathings of the cruel monsters, not fifty yards away. Fortunately, there was no wind to carry the scent from him to them, and so they did not detect his stratagem. When about half of them had passed, with a dash and a shout he was off. So completely taken by surprise were they that those nearest to him made no attempt to stop him. The two or three in the rear savagely tried to block his way and sprang at him, but signally failed to reach him, as Alec skillfully skated round them and sped onward toward the lake. Furious indeed were those that had passed him and felt themselves robbed of their victim. Outwitted were they all, but not yet discouraged. Wolves can run with great swiftness on the smoothest ice, and although, as we have seen, they cannot turn quickly, and can be dodged by a clever skater, yet for a straight go-ahead pace they are not to be despised by the swiftest runner. Then their powers of endurance are very great, and so it was evident to Alec that they were resolved, by grim endurance, to run him down.

Firmly convinced that there were none ahead of him, and that it was now to be a long race, he wisely resolved not to so force himself that he could not, if need be, keep up a good rate of speed all the way to the abode of Mr. Ross. It did not take him long to again reach the river mouth, and as he flew past the spot where, a few minutes before, his enemies had waited for him he could not but see the sagacity with which they had selected the place. He was grateful for his deliverance thus far, but he knew that there was no time for investigation, for the yelps and howlings distinctly heard told him that his foes were hot on his trail and not far behind.

Out on the lake he dashed, and still on they came. Alec is hot and excited now. The strain on him is beginning to tell, and he feels it. He knows that he could put on a desperate spurt and get far ahead, but would they not, with that long, steady louping of theirs, gradually creep up again, and, finding him about exhausted, make a desperate spurt, and thus run him down? But he is resolved to succeed, and so he nerves himself and carefully speeds along, while perhaps not five hundred yards behind are those merciless pursuers that will not be shaken off. In this way about ten miles are passed since the mouth of the river was left. Still on and on they come. The moon is now sinking low, and the shadows are weird and ghostly. Auroras, phantom-like, flit in the northern sky, while some of them seem like frightened spirits flying before avenging enemies. The sight is depressing to Alec, and so he turns his eyes from beholding them while still on he speeds.

Hark! What is that? It is like the bark of a dog that is instantly hushed. To Alec it seemed a dream or an illusion; and yet he could not help putting on a spurt of speed and veering a little out of his course to see the rocky islands, surrounded by the smooth ice, from which the dog's bark seemed to come. As he swiftly dashed along, how suddenly all things changed to him, and quick and swift was his deliverance. There was Mr. Ross with his three Indians and a number of dogs.

Alec was saved. He had fairly run into his deliverers. But no time was to be lost. Fortunately, a high rocky island for a moment hid the wolves, that were now following wholly by the scent.

With their double-barreled guns, loaded with balls, the three Indians rapidly scaled the rocky isle, on the opposite side of which they would be hid and yet within easy range of the wolves as they came along on Alec's trail. Mr. Ross and Alec had all they could do to quiet the dogs and keep them still, as some of them were eager to follow the Indians. Only a few minutes elapsed, as Alec's spurt had only put him a half a mile or so ahead of the wolves, when the guns rang out once, and then again as the second barrels were fired. Let loose the dogs now, and let everyone shout for the rescue and the victory! Five wolves were killed outright, and one was so badly wounded that the dogs soon ran him down and dispatched him. The other wolves turned and fled. Mr. Ross would not, at that hour, allow any pursuit of them.

The morning star was shining ere home was reached, and Alec was the hero of the hour.

CHAPTER V.

The Invitation to the Indian School Examination and Sports—Trapping Experiences—The Cunning Cross-fox—Frank Seeking Aid from Memotas—Method of Successful Trap-setting—Joyous Trip to the Mission—An Abiding Christian Civilization for the Indians—Sam's and a Young Indian's Novel Hunting Methods—Wild Cats Captured—The Queer Battle Between a Fox and a Wild Cat.

WHEN the boys returned home from a splendid outing on their skates they were greeted by Mr. Hurlburt, the missionary from the Indian Mission, who cordially invited them all to the half-yearly examinations at the school, which were to be held the Friday before Christmas in the forenoon, and then would follow the usual games among the Indian boys in the afternoon.

The boys soon found that Mr. Ross and the missionary had been long discussing the matter, but had as yet come to no decision as to the different games in which the white boys might, if they so desired, compete with the Indian lads.

Alec, of course, wanted to enter for the dog-race and the skating. Frank wanted to try his skill with the snowshoes, but Sam gravely shook his head and said he feared he would be lonesome ere the race ended.

"Well, what will you enter for?" said Frank, as he turned to Sam after this sally, which had set everybody laughing.

"Indeed I don't know, unless it should be tobogganing," he replied.

This also caused a good deal of amusement, as Sam's efforts in this line thus far had not been much of a success. He had caused a good deal of fun and some excitement by the extraordinary way in which his toboggan had several times shot out of the regular route and gone off on some erratic lines, perfectly oblivious to the interests of life and limb. He had one strong characteristic: he would hang on no matter which way or to what place his toboggan, under his erratic steering, flew with him. Once, in the middle of a hill, it shot off at a tangent and ran over an Indian woman. So unexpected was the attack, so deep was the drift into which she was hurled, and so rapidly did the flying toboggan get out of sight, that the poor, superstitious old woman ever after declared that it could have been no other than the Muche Manetoo, the Evil One, that struck her.

As a couple of weeks would elapse ere the day for the examinations and sports would arrive, the matter was left in abeyance as to the sports in which the boys should enter. A cordial acceptance of the invitation was of course intimated.

In talking the matter over afterward it was decided that only in one race or sport should each of the white boys enter. The number was limited as the Indian boys were numerous, and it might perhaps cause jealousies. So it was finally decided that Alec should try with his dogs in the four-dog race, Frank should be a competitor in the skating match, and Sam, with Spitfire, should contend in the one-dog race, or else enter in the skating backward contest.

From knowing the skill of the Indian boys in everything else, Mr. Ross felt that in these selected were their only chances of success. Of course, it was felt that Alec should have been in the skating contest, but as it was essential that each owner should drive his own dogs, and Alec had such confidence in his now splendid team and was so proud of them, he decided in favor of his dogs.

Mr. Ross's advice to them all was to keep themselves in good trim for any sudden emergency that might turn up, especially if it should happen that the young gentlemen in the Hudson Bay Company's service should decide to compete, or should themselves challenge them.

Full of most exhilarating sport as had been the bright sunny days since winter had set in nearly two months before this, the incentive of the coming races gave a new zest to their sports and pastimes, and so there was snowshoeing by day as well as rapid dog-traveling under auroral lights by night.

Among other things, it was arranged with Memotas that, as his hunting grounds began not many miles away from the place where Sagasta-weekee was built, the boys should have the privilege of hunting in all that section of the country under his guidance when necessary, and as much alone as they desired. Mr. Ross secured for them about a dozen steel traps apiece, and either he or Memotas instructed the lads in the methods of setting them for the different fur-bearing animals, such as mink, marten, otter, wild cat, and especially for the different varieties of foxes that were so abundant in those regions. In addition to this they were taught how to make the spring snares of fine twine for rabbits and partridges. Thus they learned much of the habits and instincts of various animals, and were delighted and profited by these lessons learned out in the school of nature, amidst such favorable surroundings.

When the boys saw the great number of tracks of the various wild animals that so speedily packed down the snow in runs in various directions through the forests, they were sanguine that great success would attend their hunting efforts. But as they drove in day after day with nothing more valuable than some rabbits or a few ptarmigan, or some other kind of partridges, they were half-discouraged, and told Mr. Ross they were surprised at their poor success.

Frank was especially mortified at his ill success. He had for days set his trap for a beautiful cross-fox that he had once or twice seen. Nearly every day he found his traps sprung and the bait gone. That it was the same fox Frank discovered by the fact that he had lost part of one of his hind feet. This Mr. Ross said doubtless happened long ago in the trap of some hunter. The fox had not been quick enough to spring away, and had thus been caught by part of his foot. If it were in the winter time when he was thus caught he doubtless ate the part of the foot that was held in the teeth of the trap without feeling any sensation of pain, as the cold would quickly freeze it solid. If he were caught in the summer time he would use the most desperate efforts to pull himself loose ere he would use his teeth, and then, of course, he would suffer much in the operation. Hence in the winter time a fox, as a general thing, if only caught by one foot, cuts himself off in a few hours, but in summer time he has been known to remain in a couple of days. Indians often talk of clever three-legged foxes in the woods.

One pleasant day Frank persuaded Memotas to go out with him and help him set his traps for that old fox that had so long tantalized him by his tricks and was getting fat on his bait. This the old man did with pleasure, for he had become very much attached to Frank. When they reached the place, to which they had come on Frank's dog-sled, the Indian very carefully examined the region around for quite a distance. He told Frank where the fox's den was, and said that now that he had become so well acquainted with Frank perhaps a stranger might get hold of him. He asked Frank to show him how he had generally set his traps that had been so unceremoniously sprung and robbed of the bait. This Frank proceeded to do, and, as he thought, very quickly and cleverly sprung back and baited them. Memotas watched him go through all the process, and then rather coolly took him down by saying:

"Good trap, well set, plenty of bait; might perhaps catch a puppy or old crow, but never fox."

This seemed rather rough on Frank, and he was

glad that Sam was not there to improve the occasion with some further caustic remarks.

When the Indian saw that Frank seemed so crestfallen at his comments he at once hastened to assure him that they all had to learn much about these animals, and now he said:

"You and I will go to work and see if we cannot get that fox in a trap again, even if his half foot tells us he has been there before."

The first thing they did was to decide where to set the traps.

"Not much hurry, though, about that," said Memotas. "We must first have a fire to burn all of Frank off the traps."

This was a bit of a puzzle to Frank at first, but when Memotas told Frank that every time he handled a trap or a bit of bait he left enough of himself on it for the fox to know all that he wanted to about him it was more unintelligible than ever.

At a spot about a couple of hundred yards away from where the traps were to be set a fire was built. When it was brightly burning Memotas cut a long pole, and then, springing or setting the trap, had Frank fasten a good-sized piece of meat as bait securely on with a fine wire.

"Now," said Memotas, as he carefully lifted up the set trap on the end of his pole, "we will burn old Injun and Frank off that trap and bait."

Then he held the trap in the fire until the meat fairly sizzled and the steel trap was quite hot.

"Guess all Injun and Frank now have gone up in

smoke, so, Mr. Fox, you'll not find us when you come skulking round this trap, anyway."

The old man chuckled, and Frank now understood what he had meant.

Memotas walked very carefully to within some yards of the spot where he had decided to place the trap. Again addressing Frank, he said:

"We must not even walk there, for if we did we should leave some more of ourselves through our moccasins, and Mr. Fox would then be too sharp for us."

Giving Frank the pole with the trap on it to hold for a few minutes, the old man quickly moved back to a spot where some tall, slender live balsams were growing. Cutting one down, he trimmed off all the branches except a mere broomlike tuft at the top, taking care all the time not to touch any of those remaining with his hands. Returning with this long, broomlike affair, he vigorously used it on a spot some yards away. Then he took the long pole from the hands of Frank, and there in that place, thus brushed out, he carefully and skillfully laid the trap. Then with the long brush he deftly swept back a thin layer of snow over the trap and bait.

"Now, Frank," he said, "set the rest of your traps as you have been doing these past days, but do not go near that one we have just arranged."

This operation was soon performed by Frank in the different places suggested by Memotas. In carefully investigating these spots the fox would be apt to get caught in the one that had in it, as the old fellow put it, "no Frank or no Injun."

By a roundabout route they started for home. At nearly every place where Frank had set his snares for rabbits or partridges he was successful in finding game. At a couple of places the snares themselves were gone and the snow was badly trampled down. Here Memotas's knowledge came into play, and he showed Frank where a wild cat had seized a rabbit just as it had sprung into the snare, and then both had struggled and the spring pole had been dragged twenty feet or so before the strong twine had been broken. In another place the feathers strewn around showed where a fox had been too quick for Frank and had taken the partridge which had been caught.

Thus they pushed on, and at length reached home. A good dinner awaited them, and then Frank harnessed up his dogs again, and, hitching them to a beautifully painted cariole, took Wenonah and Roddy out for a splendid ride. The day was cold but brilliant. The little folks were well wrapped up in their beautiful furs, and so the drive over to the mission and back was much enjoyed.

At the mission house they went in for a short call on the family, where they were always welcome. As they could not remain for dinner a five-o'clock tea was quickly prepared and much enjoyed. When about to begin a great jingling of bells was heard outside, and to the delight of all in came Mr. and Mrs. Ross, who had been driven over by Alec and Sam. It seems the boys had both returned from their hunting routes shortly after Frank had left with the two children. After a hasty lunch they had coaxed Mr. and Mrs. Ross to let them drive them over, and so a couple of carioles were soon attached to their different trains. Plenty of robes were put in, and now here they all were, and, as always, were most cordially welcomed.

They spent a couple of hours with the members of this delightful family, who here as missionaries were doing such a blessed work, even if it were one of self-denial and at times sufferings. But Mr. and Mrs. Hurlburt, their two young daughters, and Miss Adams, the lady teacher, were so proud of the Indians, and of their genuine kindly ways, that they were happy and contented with their lot.

During the brief two hours spent at the home this afternoon, as well as on many other occasions, the boys had opportunities to see evidences of their kindnesses and tangible love to the sick and hungry ones who looked so much to them. Not only did they find in Mr. and Mrs. Ross real friends to help them, but by their very substantial contributions they made the missionary and his family the almoners of many gifts much needed by the poor Indians.

' Genuine Christians themselves, the owners of Sagasta-weekee did much to help in the spiritual uplifting of the people from the degradation and superstitions of a cruel paganism into the blessedness and enjoyments of a genuine Christianity and an abiding civilization.

The time quickly sped by. They had some earnest chat, a few delightful hymns and songs of the homeland, and then a brief but earnest prayer for Heaven's blessing on loved ones far away, upon themselves in that land and their different work, and also upon the Indians.

Then the dogs were roused, the carioles arranged, and the passengers were soon all aboard. The boys took their places firmly standing on the tailboards of the sleds that projected in the rear. Grasping the tailropes, with which they held themselves on and guided their carioles, simultaneously they cried, "Marche!" and with a spring they were all off together.

They had three splendid trains and were not badly matched for a short spurt. So amidst shoutings and laughter in the beautiful gloaming of that lovely evening they fairly flew over the icy expanse of Playgreen Lake. But blood will tell, and it was soon evident that although Alec had Mr. Ross as his passenger, and therefore the heaviest load of the three, he was surely forging ahead. With those long, houndlike legs, these round-barreled, small-headed, keen-eyed dogs need not take any second place in that crowd, and so it is that, catching the enthusiasm of the hour, and springing in unison with each other, they respond to Alec's cheery call, and seem to pick themselves up and so fly over the rest of the route to Sagasta-weekee that in placing them all that could be said was, "Alec first, the rest nowhere."

"Well done, Alec," said Mr. Ross, as he sprang out of the cariole. "If you equal the speed of the last two or three miles in the race with the trains of the village and the fort, I think the blue ribbon of first place will be yours. But where is your cap?"

Happy Alec! He had been so excited with the splendid speed of his dogs, and the perfect unison of their movements, that he did not seem to be conscious of the fact that the capote of his overcoat was hanging down his back and that his cap had left him a mile or two back on the ice. However, his abundant curly locks had been sufficient for him during the excitement of that blood-stirring race. He speedily pulled up the capote over his head, and Sam, who had seen his cap fall and had hastily snatched it up as his cariole flew by, now came up and restored it to him.

Frank, with the children, was the last in. His heavy dogs, while the strongest, were not so adapted for rapid traveling as the others.

"Well, we had the longest ride," said Roddy; "you folks went so fast you did not have such a nice long time as we did."

This happy way of looking at it pleased everybody, and all voted Roddy to be a philosopher.

The Indian servants had the dog-fish all ready, and so it was not long ere the twelve dogs were enjoying their well-earned supper.

When they had all entered the house the boys, as usual, were anxious to know of each other's success during the day. Not only had Frank, as we have described, gone out to his traps, but Sam and Alec had also driven some miles to the places where they, apart from each other, were also trying their skill in trapping various kinds of fur-bearing animals.

Sam had gone out for several days past in company with a son of Memotas. He was a bright young fellow, and he and Sam had suddenly become very confidential. It was evident that they had some great scheme on between them. What it was nobody seemed quite able to make out, and so their curiosity was much excited, especially when Sam had been seen in close converse with the cook, and had then after a hasty visit to the cellar hurried away with young Memotas. To make matters worse, Sam had dropped a couple of large onions ere he reached his sled. Then one of the maids said she heard him asking the mistress if she had any oil of bergamot, and if there was any castoreum left in the house. They did not get much information from him that night, and, strange to say, he was the first one after dinner that proposed bed. Before daylight a trusty servant called him, as Sam had desired, and even then, early as it was when he came down, young Memotas was there awaiting him.

Mrs. Ross insisted that both Sam and young Memotas should have a good, warm breakfast ere they started out. It is very dangerous indeed to start off in the morning without a good, warm, generous meal. While the two boys were eating their breakfast a trusty Indian called out Sam's dogs, and now there they stood longing to be off. They did not return until the afternoon, and then they proudly brought in two prime wild cats which they had captured. Sam that evening told how that he and young Memotas had found the tracks of them some days before, and that they had been busy ever since making a dead fall, and the last day or so they had been decoying them to the place by the scent of onions. This would bring them into the vicinity of the trap; but he said that he remembered reading somewhere that some animals were attracted by bergamot, and so he begged a little from Mrs. Ross, and sure enough there the two wild cats were securely caught. The weight of the logs had been increased by heavy stones, and so, he added, "The animals were quite dead when we reached them. As there were other tracks around we have been busy ever since making traps of the same kind."

Alec had not accomplished much beyond finding the frozen part of the hind foot of a marten in one of his steel traps. He noticed which way the animal had gone, and so, taking a couple of dogs out of his sled, he put them on the trail, and to his surprise and delight they quickly ran it down. He rescued it from them as speedily as possible. It was quite dead, but its beautiful fur was uninjured.

Frank was eager to be off again with old Memotas to see the result of the new method, to him, of trap-setting for a cunning old fox. But Memotas, who was wise and experienced himself, said:

"Wait one day more yet. That old fox not going to walk into that trap the first day, nor perhaps the second day. You have been well feeding him on plenty of bait, and he not a bit hungry. But when he get hungry perhaps he go prowling round to see if his friend hasn't come with any more bait for him. For foxes get to know traps that seem just set for them to live from."

This was all rather hard on Frank, but he had come to see that it was all true, and so he patiently waited until the old man came in and said he thought perhaps they might go and see if that fox was still playing any of his tricks. The train was soon harnessed, and away they flew over the icy lake, and then into the forest trail. On and on they went, until they came near the spot where the traps had all been set. Every one that Frank had set was sprung and empty, and the one that Memotas had set with such care was missing! Nowhere could Frank see it or any trace of it. Memotas quickly stepped out a hundred feet or so, and then began walking in a circle around the spot. He had not more than half completed the circle before he quickly called to Frank, who at once hurried to his side. Pointing to a peculiar spot in the snow that had been much disturbed, Memotas said:

"I think fox caught with both fore legs in the trap. He is now walking away on his hind legs and holding up the trap in his mouth. See, there he walk on two legs! See, there he rest!" And the old man began to hurry on, closely followed by Frank, to whom he explained every movement the fox had made.

"Must be a fine big fox to get away so far with the trap on both fore feet," said Memotas. "But listen!"

A strange snarling-like sound fell on their ears, and with it something like the fierce yelping of a fiery young dog. Memotas had quickly dropped flat on the ground in the snow, and Frank crouched beside him. The old man whispered to Frank to give him his long hunting knife.

"Some other animal, wild cat perhaps, meet fox, and they fighting. Keep still, I must go back to the sled for the gun."

Without making the slightest noise the old man glided back, and was soon lost to sight.

Fortunately, there was a dense clump of evergreen balsam or spruce trees between the contending animals and Frank. Then they were so absorbed in their own quarrel that they were not very alert in watching for others. However, Frank knew enough to keep perfectly still, although he confessed he clutched the knife several times more firmly as the blood-curdling snarls of the wild cat pierced the air so near. Soon Memotas was back again, and then the question was to get a successful shot at the wild cat, as it was evident the fox was sure enough. At first Memotas crawled forward closer to the trees, the branches of which, laden down with snow, reached to the ground all around. Carefully peering through the dense branches, he gaxed intently for a time, and then he silently beckoned Frank to come. Noiselessly he crawled up beside Memotas, and after his eyes had become accustomed to the work he was able to see the two animals not more than two hundred feet away. The two fore legs of the fox were securely fastened in the steel trap, which seemed to have closed on him about four inches up from his feet. The wild cat was a fierce old male, and was doing his best to get a good grip on the fox. This the fox was resolved not to let him have, and so he kept his face toward his foe, and whenever the latter would spring at him the fox would suddenly raise himself, and, throwing up the trap so securely fastened on his fore legs, would bang it down with a whack on the head of the wild cat. With a snarl the cat would suddenly back off and arch up his back and snarl worse than ever. It was the queerest battle that Memotas had ever witnessed, and every time the trap rattled on the head or body of the wild cat the old man fairly quivered with excitement and delight. To Frank the sight was also the oddest and queerest he had ever even heard of. At one skillful parry the fox, although so terribly handicapped, was able to give the cat a whack that sent him fairly sprawling in the snow. At the sight of this Frank had to crowd his fur mitten into his mouth to prevent him from fairly shouting out:

"Well done, old fox!"

Why they remained so in this one open place, Frank now saw, was because the fox was fearful that if he got in among the fallen logs or the rocks the wild cat would have the advantage, and thus succeed in springing upon his back, while he, so hampered, could make but little resistance. All at once Frank saw the animals cease both the attack and their noises. Memotas, quick and alert, suddenly brought his gun into position, and the next instant, as Frank heard the jingling of distant bells, there also rang out the report of the gun, and the wild cat tumbled over dead.

Springing up, Memotas called Frank to follow, and together they quickly hurried after the fox, that was now again desperately striving to get away.

Memotas did not wish to injure the valuable skin by piercing it with a ball, and so, picking up a heavy clublike branch of a tree, he quickly killed the fox without breaking the skin.

A few minutes after Alec drove up along the trail. He had visited his traps and snares, and had decided to take this trail on his way home. His bells were the ones heard by the two fighters. Well was it that Memotas's quick ears also heard them, and that he was able to fire before the wild cat had fled into the forest.

They were soon all on their way home again. The fox was a great beauty, and although it was a cross, yet it was so nearly black that a large sum was given for it.

For many a day after Frank talked and laughed about that oddest of all fights, the one between the trapped fox and the fierce old wild cat.

CHAPTER VI.

The Winter Birds of the Great Lone Land—The Whisky Jack—The Ptarmigan—Their Beds in the Snow—Mission Visits—Cupid's Darts—The Wood Supply—Primitive Way of Capturing Partridges—Great Snowy Owls—Methods of Capture—Sam's Experience—The Fearful Grip of the Owl's Claw.

"Where are your singing birds?" said Sam one morning as he came in from having taken Wenonah and Roderick out for a drive with the dogs. "We have traveled over a dozen miles and have not heard a single bird song."

"Only a whisky jack," said Roderick.

This reply of Roderick's made everybody laugh; for the shrill, harsh cry of the Indians' sacred bird, called by the very unpoetical name of whisky jack, is not very musical, but just the reverse.

"Our singing birds are all in the sunny South Land during these cold months," said Mr. Ross. "We have multitudes of them during our brief summer time. Then, at the first breath of the Frost King, they flit away and leave us so still and quiet."

"What about this saucy bird, here called whisky jack, that we meet with on all of our wintry journeys?" asked Alec.

"Well," replied Mrs. Ross, "you see, in the first place, that he is not very handsome. His bluish-gray plumage is not very attractive, but he has an inner coating of black down, and if you could strip him of both of these jackets you would find him to be a very small bird after all. The Indians used to call him their sacred bird. They never kill one, no matter how hungry they may be. They have some beautiful traditions associated with him. His voice, so harsh and loud, is, according to some legends, the cry of a fair maiden who, fleeing from a hateful suitor, was lost in a blizzard. In vain she called for her own sweetheart, until her once musical voice became so harsh and rough that it lost its beauty. To prevent her from falling into the hands of her hated suitor, just as he was about seizing her the magicians changed her, in answer to her prayer, into a bird, and this is the whisky jack."

"Our next most interesting winter bird," said Mr. Ross, "is the ptarmigan, or white partridge. The colder the winter the more numerous they seem to be. They are easily snared, like the rabbits, as they have certain favorite runs, and do not seem to observe the twine or wire loops into which they so foolishly run their heads."

"Where do they sleep at nights?" asked little Roderick.

"Faith, and I know," said Sam; "for was I not fairly frightened out of my wits by a lot of them one night when traveling late to the camp to drive over a snowdrift into which they were burying themselves? I saw them fly up high in the air, and then, like a stone, they just shot themselves down and buried themselves out of sight of myself and those who were with me."

"Yes," said Alec, "and I well remember how they startled me several times as they were getting up out of these queer beds in the deep snow away out from the dense woods. It always occurred very early in the morning, shortly after we had left our camps in the woods, where we had spent the night. I could hardly get used to the start they gave me, as sometimes they flew right up from under the feet of my dogs. They seemed like wee ghosts, they were so very white, and my dogs as well as myself were disturbed by their uncanny ways."

"Do they go back to the same snowdrifts night after night?" asked Frank.

"No," said Mr. Ross; "they are birds that move around a good deal, and as far as the Indians' observations go the same flock or covey never sleep twice in the same place. If they did the foxes and other animals that are very fond of feeding on them would soon discover their retreats, and would make short work of them."

Thus the days and weeks passed by. Sometimes all the boys, with Mr. Ross and a number of Indians, would be away on some great excursion after the bears or beavers. At other times shorter trips would be arranged, when but one or two of the boys would go.

Then there were the home sports and frequent visits to the traps and snares. The dogs were kept busy, and the skates and snowshoes were not forgotten.

The visits between Sagasta-weekee and the mission were very frequent, and it began to appear as if Cupid had donned a fur ermine coat, or a feather mantle, and had made a flying visit and fired a couple of his darts into the hearts of Frank and

Alec, and on these darts were the names of the two lovely daughters of the missionary. Whether this be true or not, or only a rumor brought by a relay of gulls, we cannot say, but Mrs. Ross affirmed that never since their arrival at Sagasta-weekee were these two young gentlemen so particular about their personal appearance, or so anxious to find some good and valid reason why they should be sent over to the home of the missionary. It was also remarked, by those who saw their two beautifully painted carioles made ready for the trip, that an extra soft fur robe or two were placed therein. Their skates were sometimes also carried along with them. It was also further remarked that they generally preferred starting early in the day, and it was an actual fact that, although the whole round trip need not have taken more than three or four hours, they generally did not return until long after dark. Rumors also reached Sagasta-weekee that on several occasions two beautiful carioles, with lovely white young ladies cozily wrapped up in costly furs, and driven by handsome young gentlemen, had been met with, fairly flying over the great icy routes, while the air was full of happy laughter that sounded very much in unison with the music of the little silver bells that hung on the collars of the splendid dogs. And furthermore, it was well known that among the skating parties Frank and Alec were generally found skating with these same two young ladies. Their explanations were that their skates seemed to glide more in unison with each other, and in fact that there was a sort of affinity between them. Then their joy was complete when Mrs. Ross invited the whole family from the mission to come early and spend the day with them at Sagasta-weekee. It was remarked that these two young gentlemen generally had word that the devoted missionary had been using his dogs very much lately on his long trips among the distant bands of Indians, and it would be a capital idea for some of them to drive over with their fresh trains and bring back some of the family. This happy suggestion was of course carried out, but it was observed that the carioles of the aforesaid young gentlemen, when they returned, only had in each of them a sweet-faced, beautiful young lady, and they said that the trip had been "perfectly lovely!"

What happy days those were! To Frank and Alec had come their first young lovedreams, and they were pure and sweet and stimulating. Cynics and crusty, disappointed old bachelors might make fun of these youthful lovers and make some sarcastic remarks; still, after all, where is the noble, healthy, splendid young man of fifteen or sixteen that has not safely passed through these same ordeals and as a general thing survived? So let Frank and Alec have these daydreams and thus enjoy themselves. They will be none the worse, but rather the better, when the ordeal is over, as it is with those who safely get through with a lingering attack of the measles or scarlet fever.

One day Mr. Ross sent old Mustagan out into the woods to select a place where the next year's supply of wood could be obtained. His instructions were to find a dense forest of tall, symmetrical trees from which a trail or road could be easily made to Sagasta-weekee. Then choppers would be sent in, and some acres of this forest would be cut down and there left to dry for twelve months. The result would be that at the end of the year's time the trees would be in splendid condition for firewood. The next operation was to have these trees all cut up in lengths that could be easily handled, and then dragged home by the dogs on their long sleds when there was abundance of snow on the ground.

Sam asked for the privilege of accompanying Mustagan. As the walk was only a few miles, the old Indian was pleased to have the bright young paleface go with him. As they were to go through the forest, where there was not as yet the first vestige of a trail, they at once strapped on their snowshoes. Mustagan's only weapon was his ax, while Sam carried a small rifle. Very much sooner than they had anticipated they found a suitable grove, the limits of which Mustagan at once proceeded to mark off with his ax. These few marks thus made on some of the trees were all that was necessary to secure the property.

They had seen but little game, and so all that Sam had fired at had been a passing rabbit or ptarmigan. While on the home trip a beautiful covey of partridges came flying by them and lit in a large balsam tree but a few hundred feet in front of them.

"I wish I had brought a shotgun instead of this rifle," said Sam. "I think we might have had more than one of those partridges."

"Suppose we try and get them all without any

gun," said Mustagan, in a tone that seemed to indicate perfect confidence in the experiment.

"If we get two of them before they fly I will be delighted," said Sam, as he raised his gun and tried to get a shot at two in a line. However, before he could fire Mustagan quickly stopped him and said:

"No, no, not that way. I will show you how. Step back and keep still, and see how our fathers used to get them before the white man's gun came into the country."

Sam naturally thought of the bow and arrows, but as Mustagan had none along he wondered if the old man was going to quickly try and make some. In the meantime Mustagan had quietly slipped back into a grove of tall, slender young trees that grew up like great fish poles. Here he quickly cut down one that could be easily handled by a strong man. This he rapidly trimmed of all its branches, and then quietly returned with it to the spot where Sam was watching the birds. Stooping down to one of his moccasined feet, Mustagan untied the deerskin string with which the moccasin had been securely fastened around his ankle to keep out the snow. Cutting off a piece about two feet long, he again fastened up his shoe, and then, with the string thus secured, began to make a snare out of it. He first tied one end of the string securely to the smaller end of the long pole; then in the other end of the string he made a running slip noose, which he arranged so that it would be about four inches in diameter. Then began the strangest part of his proceedings, and one only possible in a land of such intense cold. Taking his hand out of his mitten, Mustagan wet his fingers with his saliva and then immediately rubbed it on the deerskin string. As fast as it was thus wet it froze as stiff as wire, and stood straight out from the stick. Rapidly did the Indian thus wet the whole string, the loop of the slip noose included, until the whole stood out as though made of steel wire. Then, cautioning Sam not to move, Mustagan, carrying his long pole with this uniquely formed noose on its end, moved cautiously and quickly under the tree in which the partridges were still sitting. Carefully he began raising up the pole until it was higher than the head of the partridge nearest the ground. Then he deftly brought it so that the noose was directly over the head of the bird. With a quick jerk he pulled the pole down with the head of the bird in the noose of the string, which, of course, tightened with the sudden jerk. Mustagan quickly killed the bird by crushing in the skull. Then, loosing it from the string, he rapidly went through the whole process again of moistening the string with his saliva and arranging the noose as before. In this way he succeeded in securing the whole covey of those partridges. From his favorable position Sam watched the whole operation, and was much delighted with the success of the old Indian, who had in this way, without the loss of one charge of powder, or even an arrow, secured ten or a dozen fine, plump partridges. On their way home, in answer to Sam's many questions as to his reasons for adopting this method of capturing the partridges, the Indian stated that the secret of his success in getting them all was the fact that he began by catching in his noose the bird lowest down. "When you do that," he added, "the birds above think that as those below them go down they are just flying to the ground to see what they can find to eat. Never take a bird that is higher up in the tree than any other. If you do you get no more. The rest will at once fly away."

Another bird that remains all winter in those cold North Lands is the great snow-white owl. His wonderful covering of feathers, even down to the toes, enables him to defy the severest frost. He generally sleeps by day in some dense balsam tree, and then is ready, when the sun goes down, for his nightly raids upon the rabbits and partridges. He is also fond of mice, and as there are some varieties of these active little creatures that run around a good deal even in the winter, and at night, the owls are ever on the lookout for them, as well as are the foxes. Sometimes these great white owls in their night huntings fly far away from their usual resting places. Then they are in great trouble, especially if there are no trees with dense branches among which they can hide. If the bright sun happens to peep up over the horizon ere they are safely stowed away in some shadowy place, they are at the mercy of any foe. Sometimes they alight on the icy or snowy surface of the lake. They are then easily captured. When a clever Indian dog-driver sees one thus standing out on the ice he quickly stops his dog-train, and, running toward the bewildered owl, gets on the side on which the sun is shining. Then he makes sufficient noise to keep the owl excited and looking toward him. In doing this the owl has to let the bright, brilliant rays of the sun shine right into his great, staring eyes. The man, with nothing but his long whip in his hand, keeps approaching, taking care, however, that his shadow does not fall on the bird. If he did, that instant the owl would be off. So the man keeps enough to one side to have the owl always in the brilliant light. The result is he does not see the approaching man. When near enough the man uses his whip in such a way that the long lash winds itself suddenly around the neck of the owl, and he is thus captured.

When better food is scarce these large owls are eaten by the Indians. Some are so fond of them that they are ever on the lookout to capture them. They have several methods by which they catch them. One is to fasten an upright pole securely in the ice. On the top of this is nailed a little board, and on this is set a steel trap or snare. The owls get tired with their constant flying about, and, seeing this handy resting place, are then quickly caught as they alight upon it. Another method was explained to Sam by an old Indian hunter, and with some help in securing the material they had a great deal of fun in trying it. The first thing they did was to make a great black rag mouse about as big as a beaver. To this was added a tail about five feet long. Then to the nose of this great bogus mouse was attached one end of a large ball of twine. This was the whole outfit, except, of course, the guns. One evening an Indian arrived with the news that at a certain place the great white owls had been seen in numbers, and perhaps it would be a good place to go and see what could be done in capturing some. As it was a very pleasant evening and the place mentioned was not very far away, Sam had little Roderick packed with him in his cariole, and with the mouse, ball of twine, and gun, and attended by one of the Indian servants, they drove over to the spot. The big mouse was placed on the snow as far out from the shore as the string would allow. The dogs with the cariole were driven into the shadow of a large spruce tree that grew on the very edge of the lake. Here the Indian, with Sam and Roderick, although completely hidden in the shade, could see distinctly everything outside, for the moon was now up and shining with wondrous beauty. For a time they remained there under the tree in complete silence. Then the clear vision of the Indian enabled him to be the first to detect the presence of an owl.

"Hist!" he quietly uttered, and then as he pointed out the object they were able to see a great owl sailing round and round up in the air, perhaps fifty feet directly over the big black bogus mouse. Suddenly he made a swift dive down for it. But at that instant the Indian, who had hold of the end of the cord, gave it a sudden jerk and pulled the mouse in a dozen feet or so nearer to them. This apparent big jump of the mouse seemed to disconcert the owl, and so he quickly flew away. But it was only for a moment, and then back he came. Round and round in circles he flew, getting nearer and nearer all the time, when once more he dashed down on the big mouse. But another sudden jerk had pulled the mouse out of his reach, and so the owl failed once more.

"Get your gun ready," said the Indian to Sam; "he will be mad now, and so we will soon have him near."

It was just as the Indian had predicted. The owl seemed angry at having been fooled the second time, and so when he rose up again and saw that great big mouse, which would, to judge by its size, make him such a famous supper, he dashed at it again most savagely. But once more it jumped away from him, as now the Indian kept pulling it in like a mouse running away. Seeing this the owl lost all caution, and was soon within range of Sam's gun, which speedily rang out its sharp report, and the great ghostly bird fell suddenly on the ice not more than forty or fifty feet away.

"Look out for his claws," said the Indian to Sam, who had at once rushed out to secure his game. But the warning came too late. Sam, seeing only the beautiful mass of white feathers and the great staring eyes, had reached out his naked hand, from which had dropped his mitten, to seize hold of the owl. But the savage bird lying there on its back was only wounded, and so when Sam's hand was reached out to seize it the very opposite happened, for the owl, with one of its terrible talons, closed on Sam's hand with such a grip that the poor boy fairly howled from the pain. The sharp claws had pierced him to the very bone, with a grip he could not break. The Indian, however, quickly came to his rescue, and pulling out his keen hunting knife he skillfully encircled the owl's leg with its sharp edge. This severed every sinew and tendon, and caused the claws to be so powerless that they could be easily pulled out of Sam's mangled hand.

The owl was speedily killed, the wounded hand carefully wrapped up, and the return to Sagastaweekee was made as quickly as possible. For weeks Sam suffered from his wounds ere they healed, and always after, although he shot a number of owls in this and other ways, he took good care never to let a naked hand come in contact with an owl's claws.

Poor little Roderick, who had gone out that evening in great expectancy of a good time, had had his sympathies so aroused by Sam's howlings that he began crying in sympathy, and kept it up until home was reached.

CHAPTER VII.

Wounds from Claws versus Teeth Discussed—Mr. Ross's Story of the Battle with the Eagles—Their Mountain Aerie—Their Hunting Skill—Their Voracity—The Eaglets—The Conflict—The Result—The Painful Wounds.

THE next day, as Sam was having his hand dressed, quite a discussion arose in reference to which wounds were the more painful, those received from the teeth of wild animals or those from the claws. Sam's present opinion, very decidedly expressed, was that those from the claws were the worse. This was the general testimony also of the Indians when questioned on the subject, one of their reasons being that the teeth were smoother and did not make such a torn, jagged wound as did the claws. Another was that the claws were very much dirtier than the teeth, and hence the wounds of the claws were much slower in healing than were those from the teeth.

"But what about hydrophobia from the bites of the dogs and wild animals?" said Frank.

To this Mr. Ross's reply was that that dreadful disease was about unknown among them, although there were said to have been some cases occurring from the bites of the fox.

"Did not a Governor-General of Canada die from the wounds received from the bites of a fox?" said Alec.

"Yes," replied Mr. Ross. "It was a tame fox, but it was supposed that it had gone mad."

"Perhaps it had been bitten by a mad dog, and then became mad itself," said Sam.

"That is in all probability the correct solution of the difficult problem, which for a long time troubled many medical men and others," said Mr. Ross.

"Are there any other birds in this country with claws or talons equal to those of this great owl?" asked Sam.

"O yes," replied Mr. Ross, "those of the great eagle, which is the first of all the migratory birds to reach us, are more terrible. It is generally seen during the March moon, and so the Cree Indians call that moon, or month, Mikisewpesim, the eagle moon. The Indians prize the feathers of the golden eagle very highly. The magnificent war bonnets of the great chiefs are made of them, and every warrior of any note is very ambitious to have his eagle plumes. They are hunted only for their feathers, beaks, and claws. Their flesh is worthless. They are very wary birds, and it is indeed a skillful hunter who can get within range of one of them by ordinary stalking. They build their nests, or aeries, as they are called, away up on the most inaccessible cliffs, where it is dangerous for even the most experienced mountain climbers to follow. When not engaged in nesting they spend a great deal of time in circling around in the bright blue sky, at heights so great that the eye can scarce discern them, and where the arrow or bullet of the best-armed Indian fails to reach them. Indian cunning, however, sometimes enables them to capture the eagles in traps, and then their beautiful pinions, that had enabled them to soar away into the blue heavens above, become, next to the scalps of their enemies and the necklaces of the grizzly bears' claws, the proudest ornaments with which they can decorate themselves."

"Did you ever have one attack you?" said Sam.

"Or did you ever try to get hold of a wounded one's talons with your naked hand?" said Alec.

This latter question caused some laughter at Sam's expense, as at him it was evidently aimed, in view of his recent mishap with the owl. Mr. Ross's answer was grateful to Sam, as it stopped the laughter and showed that others might make the same mistake or meet with similar adventures.

"Yes, indeed," said Mr. Ross, "for I can answer both questions that way. It was long ago when my father had charge of a Hudson Bay trading post away west of this, where the Rocky Mountain ranges were not very far distant from us. I was fond of sport, and went with the Indians on all sorts of hunting adventures. Sometimes we would be gone for days together, and have all kinds of strange experiences. We hunted every kind of wild animal that roamed in the prairies, in the foothills, or in the mountains themselves. Very glorious was the scenery among these magnificent mountains. Once when out with some Assiniboines, or Mountain Stonies, as they are generally called by the whites, we saw a large eagle attack a mountain sheep with such fury that the sheep lost its footing and went whirling down the mountain side to certain destruction. The eagle, instead of swooping down on the quivering carcass, as we had expected it to do, dashed at what we now observed for the first time— a little timid lamb that its mother had vainly tried to defend. The fierce eagle, with an exultant scream, fastened its strong talons into the back of the frightened little creature, and then, flapping its great wings, began slowly rising from the rock. We watched it as it slowly flew away until it landed on a ledge of rocks away up on a mountain side near the top. As soon as it landed we observed that there was its aerie, for from a clump of sticks some little heads were outstretched for food. The eyes of my Indian attendants gleamed with satisfaction, and they said:

"'We will soon have your feathers, old Mr. Eagle, and that will stop your destroying our mountain game.'

"While the side of the mountain on which the eagles had built their nest was quite precipitous, the back part was easily scaled, so that hunters with level heads could climb, by being careful, up so high that they could really look down into the eagle's nest. The nearest point from the nest that we could reach was perhaps fifty feet away. We did not, however, at once go that near. We did, however, crawl near enough to see the fierce, savage way in which the old bird tore that young mountain lamb to pieces and fed the voracious young eaglets, that struggled and fought with each other in their mad greed. While they were thus being fed by the old male bird we saw the mother arrive with a rabbit in her talons. When she saw the feast that had been provided for the young brood she laid the rabbit on one side, and patiently waited until her mate had satisfied the voracious appetites of the brood. Then she and the other eagle tore to pieces the rabbit and devoured it, with what was left of the mountain lamb.

" 'Big dinner all around, everybody full,' said my Assiniboines; 'big sleep next, then old ones go away for a big fly, and then we set our traps for them; but while they sleep we eat and sleep too.'

"We drew back very cautiously into a ravine about a quarter of a mile down the mountain side, to a place where we had noticed some dry wood, for we were not quite above the timber limit. Here we made a fire and had something to eat. It was difficult to make the tea, as the water, although boiling, had so little heat in it at that height on the mountain. We unstrapped our blankets and lay down near the fire and went to sleep, for we were very weary, having been up some nights before on the lookout for a mountain lion that had been lurking about. I woke up after a couple of hours' sleep and found that both of the eagles had been seen by the watchful Indians to fly away from the nest. As the length of their absence was very uncertain, the Indians quickly set to work to make the snares in which they expected to entrap them. Steel traps were unknown in those days, and so the Indians had to make theirs out of their strong buffalo sinews and deerskin twine.

"When we went back to the place where we could overlook the nest it was evident that there would be some difficulty in getting down onto the ledge where the young eaglets lay quietly sleeping. After various trials it was decided that the only way was for one of our party to be lowered over and let down by the rest. As I was much the lightest one, and as the supply of material that we had with us out of which to improvise a rope was very limited, I was the one selected to go down and put the snares in position. It was decided that we would not disturb the eaglets to-day, but would leave them alone for the present, for fear the old eagles would become alarmed and suspicious, and we would fail in capturing them. The rope, such as it was, held me all right, and I landed near the nest. The young birds were so gorged with the flesh of the mountain lamb that they were very stupid, and hardly stirred. I set to work as speedily as possible to arrange the snares, so that the eagles would step into them. As they were all constructed on the running noose principle we knew that they would quickly tighten around the feet if once they were stepped into. My principal difficulty was in finding places where I could tie the other ends of the snares. Eagles are very powerful, and can drag by the foot great weights. So I knew that all our work would be lost if I did not succeed in tying them so that their most desperate struggles to get loose would be in vain. However, I succeeded at length, and then I was hoisted up and we all returned back a mile or so and there camped for the night.

"The next morning, before we reached the spot, we heard enough to convince us of the success of our scheme. Eagles can make a big noise if they try, and two captured eagles and some frightened young ones were noisy enough as we drew near and investigated. Both eagles were firmly caught in these snares of rolled and twisted sinews, which, although not much thicker than common wire, were sufficiently strong to hold them. The Indians wished to shoot them at once, but I had long had an ambition to own a live, full-grown eagle, and therefore I would not let them fire. The rope of yesterday was soon brought into use again, and I was lowered down once more to the rocky ledge, armed only with a stout club about four feet long. The noise was simply deafening that was made by these angry birds. The instant I landed they flew at me most viciously. Well was it that the strong sinews held them firmly. As it was I had a rough time of it. I would watch my opportunity and try to strike one of them a heavy blow on the head with my club. To my surprise I received in return a heavy whack from a powerful wing. Their wings were free, and the length of the string enabled them to attack me from all quarters. Seeing my difficulties, I called to my Indians to shoot the female bird, and thus leave me but one to tackle. This they did by shooting her through the head. This left me but the old male bird. I think I could have easily knocked him over the head, but my ambition was to capture him and to take him home as a trophy. I unfastened the noose of the dead eagle, and, tying it to the rope, had the Indians hoist it up to the top. Then I made the attempt to tie together the legs of the young eaglets to have them also drawn up to the summit.

What fighters they were! The way they struck at me with their little beaks, and in every way possible resented my interference with their liberty, was wonderful. My hands were sore and bleeding ere I succeeded in sending up the last of the four to my comrades. I had them throw down the snares, and with them I made a kind of a lasso which I tried to throw over the head of the vicious bird. As I threw it he coolly reached up and cleverly caught it in his beak, and snapped it in two as quickly as could a pair of scissors. I tried it again, and once more he was too much for me. Why he had not cut himself loose when in the snare was a mystery to me when I here saw how clever he was in cutting my lasso. It was looking rather discouraging, and I began to fear that he would have to be shot.

"My comrades had been amused spectators of my adventures, and now, seeing me uncertain as to what would be my best move, gave me some advice. It was this: 'Untie the other end of the long noose that holds him to the rock where you fastened it, and tie it to the rope, and we will pull him up and see what we can do with him here.' This plan struck me as a capital one, and so I immediately proceeded to carry it out. But I had decided on this plan without taking the eagle into my confidence, and so when I began handling the string he flew at me, and with beak and wings assailed me. I had foolishly dropped my heavy club, and so at first was about powerless. Fortunately, I had my hunting knife at my side, and quickly drawing it I fought for my life. The eagle cleverly warded off my lunges at him by striking me with his wings. Sometimes so heavily did his blows rain on me that it was a wonder I was not stunned. Apparently gaining courage by his success, he seemed to redouble his attacks, and for a time kept me wholly on the defensive. Making a sudden dash at him with the hope of plunging my knife into him, he so cleverly, with one of his wings, knocked aside my knife that in my stumble I found I had awkwardly cut the noose that bound him. As I knew that his talons were now free I presumed he would at once avail himself of his liberty and fly away. But he had now no such idea. His blood was up, and so with a scream of defiance, or triumph, he flew right at my face, with his great ugly talons extended, as though he would grip me up as he had done the lamb. When attacked we naturally will do anything to save the face, and so the instant he dashed at me I threw up my left hand to grasp hold of him somewhere. This fortunately arrested his dash at my face, and in the next instant I had plunged my knife under his outstretched wings into his very vitals, and he was a dead eagle. So terrible, however, was that death grip on my hand and wrist that it was not until I was hauled up with him to the top that the Indians were able to set me free, and then it was only done by cutting the sinews or muscles of each great claw and taking them out of my flesh."

"Well," said Sam, "that is a splendid story; but you must have suffered much more than I did, and so as regards my little experience with the owl, well, I think I'll *ould* my tongue."

And so he did.

CHAPTER VIII.

Sundays in the Great Lone Land—Services at the Mission—By Skiff or Canoe in Summer—By Dog-train in Winter—Napoleon, the Tame Bear, and His Load—Services at Sagasta-weekee—Missionary Journeys—Native Ministers—The Queer Sermon—Happy Christmas Times—New Year's, the Great Day—Oo-che-me-ke-se-gou—The Kissing Day—Varied Experiences—The Great Feast—Happy Indians—Thanksgiving.

SUNDAYS in the North Land! Yes, there are such days, and they come once in seven in the wild North Land as elsewhere, and right welcome they are; for they are days of gladness, not sadness—days in which loving homage is paid to the loving Father who is also the God of nature; and as nature rejoices in his bounteous care and infinite wisdom, why should not those in his kingdom of grace also be happy in the sunshine of his love?

"Serve the Lord with gladness," was the motto of Mr. Ross's religious life, and everyone under his influence or care felt that he was a genuine man and a safe leader to follow. His religious life, while decided and settled, was unobtrusive and kindly. It embraced the two commands, love to God and love to his fellow-man.

The mission some years before established among the Indians had been very successful, and a capacious church was there built. Every Sunday a large portion of the family went from Sagasta-weekee at least once a day, and there worshiped. The morning service was conducted in the English language.

This was done for two reasons: one was for the instruction and profit of all who spoke that tongue; the other was that the Indians who were learning the language might become the more speedily familiarized with it. The afternoon and evening services were conducted in the Indian language. However, if a number understanding the English language only happened to be present, both languages were used with the help of an interpreter. The church was on the shore of a pretty lake, and it was a very pleasant sight to see the gathering of the congregation. It was one quite different from what is generally seen as crowds usually gather for worship at the sound of the church bell. Here were no long streets, or even common roads or sidewalks. The homes of these Indians, both houses and wigwams, had been built around the lake shore on the various picturesque points, not far from the water's edge. Every family wanted easy access to the lake for water, and none of them wished to be far away from the landing places where they kept their canoes. The result was that it looked on Sundays, when they came to the church in groups, as if there were a pathway from every dwelling place. Then, as large numbers of the Indians lived out on points and islands away from the one on which the mission premises stood, the people, in the pleasant summer time, came from their various homes in their canoes to the house of God. Very picturesque indeed was the sight, as for an hour or so before the time of service the lake seemed dotted with the well-filled canoes of the well-dressed crowds of Indian men, women, and children. In winter the scene was completely changed. The frost had hid the sunlit, rippling waves under an icy pavement, as hard as granite. Frost and snow and ice were everywhere.

For the summer Sunday trips to the church Mr. Ross had several large sailing boats and safe skiffs that would hold all who wished to go to the morning service. In one, manned by four sturdy oarsmen, Mr. Ross and his family generally went when the weather was at all favorable. In winter the dogs were all called into requisition, and the sight at the church, when on a bright day the crowds were assembling, was as pleasant and interesting as in the summer time, when on the bright waters were seen coming the many beautiful, well-loaded canoes. From the Hudson Bay trading post there were always a goodly number present both in summer and winter. The officials and clerks prided themselves on the quality of their dogs and the beauty and completeness of their carioles and harness. Then some of the Indians had very valuable trains, and it was interesting to notice the number of persons that would be crowded into or on these dog-sleds and the strength of the dogs in pulling them. Very primitive were some of their sleds, and mongrel indeed were many of the dogs attached to them. Yet it was surprising to see how rapidly even the rudest-looking sledges got over the ground. The dogs seemed to know that it was the day of religious worship, and therefore their duty was to get their masters and mistresses to the church with as little delay as possible. Then on the return trip, of course, there must be no delay in getting them back for dinner. For some winters a great tame black bear used to be attached every Sunday to a long dog-sled. He was called Napoleon, and Alec and he became great friends. When ordered to start he would dash off in his rough galloping way and keep up the one steady pace until the church was reached. It seemed to make but little difference, such was his strength, whether two or ten persons were hanging on the sled. At the church he was tied to a post, and there quietly remained until the service was over, when he at the same rapid rate drew his load home again. Toward spring Napoleon disappeared and was not seen for months.

It was understood that there was to be no racing on Sunday, yet somehow everybody seemed to want to go just about as fast as possible. The terrible cold may have had something to do with this. Alec was generally sent on first, or else requested to wait some time after the others had started, as his dogs had become possessed with the habit of catching up and going ahead of everything in sight.

"Supposing, Alec," said Mr. Morrison, a young clerk of the Company's service, "that it were not Sunday, I should like to run ahead of your dogs and show you what traveling is."

"Supposing it were not Sunday, I should like to see you do it," was Alec's reply.

"Supposing it were not Sunday, here goes," was the saucy challenge of this young clerk, who thought he had the fleetest train in the whole district.

"Supposing it is Sunday," shouted Alec back to

him, for they were both on the Sagasta-weekee route. "I'll just go on and tell them you will be along after a while and dine with us."

It was considerably later when the clerk arrived. That afternoon, in conversation with Mr. Ross, he gravely stated that one of the temptations of that country was a disposition to travel rapidly, to and from church, on the Lord's day. Frank and Sam, as well as Mr. Ross, had been promptly informed by Alec of the challenge and the race with this young gentleman, and so when Alec heard the remark just mentioned he gravely replied:

"Well, Mr. Morrison, you need not have any qualms of conscience about your speed to-day. We started about the same time from the church, and it was a long time after I reached home ere you arrived."

This bit of sarcasm, so well put in, so tickled Sam that he fairly exploded, and with his handkerchief in his mouth he rushed out of the room. Soon after he was joined by Frank, and together they laughed until they were sore. The hypocrisy of the young fellow was so evident that they were delighted with Alec's comforting remarks.

Mr. Hurlburt, the missionary, generally came over and held an evening service at Mr. Ross's house every second Sabbath. The alternate Sabbath evening was spent in holding a similar service at the fort. These services were very delightful. The boys often drove over to the mission services in the afternoon with their trains and brought back with them Mr. and Mrs. Hurlburt, and when it could be arranged—which was frequently done—the two sweet young daughters.

To Frank, with his powerful train, was generally assigned the missionary, who was a large, portly man; to Alec, with his beautiful fleet train, was assigned the pleasure of bringing Mrs. Hurlburt, and at first Sam had the exquisite delight of tucking the robes of rich beaver around the fair young daughters from the mission home and carefully bringing them over to Sagasta-weekee. This pleasure was, however, soon taken from him. It was indeed a happy group that assembled around the hospitable tea table those delightful evenings. The boys used to plead so hard to be allowed to drive back with the loads that they generally succeeded in having their way, although Mr. Ross always took the precaution of sending an extra team of dogs under the guidance of an experienced Indian. This was necessary, as not only did vicious, mad wolves sometimes cross that route, but blizzard storms might suddenly come up, and then it would have gone hard with the boys with their young dogs to have kept the trail.

Mr. Hurlburt generally rode home in the extra cariole driven by this Indian. This enabled Frank to take the elder of the young ladies, and we must confess that, although Frank was very fond of the missionary, he had not the slightest objection in changing him for the daughter.

Frequently the missionary, with some faithful Indians, used to make long journeys with the dog-trains to distant places where no one had ever gone before with the Bible and its sweet story of God's love to man. During his absence his pulpit would be supplied by native ministers, who, though not as yet ordained, were eloquent in their way, and were a blessing to their fellow-countrymen. Even the white people who understood the Indian language used to listen with great pleasure to some of these gifted sons of the forest as they preached from full hearts of the love of God as revealed in the gift of his Son. In after years some of these younger Indians were educated and ordained, and are now regularly settled as ministers among their own people. There were some of them, however, who aspired to be ministers who were not a success. Some were too ambitious. Some, not content with talking about what they knew themselves, must launch out into deep waters, and so speedily they came to grief. Constantly did the missionary have them under his eye, and many were the lessons he was giving them. Some would, in spite of his best efforts, get beyond him. For example, one ambitious would-be minister said in his address before quite a large audience:

"Brothers, the missionary says the world is round. I don't believe it. It is flat as the top of that stove."

As he said this he pointed to the top of the great flat iron stove in which a fire was burning, for it was in the depth of winter. Of course the missionary was informed of this daring brother's unbelief, and a good lesson in geography had to be administered to him by means of the map of the two hemispheres hanging on the wall. He manfully acknowledged to the missionary his error, and promised to make it right with the audience the next time he stood up to address them. This he endeavored to do in the following manner:

"Brothers, I made a mistake when I last addressed you, when I said I did not believe that the world was round. It is round. I have seen it. It is like two moons flattened against the wall."

Of course this would never do, and so the missionary had to take him in hand again and give him another lesson. This time he used his large ball-like globe, swung on its axis in its frame, which was supported on three feet. Patiently the minister showed him how the world was like a great ball, round in every direction. Attentively the Indian listened, and carefully examined the globe and the frame in which it hung.

"Yes," he said to his teacher, "I was wrong. I have it now. I will explain it to the people."

When the first opportunity offered he was as good as his word, and so he thus addressed them:

"Brothers, I seem to be hard to learn, but I have got it now. Yes, the world is round every way. It is not flat even one way. It is round. Yes, it is round, but then it stands upon three legs."

So another and even more thorough lesson was needed to knock those three legs away.

As a general rule the Indians who were appointed to speak kept within their own depths, and very sensible and appropriate were their utterances.

Christmas Day and New Year's Day were great times of feasting and gladness at the mission village among the Christian Indians. On Christmas Day all the men, women, and children, arrayed in their very best finery, called at the mission house, and were each treated to a large cup of strong, well-sweetened tea and a big bun. Then they went to the fur-trading post, and there received the gratuities of tobacco and other things. Many called at Sagasta-weekee, and were cordially received. The boys were very much interested in them, and took great pleasure in assisting Mrs. Ross, as on this day it is expected that the white people only will pass the tea and cakes, and with their own hands also give their Christmas gifts to the poor and needy. In such a land there are many who require a great deal of just such help. After the matters of hospitality had been attended to there were many sports on the ice, and into these all who desired to enter were cordially welcomed. The boys were in their glory in these sports, and gallantly held their own against the lighter but more agile Indians. In the evening all the trains that could be mustered were harnessed up, and everybody who could get away went over to the mission church for the Christmas services, which, on account of the elaborate musical preparations, were held in the evening this year. The missionary, aided by his musical family, had been for weeks diligently employed in teaching the Indians to sing Christmas carols and other appropriate songs for this joyous occasion. The native choir acquitted themselves admirably, and everything passed off to the pleasure and delight of all.

New Year's Day is, however, the big day to the Indians, as it is on that day that the great annual feast is held in the church. This Christian festival has taken the place of the once heathen dog feast and other pagan ceremonials that the Indians held, with disgusting rites, before the missionaries came among them.

New Year's Day is called by the Indians Oo-che-me-ke-se-gou, which literally means "the kissing day." On this day the men claim the right to kiss every woman they meet, and, strange to say, every woman expects to be kissed, and is quite offended if she is passed by without being saluted in this way, which is so much more ancient and historic than the meaningless modern one of shaking hands. This Indian definition of New Year's Day vastly amused the boys, and when in the morning Mrs. Ross and Wenonah came in they, of course, had to be saluted in the orthodox fashion. This was very agreeable, but when the Indian cook came into the dining room, in answer to Mrs. Ross's ringing, Wenonah shouted out to the boys:

"This is Oo-che-me-ke-se-gou, and you must all kiss Nahkoomah, the cook."

Nahkoomah was not at all handsome, but she knew what day it was and claimed her rights, and so when the boys made a rush to get out she blocked the way in that direction, while Wenonah bravely cut off the retreat by the other door. Seeing themselves thus captured, they gracefully accepted the inevitable. A resounding smack was given her first by Sam, which was gingerly imitated by Frank and Alec. The boys afterward said that it paid grandly to give the cook the national kiss, as from that day forward she was ever pleased to prepare them the best dishes she could.

"I say, Frank and Alec," mischievously exclaimed Wenonah, "don't you know they keep Oo-che-me-ke-se-gou over at the mission?"

This sally very much amused all, and of course gave Sam a chance to remark that it was an elegant day for a sleigh ride; that he thought Frank and Alec's dogs needed some exercise; that the road to the mission was in capital condition, and perhaps they had better be off, and the sooner the better, for fear the young ladies should wear the glass of the windows thin, looking for their coming. Mrs. Ross here interposed, and stopped Sam's voluble utterances by saying that they were all going over a little after noon, in response to a very cordial invitation from Mr. and Mrs. Hurlburt, to witness the Indian feast and dine with them in the church. This was great news to all, and as there were only a couple of hours for preparation there was hurrying in every direction.

"Put on your best bibs and tuckers, my hearties," said Sam to Frank and Alec, "for this day is the event of your lives. Rig yourselves up so gallantly and finely that the sweet, blushing lassies over beyond will be so struck with your noble presences that they will, for the day at least, imagine themselves Indian maidens enough to at least comply with the customs of the day." But ere Sam had finished his long harangue, the blushing Frank and Alec were hunting up their best apparel and selecting the warmest robes for their dog-sleds.

While all are getting ready at Sagasta-weekee let us take a look at the feast, or rather first at the preparations necessary in such a land to feed ten or twelve hundred hungry Indians. About two months before the time a great council is held. The missionary is invariably asked to be the chairman, and a clever writer of the Indian syllabics is appointed secretary. Then, as a matter of form, it is moved by the chief and seconded by some other Indian of influence, "That we have the usual feast on Oo-che-me-ke-se-gou day." This is, of course, carried amid Indian applause. Then the question next asked is: "How much will each supply to make it a grand success?" Thus there is started a spirit of emulation that would astonish some white folks.

Big Tom says: "I saw the tracks of a moose. I will give half of him, when I shoot him," he adds, while the quiet laugh goes round.

Mustagan says: "I saw the steam curl up from a bear's den. I will give the largest bear, when I get him."

Soquatum says: "I have just heard of the coming of the reindeer. I will give one."

Thus it goes on as rapidly as the secretary can write their names and promises. Those hunters famous for killing the game that is good for food promise, as these already referred to have done, all kinds of animals, from a moose to wild cats and beavers. Those hunters whose skill is in killing the rich fur-bearing animals promise to exchange portions of the valuable products of their huntings for flour, tea, sugar, and raisins at the trading posts.

Everybody was expected to promise something, and then he was to do his best to get it.

This method of getting up a feast was a unique one. The idea of subscribing bears that were in their dens a hundred miles away, or moose, or reindeer, or other wild animals that were roaming in the forests or on the barren plains many scores of miles distant, was, to say the least, very different from civilized methods. When the council breaks up every man is interested in securing what he has promised, or something better. It often happens that the man who has promised a couple of wild cats succeeds in finding a good, full beaver house. A couple of these are worth more than the cats. The man who promised a reindeer may be lucky enough to kill a moose, and thus it is. However, they all try to do the very best they can. As these various supplies are brought in they are stowed away in the large fish house of the missionary, where they speedily freeze solid, and are thus kept sweet and good until required for use. About four days before the feast the wife of the missionary calls to her help a number of clever, industrious Indian women, and from morning until night the cooking goes on. Early in the morning of the feast day the seats are all removed from the church, and long tables are improvised that stretch from nearly end to end of the building. One long table is prepared at the upper end of the church for all the whites, who are specially invited by letter to attend. As they have all contributed largely to the feast, of course, they are welcomed.

It is an interesting sight to see that happy, expectant throng. Everybody, Christian and pagan, is welcome. No questions are asked. See the piles of provisions. Surely there is enough and to spare. Well, they will need a great quantity, for Indians have great appetites, and then there are many sick and feeble who could not come to-day, and they must be remembered. There are over a thousand out to-day, and while some scores are busy preparing the feast the others skate, play football, toboggan, and in other ways amuse themselves. Of course the inmates of the mission house are busy. To the missionary and his wife the Indians all look for direction and guidance. This is necessary, that everything may go off without friction. In addition, they have to be on hand to receive such white people as may come from the various trading posts and other places.

See, here they come from Sagasta-weekee! Alec is at the head of the company. His fleet dogs are never happy now except when first in every crowd. Cozily wrapped up in fur robes in his cariole are Wenonah and Roderick. Sam has brought over Mr. Ross, and to Frank has been intrusted Mrs. Ross. The boys are now skillful drivers, and so no mishap has occurred. Cordially are they welcomed, and as it is Oo-che-me-ke-se-gou the ladies are gallantly kissed by the gentlemen. With loving tenderness Mrs. Hurlburt kissed the three boys, and said she would do so in place of their precious mothers, who would doubtless think of them on that glad day. Then she turned them over to her young folks, while she hurried off to meet the later arrivals from the Hudson Bay Company's fort.

Sam was first escorted in by Wenonah, who, as she met the young ladies of the mission, exclaimed:

"Now this is Oo-che-me-ke-se-gou, and we are all of that way to-day."

Bravely did the blushing Sam pass through the ordeal, and then Alec and Frank, in a way that seemed to come quite natural to them, saluted in a good old-fashioned way the two fair ladies who had come into their young lives and were much in their minds.

"Sure," said Sam, "that's not bad medicine to take, at all, at all."

At this there was a great laugh, for Sam had blushed and stammered and acted as though it were an ordeal of great solemnity. There was a lot of fun and pleasantry for the next hour or so among these happy young people, while the older ones were busy looking after matters pertaining to the feast. Frank and Alec entertained the young ladies' friends with the latest news that had come in by the Christmas packet. Sam, with Wenonah and Roderick, played all sorts of pranks all over the house. When later arrivals came in and gravely kissed, not only the elderly ladies of the party, but also the beautiful young maidens, Alec and Frank's faces were studies that very much amused Sam.

"Indeed," he afterward said, "I thought it was going to be pistols and coffee for four, and may I be there to see the fun."

As the tender passion had not yet struck him, he

could thus afford to be amused at the ebullitions of jealousy that rolled so ominously into the young hearts of the chums. "Black as thunderclouds were their faces," he said, "as they saw these sweet young ladies, whom they in their callow affections would already wholly monopolize, kissed by a dozen different gentlemen during the day."

"How do you like 'O-jimmy-catch-the-cow' day, or whatever you call it?" he said to Frank, as he saw him glowering at a Hudson Bay officer who had just kissed his sweetheart.

"I don't like it at all," Frank replied, with gritted teeth.

"You mean you don't like it for other folks," replied Sam. "You took your medicine yourself very well, if I am a good judge, especially when you so lovingly displayed your osculatory skill on the sweet lips of peerless Rachel, whom that young prig of a Hudson Bay Company's clerk is now approaching."

"I'll fight him," said Frank, and his hot breath and clinched fists showed that he would have loved to pitch in just then.

"No, you will not," said Sam. "Hot-headed Englishman though you are, you are too much of a gentleman to make a row in this clergyman's house, and about his young daughter. But, Frank, I will give you a bit of comfort. While the beautiful Rachel gave you her sweet lips to kiss, she only turned her rosy cheek to all the other fellows, me included. So now no more of your English, 'I'll punch your 'ead for you.'"

Here Sam's advice, helpful and needed as it was, abruptly ended, as everybody was summoned into the church to the great feast. Frank was happy once again, as he was selected to take in his sweet Rachel, while Alec had her younger sister, Winnie, as his partner. Much to his delight, Sam came in with Wenonah and Roderick. Indeed, they were almost one and inseparable on such occasions.

Of the great feast and how it was enjoyed by all we have written in other volumes. Suffice to say that there was abundance for all. In addition, great bundles of food, with packages of tea and sugar, were sent to every sick or aged or feeble person, with loving good wishes of all. The feast was pronounced a great success. At the evening meeting, where, as in former years, the Indians gathered, with the chief in the chair, and where many speeches were delivered by the eloquent ones of the village, it was observed that among the happy things said there were words of gratitude to their kind, loving missionary and his family, and to the other white friends, in every address.

It was also noticed that many of the Christian Indians, rising higher in their thoughts, saw in all these blessings that had come to them the good hand of the Great Spirit, their heavenly Father, and so to him their grateful prayers ascended, and the most frequent word uttered was "nanaskoomowin"—"thanksgiving."

CHAPTER IX.

The Indian School Examinations—The Prizes—Noble Indian Boys—The Skates to Kepastick—The Various Sports—Foot Races—The Skating Race—Tricky Clerk Outwitted—Frank and Kepastick Tie as Winners—Football—Hockey.

THE day for the examinations and sports at the mission school arrived in due time. Fortunately, it was a very beautiful day, although it was many degrees below zero. But nobody now minded that. There were no fogs, or mists, or damps, and the dry, steady cold is always much more healthy and invigorating than changeable weather in any land. Everybody invited was present, and so the day's full program was well carried out.

Mr. McTavish, a chief factor in the Hudson Bay Company's service and the chief officer at the Norway House trading post, presided at the school examinations, which began promptly at nine o'clock. The schoolhouse was packed with the children and their friends, except the large platform at the upper end of the schoolroom, on which were seated the white visitors from Sagasta-weekee and the trading posts and mission.

The children were first examined in their reading lessons in both languages, Cree and English. In their own language they used the syllabic characters, invented and perfected by the Rev. James Evans, the founder of this mission. These syllabics, as their name indicates, each represent a syllable. The result is there is no spelling, and just as soon as a pupil, young or old, has once mastered these characters he begins to read. Three weeks or a month is considered quite sufficient time in which to teach a person of ordinary intelligence to read fluently.

Mr. Evans was several years in perfecting this invention. He begged from the traders the sheet lead that is found around the tea in tea chests. Then, making little bars of this lead, he carved out his first type. His first paper was made out of birch bark. His first press he made himself. His first ink was made out of soot mixed with sturgeon oil. Many were his difficulties and discouragements, but he triumphed over them all, and now here were hundreds of Indians reading in their own language the word of God.

The whole Bible, with some hundreds of hymns and a few volumes of good books, *Pilgrim's Progress, The Path of Life,* and others, have been translated and printed in these syllabic characters. The old Indians prize them very much, but it is interesting to note that, just as soon as the younger Indians understand English and get to be able to read in it, they prefer it to their own language and books.

The examinations in arithmetic, grammar, and geography were rather limited. It could not have been otherwise in such a place. All were, however, delighted with the splendid examination each class passed through in Bible history. The Indians have wonderful memories, and here the children delighted all with their knowledge of events from the creation down, and the accuracy with which they could quote long portions of the sacred book. The writing also won a great many complimentary remarks from all, and it is safe to assert that very few schools among white people could have made a better showing. The recitations were good, considering that they were uttered in a foreign tongue. The singing was delightful. The children sang in the two languages, and the soft, sweet, liquid Cree did not suffer in pathos and beauty in comparison with the more vigorous English. Of course, a number of prizes were given. A beautiful incident occurred when the prizes for the best recitations of the fourteenth chapter of St. John's gospel were being distributed. Among the competitors was a poor lad who when a babe had been so bitten in the hand and arm by a wolf that the arm had to be cut off near the body. Competing with him were several other bright boys. The chief prize was a splendid pair of new skates, which Frank had generously given for this competition. So even had been the boys, or rather so perfect were they in reciting, that the judges hesitated about selecting the winner of the first prize. When the boys who were well and unmaimed observed this there was a short, quiet consultation between them, and then one rose up and, respectfully addressing Mr. McTavish, said that the boys who had two hands, as well as two feet, had more ways of having sport and fun than Kepastick, who had only one hand, and so they asked him to have the judges decide that Kepastick should have the skates. Noble fellows! but that is just like young Christian Indian boys. The white people present were much moved by this beautiful incident of quiet unselfishness, and soon arranged that those kind-hearted lads should not go unrewarded.

By twelve o'clock the most successful examination of the school, up to that time, was over. The prizes were distributed, and while all the white people, as was customary, accepted the missionary's invitation and dined at the parsonage, the Indians sped away home for a brief dinner, and were then soon all back again, to compete in or to witness the sports.

The first races were run by some little girls. The distance was only a few hundred yards and back. These races caused a lot of fun and enjoyment. The prizes were little handkerchiefs, strings of beads, and other trifling things in which little Indian girls rejoice, and of course every little competitor must have a prize. Then there were races for little boys. It was great fun to see the sturdy little fellows so gallantly strive for victory. Meanwhile arrangements were being made for the more important races of the day. The courses had been marked out previously with flags, and so every class knew its course and ran accordingly. The fleetness and endurance of some of even the small boys were wonderful, and great was the interest, and even intense at times the excitement, when several well-matched competitors gamely struggled on for victory. In the races open to all comers the larger Indian boys were disappointed that none of the whites had entered, as they were anxious to test their own speed against them. There were races worth going across a continent to witness, and genuine and hearty was the applause that greeted the winners, who came in at such a rate that the white boys, while cheering as heartily as the others, saw how wise they had been in declining to put themselves against such runners as White Antelope or Spotted Deer, the winners.

When the skating matches were called Frank promptly entered the lists. His appearance was received with applause. Even the quiet Indian lads tried to make a noise to show their pleasure in greeting the handsome, manly fellow whose splendid gift had gone to Kepastick, the one-armed lad. Two or three young clerks or fur traders also entered for the race, one of them being the young man who had so abruptly left Alec the night of his fearful race with the wolves. The route marked out for the skaters covered in all about ten or twelve miles. It, however, so twisted in and out among the islands on the frozen lake, that many of the competitors would be in sight nearly all of the time. That the intending skaters might thoroughly understand the route, it had been marked out a week or ten days before the race, and it had been thoroughly understood that any of the competitors were at perfect liberty to skate over the grounds and get familiar with the different turning places, marked by little red flags.

Frank, with Alec as a companion and trainer, accompanied by one of Mr. Ross's servants, who was also a splendid skater, had gone over the route two or three times, and so was quite familiar with it. A little before the race began he was quite surprised to have this Indian skater call him aside and tell him to be careful and keep his eye on the correct route, and also to guard himself against that young white man who had deserted Alec. He then added:

"Watch the Indian with one arm; his heart is good toward you."

Then, putting his fingers to his lips as a sign of caution, the Indian quickly slipped away among the crowd. This very much perplexed and bothered Frank, especially when Mr. Ross said to him:

"Keep your eyes on the lookout for the flags—the Indian lads are so familiar with the route that they will not bother to notice them; and look out for tricks from those whose faces, like your own, are white."

There were perhaps twenty competitors in the great race. As the distance was so long it was not very essential that they should get off at the same instant. There would doubtless be those who depended on rapid bursts of speed to carry them to the front, and so a second or two made but little difference at first. . At the report of a gun away they flew. They had all sorts of skates and all kinds of styles. With ten or twelve miles' work before them, none, except some of the younger lads, tried to do their very best at first. Frank naturally wished to skate in company with his white companions, but they sullenly refused the offered society. Insulted and annoyed at this conduct, and remembering the warning words of Mr. Ross and also of his faithful servant, he just made up his mind to be on the alert, and if it were possible he would be in the first of the pale-faces. On and on they sped, until a couple of miles at least were covered. Then they had reached a spot where the route lay between two rocky islands not a hundred feet apart. The ice here was beautifully smooth, and being well sheltered was as clear as glass. With a wild whoop the Indians dashed on across it, and at the same time, rather to Frank's surprise, one of the clerks, putting on a rapid burst of speed, dashed directly in front of him, in the center of this narrow place. Frank, with his suspicions all aroused, keenly watched him, and to his astonishment saw him deliberately but cautiously let slowly trickle from his hands fine streams of the white crystal quartz sand of that country. To have skated over it would have so dulled his keen-edged skates that anything like victory would have been impossible. There are times when the mind works rapidly, and so it did here with Frank. The first thought was to shout out and expose the villainy. The next was to evade the trap and for the present say nothing about it, and see what trick would next be tried. So, quickly veering to the windward side sufficiently to make it sure that he would escape the sand, he rapidly sped along, humiliated and indignant that a white man would try a trick that an Indian would scorn to do.

On and on they flew. The route turned and twisted, and in several of the windings it brought them in fair view of the excited group on the mission hill who watched their progress, for now more than one half of the route was covered. They were now entering a kind of a maze among the islands, where persons not thoroughly acquainted with the route required to keep a vigilant eye on the different flags. In the front group was Frank, and closely edging beside him, he noticed with pleasure, was Kepastick, the one-armed lad, with his beautiful new skates, now serving him grandly and well.

"Chist!" said the Indian lad quickly, and Frank knew by the way that this word, which means "look," was uttered that there was something meant. Letting the boy glide just ahead of him, Frank caught the meaning of his words, though uttered in broken English:

"Some bad hearts change flags to bother Frank. Frank keep near Kepastick. He knows the trail."

These friendly words were uttered none too soon, for Frank saw at once that even some of the Indians, trusting to the flags, were perplexed and some had gone hopelessly astray. With a rush and a jeer of triumph a white clerk made an attempt to fly by, for once out of that labyrinth of crooked icy channels the home stretch was as straight as an arrow. Frank was for responding to his spurt with an effort equally desperate, when Kepastick checked him with:

"One Indian, good heart, meet clerk's bad heart; all right yet."

Frank, now completely bewildered, yielded himself implicitly to the guidance of Kepastick, who moved on with all confidence and paid not the slightest attention to the flags.

Look! Away beyond the islands, in the distance, shining in the sunlight, is the steeple of the mission church. Just a few more windings in these tortuous channels, and then the two miles' dash for home. Most of the Indians—for their skates were poor—have fallen in the rear. The one white man whom Frank despises is perhaps a hundred yards ahead, and not far behind him are his companions. With intense interest Kepastick is watching them.

"Chist!" he cries again, and his dark eyes flashed with excitement; "the trail is ours!"

It seems that there ran out from that place two channels that looked very much alike. The correct one had been flagged several days before, but the previous evening the clerk had skated over and had flagged the wrong channel. Sharp eyes had been on him and had discovered his trick, and these misplaced flags had been replaced at their proper positions, while the others had been left as the villain had placed them. Thus thrown off his guard, he blindly dashed into the wrong channel. The rocky shores were high and abrupt, and so Kepastick and Frank shot by the trap and into the correct channel, and were hundreds of yards out on the now open lake, with their faces toward home, ere the plotters discovered, to their dismay, how they had been completely foiled. As rapidly as possible they turned, but the distance could not be made up, and so to their chagrin they not only found that Frank and Kepastick had tied first, but that six or seven Indians, some with home-made skates, had wholly beaten them.

As the miserable trickster passed Frank on the shore some time after, in the presence of the chief factor, Mr. Ross, and several others, Frank sternly looked at him and uttered the one word "Sand!" None but the two then knew what was meant, but the guilty rascal paled, and so trembled that it seemed as though he would fall to the ground. Very soon was he out of that company. Next day he asked to be transferred to another post, which request was cheerfully granted. It was a long time before Frank told of his contemptible conduct. When Mr. Ross at length heard of it he communicated at once with the head officers of the Hudson Bay Company in reference to conduct so dishonorable, and the result was that the poor fellow, who had not improved over such actions in other places, was ignominiously expelled from the service.

Meanwhile the other sports were progressing finely. The football teams crowned themselves with many honors. The games were not fought on any strict Rugby rules. The goals were set in the ice, about four or five times as distant from each other as is the case in civilization. Then two captains were named, and they selected their men and boys alternately, until all who wished to play were chosen. Then each side was lined up at their own goal. The ball was placed away out in the center between them. At the firing of a gun there was a wild rush, and the side that had the fleetest runners thus secured the first kick. The ball was not to be thrown or carried. It was to be kicked, and could be struck with the hand or head. The game was fast and furious while it lasted. It was always in ground, and there was no hold up until it went between the poles of one or the other side. The cries of "Foul" were never heard, and umpires were only needed at the poles to shout out when a goal was won. It was a jolly, lively, easily understood game of football, enjoyed by all. Generally five wins in nine plays was the rule.

The hockey games were like those played by men and boys in civilized lands, only here everybody who wished to play was paired with somebody else, so as to keep the sides even. Everybody not otherwise engaged enthusiastically took a hand in it, and the fun was very great. Mr. Hurlburt, Mr. Ross, Hudson Bay officers, as well as all down to the smallest Indian lad who could handle a crooked stick, had a share in this game. The day was so cold, and the smooth ice expanse so great, that the vigorous exercise did everybody good.

The tobogganing games were given over entirely to the girls to compete in, and skillfully and well did they acquit themselves. The other minor games also gave great satisfaction, and afforded any amount of amusement.

We reserve for the next chapter the story of the great race of the rival dog-trains, which for long years after was talked about in many a wigwam and at many a camp fire.

CHAPTER X.

The Great Race with the Dog-trains—Careful Preparations by Alec—The Different Breathing Places—The Treacherous Half-breeds—Their Signal Failure—Alec's Triumph.

AND now for the races with the dogs. These were looked forward to with the greatest interest. All sorts of rumors were afloat of some wonderful surprises in store. Fortunately for all parties concerned, including the dogs, there had been a great abundance of fish during the last few years, and so every Indian wigwam and house fairly swarmed with dogs, of all sizes and degree. In other years, when fish failed and the herd of reindeer came not, as a last resort against starvation the dogs went into the soup pot. But they had fared better lately, and so now they were all in the finest trim, and the trained ones were as eager here for the races as were their masters.

There were about a dozen trains that contended for the victory in this next race. There were to be four prizes given. Alec, with his splendid houndlike dogs, seemed a certain victor. However, as from different parts the dogs came into position and were eagerly scanned by those present, it was seen that there were many trains that would make a gallant race ere they or their magnificently developed drivers would even take a second place. Alec and a young clerk were the only whites in the race. Then there were three half-breed fur traders, and the rest of the competitors were pure Indians.

The Indian carpenter at Sagasta-weekee had made for Alec a splendid birch tobogganlike sled for this race. It was very light, and so the maker had sewed and resewed it, and so stiffened it with the sinews of the reindeer that it was as strong as a piece of steel. He had fastened a seat in it so cleverly that if the sled went over the seat collapsed like a rubber ball and as quickly resumed its position when the sled was righted. Old Memotas had especially manufactured the harnesses for this event. He made them out of the softest and lightest mooseskin that Mr. Ross could buy for him. It took Memotas a long time to get the right kind of traces to satisfy his experienced eye. After testing a good deal of leather he settled down on a set of very long ones, that would not at all interfere with the long, springy movements of these beautiful houndlike dogs.

The start was to be from the foot of the mission hill on the ice. The route marked out, and along which Indians had now been stationed, was first to be the trading post, a distance of two and a half miles. Here each train would be detained exactly five minutes. At the expiration of the five minutes the next part of the race would begin. This was to Sagasta-weekee, a distance of perhaps five miles. Here there was to be a compulsory wait of ten minutes for each train, and then the dash back by the straight route to the mission, a distance, say, of six miles. Some of the Indians wanted the distance to be at least doubled, but this could not be allowed. These races and prizes were only designed to encourage the Indians to be kind and careful with their dogs, as only by such treatment could they be brought to be of the highest use to them in that land where they are so much needed.

Amid a good deal of barking, and some growls from some of the more quarrelsome dogs, the cry of "Marche!" was shouted, and they were off. Some especially clever Indian trains were the first to respond to the call and sprang to the front. Some of the drivers were going to run; others, like Alec, intended to ride, while perhaps the greater number would ride or run as they judged best in the excitement of the race. Each driver, Alec included, had a splendid dog-whip, but it was a long time since a dog of Alec's was struck. Indeed, the first one to receive a powerful blow was the leader dog of a train beside which Alec was running. As Bruce came alongside, and was slowly forging ahead, the vicious brute made a spring at him. Quick as it was, it was observed by his Indian master, who, although more than twelve feet from him in the rear, sent out so speedily and accurately that long, heavy, snakelike whiplash that it caught the brute on the nose with such force that, with a howl of pain, he turned to the front before any damage had been done. A few seconds later Alec and this Indian driver sped on right and left of a couple of trains mixed up in terrible confusion, while their drivers, a white man and a half-breed, were in anything but a pleasant mood. On and on they fairly flew. Alec had been warned to guard against running into some of the vicious dog-trains, as some of them had teeth like wolves, and one fierce attack might easily disable one of his lighter dogs.

Without mishap Alec reached the fort, and found that five trains were there ahead of him. In a minute or two most of the others arrived. Even those tangled up had speedily unloosened, and had not lost more than a couple of minutes by their collision. Exactly as each train's five minutes expired, away they flew for a long run for Sagasta-weekee. The ice was in fairly good condition for traveling, although there were long stretches where it was so absolutely smooth and glassy that some of the dogs would slip and slide in spite of their best efforts to the contrary. On this smooth ice the Eskimos and the mongrels had the advantage, as they had such hard feet that they very seldom slipped. The feet of Alec's dogs were perhaps the worse for these smooth icy places, and so he found that it was necessary, where the traveling was good, for him to urge his dogs more than he had intended, to make up for what he lost in the glassy places. Thus on they sped, and when Sagasta-weekee was reached Alec found three trains ahead of him and a couple alongside of his own and others close behind him. Ten minutes was the time allotted for the rest here. The instant Alec had arrived Memotas was at his side, and with him at once examined his dogs and compared his train with those that had thus far kept ahead. Memotas was delighted with the inspection, for, while the other trains seemed about exhausted at the terrific rate their drivers had pushed them, Alec's were as playful and lively as though the race had only begun. So, barring accident or foul play, there seemed to be no reason why Alec should not win with flying colors. Two of the half-breeds with very vicious trains now pushed on with four minutes of a start. An Indian followed two minutes after, and then in four minutes more Alec and those who had arrived at the same time as he did were again ready for the final run of the six-mile home stretch. Just as Alec was leaving faithful, alert Memotas said to him, as he tucked him in:

"Be on your guard against those two half-breeds and their vicious dogs. Try and not pass them in a narrow place. There is mischief in their hearts. Be wise."

"Marche!" and he was off.

For the first time now his blood began to tingle, and he entered into the wild, joyous enthusiasm of the race. He had become an expert in the use of his whip over the backs of his splendid dogs. Skillfully he whirled it, and its pistollike report rang out over them, but not once did it inflict a stinging blow.

"Ho! ho! my gallants! With Scotland's best staghound's blood in your veins, and Scotland's names, my bonny dogs, for Scotland win the day!"

He must needs hurry now, for fleet trains are around him and some ahead of him, with drivers just as keen and eager to win as he, and every one of them accustomed to dog-driving for years. Victors are some of them in previous contests, and not one of them is disposed to see a white lad from across the sea come and wrest their honor from them. Whips are flying now in earnest, and the dogs of other trains are waking up to realize that there is fire in their masters' eyes and strength in their arms and a burning sting at the end of the heavy lash. With terrific rushes they make their desperate efforts to forge to the front. Alec, excited now to the highest pitch, calls as never before to his dogs:

"Marche! Bruce, up! Up, Wallace! and you Gelert, and my bonny Lorne. Ho! ho! Away, away, my bonny dogs! Away! away!"

Grandly did they respond. They too have caught the enthusiasm of the hour, and as in clocklike unison in those long, light traces they stretched themselves out and fairly flew over the icy surface, they seemed to lift the light sled and its driver as a thing of naught.

Steady, Alec! Keep well balanced now. You have shaken off every sled that started in this last dash with you, but there are stubborn competitors ahead, and there are rough places where an upset at such a speed means disaster as well as defeat. But he thinks naught of these things; his Scottish caution has gone to the winds, and with dauntless courage he keeps up his cheering cries. Rapidly does he gain on a powerful train ahead of him, and just as he begins to fly past it the vicious leader turns and springs at Bruce. He fails in his attempt on account of the slippery ice, and falls directly in front of the oncoming train.

"Marche! Bruce!" shouts Alec, and with a mighty bound the gallant fellow responds and springs directly over his prostrate assailant. Quickly follow

Wallace, Gelert, and Lorne. With a stunning blow Alec's sled hits the still struggling brute. Well now is it for Alec that the cautious builder of that light sled had strengthened it with deerskin sinews till it was tough and strong. And so it stood that fierce shock, and, with its sturdy occupant unseated, over the great dog, with undiminished speed, it goes. Before him now are the two great trains of the half-breeds. These are the men and trains about which Memotas whispered his words of caution. And well is it for Alec that he was put on his guard. Before them for a mile or so is the narrowest part of the route. The good ice in places did not average more than from fifty to a hundred feet across. Plenty of room anyone might say for three dog-trains to rush by in at the same time. Yes, if all are fair and honorable, but not wide enough for the safety of the third if the other two are determined to stop him at all hazards.

If there was one thing more than another in which Alec had carefully trained his dogs it was for them to respond to his voice, and quickly move to the right or left, as he spoke to them. Like some other drivers, he had them so well trained that no horse responds to the pull on the reins more promptly than did his dogs to his voice. As Alec rapidly gained on these trains he observed that they were running about parallel to each other, and that the width of the ice was about the same between them and each shore. This so equally divided the ice that it made it difficult to decide whether to try and pass between them, or on one side or the other. Alec's first wish was to see if they were really working together against him, and so he shouted to his dogs as though he would dash in between them. At once they began to close up from each side to block his way. Quickly checking his dogs before there was a collision, he then tried the call to the right hand, and here the same plan was again pursued. It was evident, seeing that they would both be beaten in a fair race, they were resolved, by sacrificing one train, that the other should win at any cost from this white lad. Their dogs were large and fierce, and at one word from their master, if a collision occurred, would fasten on the lighter and younger dogs of Alec, with disastrous results. So Alec, who saw the plan, resolved that there should be no collision with his train if he could help it. All this time the speed was fairly kept up, and alert and watchful was each driver, although not a word was spoken among them. After a little more maneuvering from side to side Alec observed that his dogs were quicker to respond to his voice than were theirs, and so he resolved to try and confuse them and throw them off their guard. In this he at length succeeded. When, with a great show, it appeared that he was going to dash between them he suddenly checked his dogs just as the other two trains closed in to block his way. Quickly they saw their danger, and tried to avert it, but they were too late. Their own fierce, excited dogs sprang at each other as they met, and ere their masters could separate them Alec had skillfully veered to the right and was by them. The coast was clear now, but fleet trains were close behind. The blocking of the way had necessarily somewhat lessened the speed, and swift trains had come up dangerously near. But what now cared Alec? Springing to his feet, he swings his whip and calls to his gallant dogs. The distance is now only a couple of miles, and direct is the route. How those beautiful dogs do go! In perfect unison they spring together, while Alec's cheering voice rings out:

"Marche! Bruce, my hero, my leader! and you, Wallace, true to the end, and Gelert the avenger, and Lorne the fortunate! Gallant Scots ye are, and this is our Bannockburn!"

Thus on he drives; and now before him in the distance is the expectant crowd, who, having finished all their other sports, have gathered on the sloping banks to watch the return of the dog-trains. The day is drawing to a close, but there is one of those marvelous gloamings of the Great Lone Land, and so the whole scene is as visible as at noonday. The speed at which Alec travels soon brings him near, and as the sharp eyes of many tell them that he is the victor, and far in advance of any other train, there is, for an Indian crowd, a great deal of cheering, or rather a shouting of what sounds like "Hi! Hi! Ho! Ho!" from many a dusky Indian's lungs. For Alec is very popular among them, and they rejoice at his victory. The few whites are also very much interested, and add their full share to the noise and excitement that tell of Alec's triumph. Of course, Frank and Sam were wild with delight— so much so that they could not even shout. Sam in describing their feelings afterward said:

"We could only yell, but that we did in right good earnest."

As Alec dashed into the midst of the cheering crowd warm indeed was his welcome. Stalwart arms seized him, and hoisted him up on the shoulders of a couple of gigantic Indians, who at once began their march to the front of the mission house, where amid the cheering of the crowd a blue ribbon was pinned upon the breast of his coat by the trembling fingers of an equally happy maiden, and her name was Winnie.

CHAPTER XI.

Pasche Disappears—The Search—Big Tom and Mustagan—The Whisky Jacks—Pasche Found in a Hollow Tree—Chased by an Angry Moose Bull—Pasche Rescued—His Quaint Account of His Adventures.

THERE was great excitement at Sagasta-weekee one morning when word came in that the stableman who looked after the cows was missing. In fact, he had not been around for three days, and the boy who helped him in the stables was scolded for not having reported his absence. The name of the missing man was Pasche. He was a French half-breed who had come up from the Indian settlement near Montreal, several years before, in one of the canoes of the famous Iroquois brigades that annually made the trip up the Ottawa and other rivers into Lake Superior to Thunder Bay, and from thence by Lake of the Woods and still other rivers until they reached Lake Winnipeg.

Poor Pasche was ignominiously discharged by the despotic governor of the Hudson Bay Company, as being unfit for the laborious work of a canoeman in one of those large canoes. The fact was that it was only the most vigorous and muscular men who could perform the tremendous task assigned them by that tyrannical man, who drove his men on and on with all the cruel, callous persistency of a slavedriver. No wonder poor, weak Pasche gave out where many a stalwart man has also failed. He had been a sailor for some years on the St. Lawrence, and had the agility of a monkey in climbing up to the top of the masts. The unfortunate fellow was left stranded in that wild country, and so out of sympathy for the poor exile Mr. Ross had given him work and a home until he could return to his own people. The kindness of his new master made him quite contented where he was, and so year after year he had remained, and to him had come the care of the cows both in the summer and winter.

Now he was missing, and had been for three days. The family was alarmed, as it was such an unusual thing for Pasche ever to be away over a night. Mr. Ross at once called into the kitchen all who had lately seen him or knew anything of his latest fads. Of these the poor fellow had quite a number, and while some of them were sensible, others of them were generally laughed at by his friends. The latest one was that he imagined himself a great hunter, and had secured some traps and had set them in the woods in various places, most of them several miles away. The last time he was seen by the stableboy was when he had finished the morning work at the stable. Then he had taken his gun and ax and started off to visit some of his traps. When Mr. Ross chided the boy, who had industriously attended to all the stable duties alone, he said that Pasche had made him promise to say nothing about his huntings, for fear he would be laughed at.

A heavy fall of snow had completely obliterated all tracks, and so there was no possibility of following him up in that way. A messenger was sent for old Mustagan and Big Tom, both famous Indian guides, and a consultation was held with them. They smoked their stone pipes and talked the matter over, and then went out. After closely questioning the stableboy they returned to the Indian village. Here they secured a couple of sharp, bright little beaver dogs. With them they returned to the stables, and there, showing the dogs a coat that Pasche was in the habit of wearing, and making them thoroughly smell it, they tried to get them on his trail. All, however, the dogs would do was to get back out of the deep snow as quickly as possible and into the shelter of the stables. The plan was not a success. These dogs were too small for the deep snow, and soon the old Indians gave up this plan in disgust. Then they strapped on their snowshoes and made a long circuit around the place, and thus tried to find out some clew or trace of the missing man. Failing in this, they returned to the house, and after a hearty meal they equipped themselves to find that lost man. They had but little to work on, as Pasche had never revealed to anyone the whereabouts of his traps. However, Indian eyes are sharp, and so, unknown to him, keen hunters had observed his doings, and could tell the locality of every one of his traps and snares. Those who had any knowledge in this direction were summoned, and then, with the information thus obtained, the two old men set off on their snowshoes. It was not long ere they reached his first trap, but the snow covered everything there. Then on to his next resort, still no success; and thus it was throughout the whole round.

The Indians were puzzled and perplexed, and as they had now been on the go for hours they kindled a fire and awaited the arrival of some of the sleds with supplies that were to meet them here at this designated spot. The boys, who were equally grieved and excited with the rest at the loss of Pasche, with whom they had had a lot of innocent fun, had harnessed up their dog-trains and joined the party who brought out the supplies. The meal was quickly prepared on the big, roaring fire, and vigorous appetites made heavy inroads on the abundant supplies which Mrs. Ross had sent. They all noticed, while at the meal, the unusual number of whisky jacks, the Indian's sacred bird, that were at once attracted by the fire. They were all very noisy, and seemed unusually excited. The Indians are quick to notice the actions of even the most insignificant birds when on their hunting or warlike excursions. Many a lurking warrior securely hid from the keenest human eye has been given away by a noisy blue jay or a suspicious cawing crow, and has thus failed in his attempt to surprise his enemy, and has been obliged to make a hasty retreat.

In answer to Frank's question, Big Tom told the boys how some of the wild animals are warned by the birds of the approach of the hunters, and are thus the more difficult to reach. So here the whisky jacks, noisy at any time, but unusually so now, attracted the curiosity of those alert, watchful old Indians, as well as much amused the boys with their saucy ways. The birds, as usual, clamored around the fire, and as long as a crumb or bit of anything could be obtained were very saucy and persistent in their begging. It was great fun for the boys to feed them, and to even catch some of them by their feet, so bold and venturesome were they. They were all, however, speedily liberated, as Mustagan and Big Tom were anxious, if possible, to learn something from them. So the remains of the meal were speedily scattered, and while the boys wrapped robes around themselves and sat near the fire to keep warm, the Indians, lighting their pipes, sat down on a log near the fire to watch the actions of the birds. For a time they fluttered around and scolded in their pert, boisterous manner. Then, seeing there was nothing more forthcoming, they began flying about in the woods, but occasionally came back to see if the next meal was being prepared. Seeing no signs of it, they flew further and further away, and now principally in one direction.

After a while the quick ears of Mustagan detected a series of unusual cries of the birds. He at once called Big Tom's attention to it, and they both decided that there was something unusual to cause them thus to act. Not knowing but it might be a wolverine or a wild cat at which the birds seemed to be so angrily scolding, while the boys and the rest of the party remained near the fire they took their guns and carefully made their way through the woods to a spot where, without being seen themselves, they could observe the birds. To their keenest investigation nothing unusual was visible. The new, trackless snow was as yet unmarked by step of man or beast. Still excitedly the birds acted, and incessantly scolded. Soon the two men noticed that the center of their whirlings was a large dead trunk of a tree that had been broken off between thirty and forty feet from the ground. Around this stub of a tree the birds whirled and scolded, and occasionally some of them would light on the rough, jagged edge of the top and seemed to be peeping down into the heart of the dead tree. The curiosity of the men was aroused, and they wondered what animal the birds had there discovered. Immediately they started for it, keeping their guns in readiness to fire if it, whatever it was, should attempt to escape. When they reached the spot there was not a track visible of any animal. The birds whirled around if possible more noisily than ever, and so it was evident to the men that there was something in that tree. Drawing his ax from his belt, Big Tom made ready to pound against the side while Mustagan, with pointed gun, was on the alert to shoot any animal that the noise should disturb and cause to attempt to escape. With lusty vigor Big Tom pounded away at the old tree, while carefully Mustagan watched the top. In an instant after there were two very much amazed Indians. For from the interior of that old tree thus vigorously assailed there came the faint cry of a human being! What his first words were neither man was particular to inquire. It was enough for their quick wits to tell them that they had found the lost man for whom they were seeking and that he was still alive!

At once they lifted up their voices and shouted words of cheer and encouragement to the imprisoned Pasche. Then they called to the rest of the party who were at the fire to hasten to them. Neither the boys nor the men required a second call. They were speedily at the side of the two old Indians who, for such people, were very perceptibly excited.

At first the boys could hardly take in the situation, but quickly it dawned on them that here was an imprisoned, half-starved man who must be helped out of his dangerous predicament. What had best be done was the question that Mustagan, Big Tom, and the other Indians were discussing. Some suggested cutting down the big tree at once. This was discouraged by some, who said that the blows of the ax on the dead tree would dislodge so much dry, dusty, rotten wood that it would about smother the imprisoned man. So it was quickly decided that he must be pulled out of the top where, it was quite evident, he had fallen in. At once the tail ropes of the sleds and the packing and tie lines, which are also made of leather, were fastened together, and an effort was made to get one end to the poor fellow inside. In the meantime, while these preparations were being made by the Indians, the boys endeavored to hold some kind of conversation with the imprisoned Pasche.

"Arrah, my man," shouted Sam, "and what are ye doing inside there?"

"I fell in," faintly came back to the listeners.

"Were ye looking for the cows?" persisted the irrepressible Sam, who was a great favorite with Pasche, although he often unmercifully chaffed him.

"No, but a moose bull was looking for me."

This answer was the explanation that told the whole story; but, while the old Indians were able to now understand at once the whole matter, they left it for Pasche, when rescued, to tell his story. So in the meantime the question was how to liberate him as speedily as possible without injury. They first tried by fastening a stone to one end of their improvised leather rope to so throw it up that it would drop into the hollow tree as into a chimney. But although they succeeded several times in getting the stone to fall in, yet so jagged was the edge of the broken wood that the rope would not slide down. This plan failing, the next one tried was to cut down as large a young tree as the whole party could handle, and then carry it and lean it up against the hollow tree in which was the imprisoned man. Alec, who was a daring climber, at once volunteered to climb this, and thus carry up one end of the rope, which could then be easily lowered down to Pasche. Ere he started Mustagan handed him a ball of deer-skin twine, and told him to put that into his pocket, as he might need it before he came down again. Taking off his overcoat, and tightly fastening his leather coat around him with his sash belt, Alec gallantly began his difficult task. It was no easy work, as the tree was in some places quite icy and it was hard to grip with his hands, which soon began to feel the effects of the cold. But he gallantly persevered, and, cheered and encouraged by Sam and Frank, he at length succeeded in reaching the top. Here for a time, after a cheery shout to Pasche, he rested, while he warmed his nearly frozen hands in his warm mittens, which he had stuck in his sash belt. Then, hauling up sufficient length of line, he carefully dropped it down to the poor fellow at the bottom. But now another difficulty presented itself to him. He alone could not haul out the imprisoned man, and the men below could be of little service, as the rope if pulled on would surely get caught in the ragged edge of the rotten tree. It was now that Alec saw the value of Mustagan's forethought in giving him that ball of deerskin twine.

Calling up to him Mustagan said:

"Hold on to the end of that twine, and let the ball drop to me."

This Alec at once did. Then Mustagan fastened a good solid green birch stick about four feet long and five or six inches in diameter to the string, and then said to Alec:

"Now draw it up and lay it across the top of the tree, where it will rest firm and strong."

This was quickly done. Then calling to Pasche to tie the end let down to him about his waist, and then to hold on, he placed the rope over the strong, smooth green stick he had pulled up, and then gave the word to the men below to haul away. No second order was necessary, and soon Pasche was pulled up to the top. He had no difficulty in slipping down the inclined tree, weak as he was. Alec also safely reached the ground. Poor Pasche was quickly placed on a dog-sled, and they all hurried back to the fire, where some tea and food were hastily prepared for the hungry, half-frozen man. He was so weak and exhausted that it was thought best not to trouble him to tell his story until they had all returned to Sagasta-weekee.

The journey home was soon made, and there was great rejoicing at the recovery of the poor fellow. The following is his quaint story of his adventures:

"Well, you see, I was emulous. Les garçons—the boys—they succeed. They capture le renard—the fox—the wild cat, and other animals. And still they not natives. So I think it over when I milk la vache, and Sam he pushed open la porte and he show me fine cross-fox he caught, and that make me emulous. So I take my wage le maître he give, and I exchange for the traps. When my work is done, en avant, on I go to the great woods. Aller à pied—I walk—I carry my traps, I set them with much bait. I get nothing. Le chien—the dog—he follows, he gets in the traps. Then I try again. I go far away this time. I set my traps, I await with tranquillité. It is far in the woods. I wait trois days. Then I go to see if le renard, like Sam's, is in my trap. Aussitôt que possible—as soon as possible—I reach my traps. There is no renard. So I return home. Il fait nuit—it is night. Then I say, A quoi bon?—What good is it?—and I stay with my cows. But Sam he comes again and he say great things about la chasse—the hunting—and so I say, I try again; and this time I take the great wolf trap that hang in the stable, and I start early, and I go far in the woods, and I set my traps, and I put the big one, the wolf trap, set with a log made fast to the chain, and then I retourner—return—to my duties. Three days pass, then I advance again in the woods. It is far. Il fait de la neige—it is snowing—when I draw near. I hear a great noise. I draw nearer still. I see the great moose bull, with his hind foot in the wolf trap. He also sees me. I raise a great shout. A quoi bon?—What good is it? He comes for me. Voulez-vous?—I say. So I fire my fusil—gun—at him. Still he comes, for now I remember I only had shot for partridge in that gun. J'ai chaud—I am hot. He makes me so, he looks so fierce. His great ears, his long face, all his hair point toward me. I turn, I run. So does he run, but it is toward me. Still he comes. He has still the wolf trap on his foot. The log is fastened to the chain, so it troubles him. Still on he comes. I can keep ahead, on account of the log, but the log slips off the chain. So now he comes faster. I run, I fly. I see him draw near. He looks diabolical. I despair. I see this tree like the mast broken off in the storm. I learn to climb well when I sail on the ship I rush to the tree with the moose bull close behind me. I drop my mittens, I seize hold of the rough bark, I climb up just as that animal, like le diable—the devil—he rush up, and he strike his great horns against the tree where I was, but I not there, I just above, out of his reach. I dare not go back. So up and up I climb like the sailor as I was, and when I get to the top I find plenty of sticks there, where some time ago the crows they make the nest, and it seem strong, and as I could not hold on at the sides of the tree I pull myself up and I try to stand on those sticks, and they break sudden and

I drop, I fall, I sink down into the tree. I throw out my arms to catch hold, but the tree is rotten wood inside, so I lose my grip. The wood it come down with me. I sink into the depths, and there I was. The rotten wood made a great dust as down I slide. It nearly choke me. I cannot call out; my mouth, my eyes, my throat all full. There I stay. I could not climb out, the place too small. I could not work up my knees, so there I stay. My heart gets very sad soon. Il fait nuit—it is night. I am lost. Good-bye, I say, to all. I weep and then I sleep, I wake up with a start, then I sleep again. When I wake again, il fait clair—it is light—above and I rejoice. The dust is all out of my eyes and mouth. I can move back my head enough to look up and see the blue sky. Then I call aloud, but there is no response. I then remember I have some food in my pocket. It is difficile to get at it, but I succeed. I eat it, it is very good. Then I find I have my knife in my pocket. I call again and again. I think I hear a reply; but it is only the birds, the whisky jacks. They fly across my vision at the top; they look at me, they scream, they mock me. Never mind, I have my knife; so I will hope to cut my way out. It is easy cutting in the rotten wood. But the dust affects me. I cough much. I can work but little. I have to wait for the dust to settle. The air is bad. When I get to the hard outside wood I can do nothing, my strength is gone. It is hard to breathe when I keep still. It is worse when I try to work. So I give myself up to die. I call out at times, and I try to think of my friends, and I try to pray, and that comforts me best of all. Thus passes this second day, and now I am very faint. I can just easily move round in my prison, but I cannot sit down or lie down. I am very tired. Still I call, and more and more the whisky jacks come and mock me. They seem angry I have nothing for them, and so they scold, as they do at the camp fire when we feed them nothing. To-day for a time they left me, and then they came back and seemed to laugh at me, and then I heard Mustagan and Big Tom call, and I was rescued.

"Je suis fâché—I am sorry—I went hunting. I will go no more. Sam may continue."

CHAPTER XII.

Kinesasis's Wonderful Story—How He Wooed Shakoona—Their Youthful Days—Miskoodell Rescued from the Bear—Oosahmekoo with His Gold—Kinesasis's Successful Hunt—His Furs Stolen—Marries Shakoona—Conflict with the Old Warrior.

THE romantic and thoroughly characteristic Indian way in which Kinesasis had obtained his Indian wife was one that had very much interested Mr. and Mrs. Ross. They had known him for many years, and had ever been pleased with the kindly, helpful way in which he had always treated his wife, whom he called Shakoona. "Shakoona" means "the snow-white one," and those who knew her well, and studied her quiet, gentle manner, said she was well named. The terrible loss of her children had been such a shock that her once black, luxuriant tresses had become as white as the snow, making her name more impressive than ever before.

The story of how he had obtained his wife Kinesasis was induced to tell one evening at Sagastaweekee, when fierce winds were howling around the place and at times seemed to strike with such fury against the house that they appeared like wild beasts shrieking for their prey. As a general thing Kinesasis was not very communicative on matters relating to himself, but as Mrs. Ross, who had some knowledge of how he had obtained his wife—indeed, her mother had a little to do with its consummation—had asked him to tell it for the pleasure of the boys and some good friends who had come over for a day or two from the mission, he could not refuse.

The great log fire roared in the large fireplace in the dining room, while round it gathered the expectant listeners. Mrs. Ross had sent over to Kinesasis's little home and had brought from thence Shakoona, his wife. She was now, like Kinesasis, getting up in years, yet she was the same shy, clever, modest, retiring woman she had ever been, and yet, as will be seen, there was that latent courage in her that mother's love can best bring out. The inevitable pipe had to be produced and gravely smoked by Kinesasis, and those who would smoke with him, ere the talking could begin. When this ceremony was over Kinesasis, looking kindly at Shakoona, began:

"We had been children together in the forest. Our fathers' wigwams were not far apart. With other Indian children we had played in the wild woods, among the rocks and on the shores of the great lakes. When large enough to help I had to go and try my skill in setting snares for the rabbits and partridges and other small game. The trail along which I used to travel each morning, as I visited my snares and traps, was the one in which I often found little Shakoona getting sticks for the fire in her father's wigwam. He was a stern man and cruel, and very fond of gain.

"The years rolled on, and I was now a hunter, and could use the bow and arrows of my forefathers, as well as the gun of the white man, which was now being brought into the country. Shakoona was now grown up, and was no longer a child. We often met, and let it be known that we loved each other. Shakoona's mother and the other members of her family were my friends, and they all had good reason to be my friends, for one summer, some years before, when Miskoodell was a little child, I saved her from the paws of a bear. Her mother had gone out to gather moss and dry it for the winter use. She had Miskoodell strapped in her moss-bag cradle, with its board at the back. While the mother was at work she left her little baby girl in her cradle standing up against a tree. As the moss was not very good just around that spot the mother wandered off quite a distance to find where it was better. While she was thus hard at work a large black bear came along from the opposite direction. I happened to be out in the woods with my bow and arrows shooting partridges and what other small game I could find, for I was then only a boy.

"Where this moss grows the ground is very damp, and it is easy to walk very still. I came along, not being far behind the bear, and there the first thing I saw was that big bear with that baby, cradle, and all in his forearms. He was standing up on his hind legs and holding it awkwardly, like a man does."

This last remark created quite a laugh at Kinesasis's expense; but Mrs. Ross came to his rescue, and declared that the expression was correct. "For a man," she said, "always awkwardly holds a young baby—the first one, anyway." she added, as she saw her amused husband laughing at her.

"Go on, Kinesasis. You said last that the bear was standing on his hind legs, and awkwardly holding the baby, as a man does," said Mrs. Ross.

Thus encouraged by the lady whom he so greatly respected, he went on, and only modified his statement by saying:

"Indian men do, anyway. Well, there I was, not very far behind and well hid behind the trees, and I watched that bear, and I think if I had been a white boy I would have laughed. Strange to say, the baby did not cry, but seemed pleased to have some one lift it up in the cradle. The bear would put his big nose in the baby's face very gently, and it seemed to like to feel this cold nose. All at once I saw by the fine bead work in the cradle that it was the child of the mother of Shakoona, whom I loved, the little Miskoodell. Then I thought the mother of the child must be near, and while the bear is kind to the child, as bears of that kind always are, it will surely attack the mother when she comes. So, boylike, I resolved, in my great love for Shakoona, to try and kill that bear. It was well for me that I had some steel-pointed arrowheads, obtained at the traders' shop. These I had not been using, as they were too valuable to risk losing in shooting small game. However, here was game big enough. So I at once removed the flints from three of my best arrows, and quickly lashed on these long steel points with sinew.

"All this time the bear was still fooling with that child. He would turn it round and round, and then sometimes he would set it down, as though he wanted it to walk off with him. At length, after failing in this, it seemed to me as if he were going to start off and carry the child with him. When I saw this I knew that I must now try and shoot him. So I crawled along on the mossy ground, and dodged from tree to tree until I was very near him. Once or twice I was going to shoot, but I was afraid of hitting the child. All at once I saw him drop the cradle and straighten himself up and listen. He had heard something that startled him. It was the mother coming back. Now in the distance I, too, could see her coming. She had a large bundle of moss on her head which she was supporting with both hands. She had neither gun nor knife.

"I could wait no longer. I drew my arrow to the head of my bow and, as the bear was standing up with his side toward me, and his paws were well up, I aimed for his side, just under the leg, and sent the arrow with all the force I could. I was perhaps twelve years old, but I well knew, like Indian boys, how to use the bow. My arrow struck just where I wanted it to. It entered his side near the heart. With a savage growl he jumped, but he had not seen or heard me. He only saw and felt the arrow, and so that was his only enemy, he thought. That is the advantage of hunting with the bow over the gun. If you can keep hidden, with bow and arrows the animals are not alarmed at your presence, but with a noisy gun the animal knows where you are and comes for you. So it was in this case; the bear only tried to get hold of the arrow that was sticking into his side. He twisted himself round and round and tried to pull it out with his paw on the opposite side, but I had sent it with such force that he could not succeed. The more he worked at it the more the blood poured out of the wound. He seemed to have forgotten now all about the child and the coming mother, so I was sure he was badly hurt. But he was far from dead, and very angry at the arrow, so I thought I would give him another one. This one I sent into the other side, as he was moving round and round. When this second one struck him he seemed to think that he was in the wrong place, and had better start for his den; and so off he hurried, coming right by where I was hid. I still had one steel-pointed arrow. With this one ready to shoot I sprang up before him. I was going to try and shoot him between the eyes, but at the sight of me he threw up his head, and so I shot the arrow into his throat. He gave one great spring at me, but it was his last, and there he lay quite dead. When we opened him we found that one of my arrows had entered into his heart, and when he made that last spring at me it did its work. The mother of Shakoona picked up the cradle in which was Miskoodell, and found her child uninjured. She was of our race, and therefore did not say much, but I knew that I had made a friend.

"Some years went by, and I brought my presents and asked the father of Shakoona for her to be my wife, but he was stern and cruel, and appeared to have forgotten that I had rescued Miskoodell. Indeed, when told the story he only said, 'It was only a girl, anyway, that was rescued.' Since we have become Christians, thanks to the missionaries, we now think as much of the girls as of the boys. But Wahbunoo, for that was his name, spurned my few gifts, for he was very selfish, and said that he that would receive Shakoona must bring many gifts, and even the 'Keche Shuneou,' the gold of the white man, ere he could have her. This was bad news, but I saw he was strong in his mind, and so I gathered up my gifts, which with all Indian ceremony I had laid at his feet, and without a word I left his wigwam. That night Shakoona and I met for a short time, and we gave our promise to each other, and vowed to be true to each other, no matter what might happen.

As I saw it was a large price Wahbunoo wanted, I plunged that fall into the forest with my traps and plenty of weapons. My object was to hunt very hard, and so be able in the springtime to bring in so many skins of the silver and black foxes, with beaver, mink, otter, marten, and other rich furs, that I could change them for rich presents, or even for gold, with the traders, and thus cause Wahbunoo to look kindly on my gifts and grant me my wish. To carry out this purpose I went far away, where I was told by hunters that but few ever hunted and that the game I was after was very plentiful. The reason why it was so little visited by hunters was that it was reported that great Windegoos, man-eaters, there haunted the deep forests, and that many hunters had mysteriously disappeared. They had gone there with great hopes of success, but had never returned. The man-eating Windegoos, that were so great and high that they could brush the trees aside as they walked along, they said, had devoured them. So it was said and believed by many. So great was my love for Shakoona that I cared for none of these stories, and was willing to run all risks for her sake; and so I made the many days' journey and reached those hunting grounds. All winter I worked hard, and met with good success.

But while I was far away things were going on at the spot where dwelt Shakoona that were to my hurt. One day there walked into her father's tent a great chief having on his face and body the scars of many battles. But while he was surely a brave warrior he was a man of fierce temper, and some of the wives he already had showed the marks of his fierce anger. The top of the head of one of them was hard and dry, for Oosahmekoo—that was his name—had in his anger, because she had not quickly prepared his dinner, rushed at her and, circling the spot with his knife, had torn away the scalp; and still she lived. This Oosahmekoo was the man who came with his gifts to buy from Wahbunoo the beautiful young Shakoona. He had gone off with another tribe in the south, called the Sioux, and in one of their warlike excursions they had attacked a band of white people passing over the prairies. They had crawled up to them in the darkness of night, and as the watchers had gone to sleep they had killed them all. Among the pillage and plunder was a bag of gold. The Sioux then knew not of its worth, so they gave it to Oosahmekoo, and as he had been much among the fur traders he knew it was valuable and carefully kept it. He had seen Shakoona as she industriously did her work, and wanted her for another wife. When he entered the wigwam his manner was so proud and unceremonious that even Wahbunoo's temper got the mastery over his love for gold, and he refused to let Shakoona be the sixth wife of a man who had no more respect for the custom of the tribe, and would thus act before the father whose girl he wished to buy. So he had to pick up his bag of gold and leave the wigwam. His having to leave in this way gave great joy to the mother of Shakoona, and to her brothers and sisters, especially Miskoodell, who was now a bright young girl herself.

"But old Oosahmekoo, although repulsed this time, was not to be easily put off. He saw that he had broken the usages of his tribe in the way that he had acted, and so, pretending to hide his anger, he found times to meet the father of Shakoona and offer his gold for her. Without letting him know the reason of their so doing, his family all seemed very indignant that Oosahmekoo should have so insulted the old father, and so they kept him in such a state that he refused the chief's offer, but not in such a way as to discourage him from persisting in his efforts.

"The winter passed away, and I prepared to return with my heavy pack of rich furs. On the trail of many days I reached the hunting lodges of some of our people, who, being near, had frequently gone to the village. There they had learned about the efforts of Oosahmekoo to buy my Indian maiden, and of it they told me. When I heard it my heart got hot, and I clutched my knife and said something, but my friends urged me to be wise and careful, for the old chief was cruel and powerful. Some of them with lighter loads hurried on, and one who was my true friend went fast and quietly told Shakoona that I was coming on the trail. And some one else had told Oosahmekoo, and had also told him that I was the favorite hunter of Shakoona, and that I was bringing home sufficient rich furs to more than equal his gold in value, to lay at the feet of Wahbunoo. The news given to Shakoona filled her heart with joy, while that given to the old chief made him furious and eager to destroy me. With the help of her mother, who remembered how I had killed the bear and thus likely saved her life, Shakoona was able to get away, and met me on the trail long before I entered the village. From her I heard all there was to know. She put her arms around my neck and kissed me, and said she would die before she would be the sixth wife of such a man. There we promised that we would rather die than be separated. We saw that we would have to be very wise and careful, as my friends had said. I was glad to learn that all my maiden's family were friendly to me. Only a little while dare Shakoona stay with me. If her stern father missed her there would be trouble, even if his love for her was only what she by her sale could bring to him. Before she left me I told her that in due form to-morrow I would enter her father's wigwam and open my pack of rich furs before him, and by their value would win his consent.

Then she kissed me and quickly hurried back again. That night following was a bad night for me."

For a time Kinesasis paused in his narrative, and seemed, Indian though he was, to be deeply moved, while his aged wife buried her head in her blanket and bowed to the floor. Mr. Ross, who knew his story, respected the old man's feelings, and for a short time said and did nothing; then he filled the calumet and gave it to him. The tobacco and the rest quieted his perturbed spirits, and handing back the pipe he continued his most fascinating story:

"Yes, that night I entered the village was indeed a bad night for me. Evil eyes had been on Shakoona. Cunning steps had followed her, and sharp ears had heard enough of our story to find out what I was going to do next day with my valuable furs that I had been eight long moons in hunting. As I entered the outskirts of the village I was met by a young Indian with the word that the wigwam of my relatives was cold and empty, as they had not yet returned from their hunting grounds, which were in an opposite direction from the way in which I had come. Very cordial seemed the invitation of that man for me to rest that night in his wigwam, which was a large one, being made of many dressed buffalo skins sewed together.

"Without any distrust I accepted his invitation, as was the manner of our people, and was glad to unstrap my heavy load of furs, as well as my gun and traps and blanket. With much more attention than is generally shown to one thus coming in, this Indian helped me in various ways. With a good deal of show he hung up my gun and traps for me, and placed my pack of furs tightly back against the leather wall of the wigwam. In the meantime fish and venison were brought in, and a good supper was prepared and eaten. Afterward we smoked and talked for some time, and then prepared to sleep. Noticing that the wind outside was rising, he showed me a place where I could spread my blanket where there would be no draft, but it was away from my pack of furs. At first I thought I would bring my furs from the place where they had been put and place them at my head, but this I saw would give offense, and now as some young children were lying down to sleep near them there was not enough room for me. Still a little fearful, I made an excuse and stepped out of the wigwam for a minute. There I saw that the snow was well piled up against the leather wall all around. This quieted my fears, and so I returned into the wigwam, and being very weary was soon fast asleep. In the morning my furs were gone! A thief in the night had cut through the leather, making a hole so large that he could easily and noiselessly lift out my pack of furs. He had left the upper part uncut, so that as quickly as he had obtained the pack he could let the leather down again and thus cover up the hole. For fear the wind should get in and disturb the inmates he had quietly laid a large deerskin over the whole place on the outside. I was in a sad state the next morning, but I kept my lips closed and said but little. The Indian family were much excited and angry at the theft. The young Indian who had invited me in made a greater ado than anyone. I suspected him at once of being the one who had robbed me, but I had then no evidence, and so carefully held my tongue. But I thought a great deal, and in time I found out that he was in the plot.

"What to do I knew not. However, refusing to again eat under the wigwam where I had been so robbed, I took my gun, blanket, and traps and pushed on to the wigwam of my friends, and to my surprise found them in it, and there they had been for some days. Then I knew that that young Indian was an enemy. To my friends I told of my success, and of my loss. We set about the recovery of them at once. Runners were sent to every trading post describing the contents of the packs and telling the traders the circumstances of the robbery. There was great indignation. Such robberies are very rare. If the thieves are found out they are generally quickly poisoned by the conjurers of the tribe. That is one of the things they are expected to do. A robber of traps or furs is soon poisoned. Then the traders themselves are down on these things. So the story of the theft was soon known, but the furs were not recovered until a long time after.

"Wahbunoo was very cold and repellent. He would not believe my story, and so refused to have me come to his wigwam. So Shakoona and I had to meet when we could, and that was not often, for the father was cruel and Oosahmekoo had many spies. Still, we had many friends. Miskoodell, the little sister, was sharp and shrewd, and helped us greatly by warning us of danger. So did her brother, Netahwatee. He was a good hunter, and had friends who had seen the furs. He had been on the alert, and had found out that the young Indian who had invited me into his wigwam had during the winter hung around the tent and had asked Shakoona to be his wife. She had repelled him with scorn, and Netahwatee had told him that she was fond of Kinesasis, and that even now he was away in the forest hunting, to bring in sufficient rich furs to buy the consent of their father. At this news from Netahwatee, he arose and left the tent, but he ground his teeth as he went out. After that he was often seen in earnest talk with Oosahmekoo, the old chief, and it was the belief of many that they had been the ones who had planned the stealing of the furs. But they were cunning, and so covered up the tracks that a long time passed ere the truth came out. But, although some of the family were friendly toward me, the father of Shakoona turned more and more against us. The gold of the old chief was offered again and again, and at length I heard that there was a likelihood that he would yield, although Shakoona still declared that she would throw herself from the cliff into the lake rather than marry him. And this I think she would have done, for we loved each other, and do still."

Here the old man stooped over and, tenderly lifting up the head of his aged wife, kissed her on the forehead.

"One day some little boys out hunting rabbits among the great rocks overheard some earnest talking. At first they were frightened, and were about running home when one of them, who was Shakoona's youngest brother, proposed that they creep to the top of the rocks and try and see who the talkers were on the other side. Noiselessly they crawled to the top, and then as they peeked over whom should they see but Wahbunoo and Oosahmekoo in earnest talk? They saw the chief with a fire bag that seemed heavy and saw him offer it to Wahbunoo, who took it and held it. Then the little boys slid down the rocks and returned to the tents. Netahwatee's little brother told what he had seen, and the brother told his mother and Miskoodell. They talked it over, and Miskoodell was sent to warn us of what was being done.

"So that very night we quietly left the village and hurried to a place where Netahwatee, who had gone on some hours before, met us with a white man, a missionary. He was pleased to hear from Netahwatee that there was an Indian couple who wanted to be married by the Book, in the Christian way, and not in the old pagan Indian manner; but," said Kinesasis, with a bit of a twinkle in his eye, "he did think it was a queer idea of ours that we wanted to be married out there in the forest by moonlight. However, as we had with us what he called witnesses, he married us. We did not then return to the village, but went off with some friendly relatives at a trading post where the Indians were all Christians. Netahwatee and the others who had been with us went back at once and told how we had met the missionary and had been married with the Book. Strange to say, when Wahbunoo heard this he said he did not care, and would not oppose us as we were married by the Book. He was very superstitious, and was afraid that evil would come to him if he seemed to be angry with anyone who had had anything to do with the Book.

"It was very different, however, with Oosahmekoo, the old chief. He was wild with anger. He made many threats. He was not as cunning as he generally was, and so he told his plans to get revenge. He was going to waylay me and kill me on the trail. Some of my friends overheard his threats, and a swift runner put me on my guard. I felt that my youth was a match for his years, and then I had won my loved Shakoona. So I had no fear. I left my wife among friends, and I started on the return trail. We met in conflict, and I was not hurt. He was quietly buried the next day."

Here Kinesasis ceased. He could say no more that night, the memory of the battle came up so vividly before him, although many years had passed away since it had occurred. Since then he and his old wife had become Christians. He paused for an instant, and then went over to the place where on the floor the heroine of his story, his true little wife, had sat during the long recital. Then tucking her arm in his, as lovingly and as affectionately as any white man could have done, they quickly slipped out of the house and returned to their own little dwelling place.

CHAPTER XIII.

Comments on Kinesasis's Wonderful Story—The Pack of Furs Recovered—Honesty of Indians—Their Different Hunting Grounds—The Golden Rule—The Dishonest Foreign Indian—His Sudden Death.

THE next morning the wonderful story of Kinesasis, which had produced such a deep impression on all, was thoroughly discussed. During its recital some one had quietly turned down the lamps, and thus the lights from the bright fireplace had full play upon him. This seemed to add to the effect of the scene, as frequently Kinesasis, in his intense earnestness and few but strong movements, stood in the bright light or turned into a shadowy place. As the story was light and shadowy itself, so also seemed in appearance this dramatic old Indian so eloquent with his theme. He had deeply stirred and excited the boys as he had moved along in his story; and not only this, but he had changed their ideas concerning him. This complete revulsion of feeling had come at the close, when the old Indian, whom they had thought was so cold and destitute of sentiment, had stooped down and kissed his wife, as he had also done before during the recital of the story. It was done in a way that was so real and genuine that it completely broke them down. They declared that morning that they would not quickly judge anyone again. They had thought him phlegmatic and unlovable, and now here had come out from the heart of this Indian, of such a rugged exterior, a story and an exhibition of love and devotion more genuine and beautiful than any that had ever been revealed to them in song or story.

"And for very many years," said Mrs. Ross, "he has been kind and true to that quiet, industrious little wife, who as a young maiden was so true to him and would undoubtedly have died rather than marry that chief."

"What about his pack of furs?" said Frank. "And did they find out the thief and put the conjurers after him?"

"I am glad you have mentioned it," said Mr. Ross. "I have heard Kinesasis tell the story of their recovery, and will give you his version of it. As regards the actual transgressors, they must have been the old chief who was killed and the young Indian whom Shakoona had refused. When the old chief was killed the young fellow disappeared and was never heard of afterward. When the leather wigwam that had been cut into was carefully examined it was found that the knife had been used on the inside, and that the great pack of furs had been handed out, so there must have been at least two persons engaged in the robbery. Weeks later some women out snaring rabbits in a dense swampy place found the pack cachéd up among the branches of a great spruce tree. It was so completely hidden in the close branches that it was a wonder that they ever discovered it. The only clew they had was that a great wolverine came tumbling out of the tree and hurried away into the dense forest. The women, like the men, knew what clever animals these wolverines are to find out where venison or other game has been hid away until needed. So, as their curiosity was excited, they carefully searched the tree, which was a very large one, and there in among the dense branches they found the pack of Kinesasis. They were not able to reach it, but reported their discovery when they returned to the village. Kinesasis and others were soon after it. It was well that they found it when they did, as the wolverine had cut through the outer coverings of deerskin and had already ruined several valuable furs. In an hour more there would have been nothing worth taking away, so terribly destructive are these animals when they thus find anything of fur or game.

"Strange to say, old Wahbunoo would not accept anything from Kinesasis. The death of the old chief had very much disturbed him, and it also gave him such an idea of Kinesasis's prowess that he had to respect him. The bag of gold also disappeared, and to this day none knows what became of it. Kinesasis carried his furs to the Hudson Bay Company's store, and received enough for them to make him and Shakoona comfortable for many a day."

"I have always heard that Indians were so honest with each other about their furs and traps," said Alec; "but this stealing of Kinesasis's whole pack seems to knock that idea over. What are we to believe about it?"

"What you have heard about the honesty of the Indians is the truth," said Mr. Ross. "This stealing of the furs of Kinesasis was not an ordinary theft for gain. The object of it was to prevent him from having sufficient gifts to satisfy the father of the maiden of his choice. The fact that the furs were hid away as they were showed this. They could not bury them, as the ground was frozen like granite; they dare not burn them for fear of detection; and the ice was too thick on the rivers or lakes to be quickly cut through. It was very evident that they did not try to sell them."

"But did not the thieves hide them there so that they could go and get them, and sell them when the excitement of their loss had passed over?" said Alec, who was a boy who had a habit of seeing things from different sides and liked to have all the difficulties cleared up.

Mr. Ross admired this trait in Alec's character, and always endeavored to meet it in a way that was helpful to the lad. So to this last question his answer was:

"No Indian who wished to preserve anything of value for future use would think of putting it up in such a place. They all know the thievish, destructive habits of the wolverines, and other animals of that kind, that quickly detect and destroy everything destructible if placed in a tree in the manner in which this was done. The wonder was that this was not found out much sooner and completely destroyed."

"Tell us, please," said Sam, "how the hunters act toward each other in regard to their hunting grounds and furs. Have they any titles to the different places where they hunt year after year?"

"They have no written titles," said Mr. Ross, "but for generations the same families have hunted in the same localities. Then some Indians, generation after generation, are noted as famous hunters of certain animals. For example, Big Tom is noted as a successful moose hunter, and so were his immediate ancestors. Others made a specialty of the beavers, others of the otter, and thus it went. These Indian families naturally had localities where these different animals abounded, although there were seasons when other varieties of fur-bearing animals swarmed through these regions, and for a time were really more numerous than the ones there generally hunted. As might have been expected, the hunters of the moose, reindeer, black bears, and other large animals that wander over immense districts had the right of following them in any direction. The hunters and trappers of the rich fur-bearing animals, however, generally kept in certain regions year after year. Sometimes a hunter in order to reach his own grounds had to pass through what we might call the preserves of three or four different families. I once accompanied a hunter to his grounds, and we saw no less than seventy traps of other Indians on the trail as we passed along mile after mile. In one of them was a beautiful mink. My Indian companion at once stopped, and, putting his pack off his back, opened it and cut off some of his bait. Then he took the mink out of the trap and reset it, supplying it with his own bait. The mink he tied to the top of a young sapling, which he bent down for the purpose. When he let go of the young tree it sprang up so that the mink hung in the air, about fifteen feet from the ground. Here it was safe from the prowling wolverines and other animals. Then the Indian made some peculiar marks upon the tree with his ax. His pack was then again shouldered, and we proceeded on our way. I was very much interested in his proceedings, and so when he had completed his work I asked him if that trap belonged to his brother or some relative.

" 'No,' he replied, 'I do not yet know whose hunting ground this is, but my duty is to do as you have seen me act. Perhaps when that hunter comes along to-morrow or next day he will find another mink in that trap. Then with two instead of one he will be the more pleased.' "

"Well done, honest Indian!" shouted the boys, when they heard this. "There is a lesson for many a white man."

"And boys, too," added Sam.

Continuing, Mr. Ross said: "This was the understood custom. It might seem a little burdensome on the man who had the farthest to go, and quite a tax on his supply of bait. But then he had the advantage when he reached his hunting grounds, in that there were fewer human footsteps, and, in all probability, correspondingly more game."

"Were there no exceptions—none who would take a mink or otter if they had a chance from a neighbor's trap, if they thought they could escape detection," asked Alec.

"I only remember of one case occurring in many years," said Mr. Ross, "and there was soon a dead man at the end of it. It was the winter after the great flood in Red River. A number of Indians who lived near its mouth were driven out by the great flood. Some of them came into this North country. The most of them were industrious and worked hard. By fishing, shooting, and hunting where no persons specially claimed the localities they did well, and got on as did the others. There were a few among them who apparently did nothing, but lounged about and lived on the industrious ones. No notice was taken of these. There was one man, however, who soon began to be talked about. He was not known to have any traps, nor was he ever seen to make any dead falls or other things to catch the fur-bearing animals. Yet he often sauntered into the trading post and brought out from under his coat a fine mink or marten, and sometimes even a splendid otter. Soon some of the hunters began to speak about strange tracks about their traps. One hunter told of how he had visited one of his otter traps and had found a quantity of hairs of an otter on the teeth, and yet the trap was set. He had also observed where somebody who chewed tobacco had been spitting on the snow near this same otter trap. Now, while these northern Indians are great smokers, they never chew tobacco, but this suspected man, who had in the Red River country been much with the whites, was nearly always chewing and spitting. Then there was the suspicious circumstance that a few days after he was offering at the Company's store a fine otter skin for sale. The Indians then were nearly all pagans, and there was no law in the land but their own tribal one. A secret council was held, and it was decided to put a watch on this man. Two or three of the cleverest Indians were appointed to watch his steps. Cunning though he was, they were too clever for him, and they so well followed him up that they saw him take a mink out of a trap. Then, resetting the trap, he hid the mink under his coat, and rapidly disappeared in the forest. The detectives did not rush out and capture him. They did not even let him know of their presence. As quietly as they had followed him, so they did return. The secret council was again summoned. A message was sent to a noted conjurer of the tribe, famous for his deadly poisons. Two days after a big Indian lay dead in the birch wigwam of one of the Red River Indian families. The burial was very quick and quiet. Not much was said. Indians do not, on some subjects, talk much, but it was observed for long years after that no hunter ever complained of his traps being robbed."

"I cannot see," said Frank, "why any honest person could complain of any such laws as those. They were certain that he was guilty, and then they quickly punished him."

"Yes," said Mr. Ross; "to some it may seem severe that he had to be killed, but the severity in this case crushed out the crime. None dare imitate him for fear of suffering his doom."

CHAPTER XIV.

Home Amusements and Studies—Happy Days at Sagastaweekee—Stories of the Early Hunters—Methods of Hunting Before the Introduction of Firearms—Wolves More Dreaded Then—Story of Two of Kinesasis's Children—Killed by Wolves—Shakoona's Sorrow—Saved by the Caresses of Little Children.

SAGASTA-WEEKEE was at all times a cozy, homelike place, but never did it seem more inviting and comfortable than when blizzard storms roared round it, or when fierce snowstorms seemed to make their mightiest efforts to see if they could not bury it in their enormous drifts of whitest snow. These terrific wintry gales sometimes made the house tremble on its foundations, and occasionally so shook the building that pictures hung on the wall would swing, and spoons in a tumbler on the mantelpiece would perceptibly jingle. But, in spite of the war of the elements outside, all was brightness and bliss within. There were endless resources of innocent amusement or work for all. A splendid, useful course of readings had been marked out for the boys, and Mr. Ross saw that this, as well as the books prescribed by their teachers at home, were faithfully read and studied. Then the rest of the time was devoted to recreation and work. A capital workshop, well supplied with tools, including a complete turning lathe, as well as fine saws for delicate fretwork, was always open to them, and in it many a pleasant and useful hour was spent.

Frank excelled as the mechanical genius of the trio, and so generally to him was assigned the work of making any difficult repairs needed on the dog-sleds or harness, for it was a point of honor among the boys to keep their own outfits in perfect condition themselves.

Sam excelled, as might have been expected from his nationality, as a reader and reciter, and during the long evenings added much to the profit and diversion of the household.

Alec had a sweet, well-cultivated voice for one so young, and particularly excelled in singing the sweet songs and ballads of old Scotland. Often amidst the hush of a still, quiet night, or even in the lulls between the roar of the blizzard or tempest, might have been heard the sweet notes of "Auld Lang Syne," "Annie Laurie," "Comin' Through the Rye," "John Anderson, My Jo," and many others that brought up happy memories of home, and touched for good all listening hearts. Another source of interest to the boys was for Mr. Ross to invite in some intelligent old Indian, like Memotas, Big Tom, Mustagan, Kinesasis, or Paulette, to tell some remarkable incident of his life, either as a hunter or traveler. Then, as there were living at the village not far away a number of Indians who had gone out with great Arctic adventurers or explorers, and had been gone for years, some of them had very remarkable stories to tell.

As Kinesasis had had charge of the dogs during the summer, and was still much employed by Mr. Ross on various jobs about the place, the boys became very well acquainted with him. He was a thorough Indian in his actions and modes of thought, and only saw things from his own standpoint. He was very observant, and had been quietly studying these three young "palefaces," whom his master, the Ookemou, Mr. Ross, had brought across the great sea. At first their active, demonstrative ways, so different from the quiet and taciturn manners of young Indians, tried him considerably. Yet he soon became accustomed to them. Then their grit and courage and perseverance under difficulties soon won his admiration. They had their mishaps, and, of course, in their endless sports and adventures they had to take their share of knocks, but under them all they were so good-natured and resourceful, as well as resolute and fearless, that the old Indian talked much about them among his own people, and said: "It was no wonder that the palefaces succeeded, if all their boys were like these three." But what completely made him their friend was Alec's terrible adventure with the wolves, and his signal triumph over their instinct and cunning by his resourceful tact and splendid endurance. Poor Kinesasis had reason to rejoice over every victory obtained over these fierce northern wolves. Some years before this they had during his absence broken into his wigwam and devoured two of his children. Some time later Mr. Ross told the story to the boys as he had heard it from Kinesasis himself. It was as follows:

"It was long ago, before the white traders had sold many guns to the Indians. Then the game was very much more plentiful than it is now in the forests. The wild animals were then also very much tamer. The bows and arrows of the hunters made but little noise in comparison with the loud report of the gunpowder. The result was that the animals were much more easily approached."

"Is it true, then," asked Sam, "that the young animals now, that have not as yet heard the firing of a gun, are wilder than the young ones were before gunpowder came into use?"

"Certainly," replied Mr. Ross. "It is well known by those who have studied it that all wild animals, and even birds, very soon become wilder and more alert and watchful after the introduction of gunpowder, and, what is stranger, they seem to be able to impart to their progeny this same spirit of fear and caution."

"I have often wondered," said Frank, "how it was that the Indians were able to kill sufficient game to keep themselves alive before they began to purchase gunpowder."

"What I have said in reply to Sam's question partly answers yours," answered Mr. Ross. "When a boy I often talked with old hunters who for many years hunted ere they fired a gun. They killed partridges with clubs, or with a noose on the end of a pole, as some of them can do yet, as has already been seen. Then they had no difficulty in crawling up to within a few feet of the deer or beavers."

"What about the more savage animals, such as the bears and wolves?" asked Alec.

"As regards the bears, as the hides of the old fellows were hard to pierce with arrows sufficient to give a mortal wound, the Indians depended mostly on the hand-to-hand conflict with the knife or tomahawk. With the wolves it was different. Before the guns were introduced the Indians dreaded the encounters with the wolves more than any other animals. It is true that they feared the fire as much then as now, but the Indians suffered from many disadvantages. Steel axes were but few, and very expensive. Now armed with guns, behind a good fire, hunters are comparatively safe. Then the wolves patiently waited until the limited wood supply was exhausted, and then closed in for the final struggle. It was then teeth against tomahawks, and the chances were more in favor of the wolves than now. Solitary hunters or single families caught by a pack were frequently overpowered and devoured. Climbing up into the trees afforded a temporary respite, as wolves cannot, like bears, there follow their victims. But the wolves were persistent besiegers, and woe to the unfortunate hunter who was thus treed by them unless help was near. For days they would keep watch, day and night, until the unfortunate one, chilled and benumbed by the bitter cold, fell into their midst and was speedily devoured. In those days the wolves were much more numerous than they are now, and more courageous in their attacks on the wigwams or even small settlements of the Indians. When distempers cut off the rabbits, or the deer were scarce, the wolves were very audacious in their attacks.

"It was one winter when the cold was terrible and the snow unusually deep that the sad tragedy came to the wigwam of Kinesasis. The reindeer had not come down from the barren plains as usual that winter, and the other animals generally hunted by the wolves were few and far between. Some of the Indian hunters had had some very narrow escapes, and the result was that very seldom did anyone venture far alone into his hunting grounds. Kinesasis was always a man of great courage and strength. He laughed at the caution of the others, and boldly pushed on to his distant hunting grounds whenever he saw a prospect of success. His wigwam, in which he left Shakoona and the two little ones during his absence, was made as warm and comfortable as such a habitation can be. It was arranged with the best of birch bark, and around outside, up to within a few feet of the top, Kinesasis piled the dry moss of that country, which grows there so plentifully. He cut abundance of wood, and left plenty of frozen meat and fish on the high staging outside. The only drawback was that the wigwam was situated on the outskirts of the village, close to the dark forest. Once a day, when the ice would be cut by the men of the village, Shakoona would take her buckets, made of the skin of the sturgeon, and go to the lake for her supply of water. It did not take her very long to make the trip, and she loitered not on the way, as she generally had to leave her two little ones alone. However, as the little girl was eight years of age and her brother only two years younger, the mother knew they were quite able to take care of themselves under ordinary circumstances during her brief absence from them.

"One day, however, when she returned she was horrified beyond all expression to find that a couple of great wolves had noiselessly crawled in from the forest and were greedily devouring her children. With a scream, but not with a faint, she threw one of the leather buckets of water on the smouldering fire which burned on the ground in the center of the wigwam. Then she instantly seized an ax, which fortunately was near the door by which she had entered. The clouds of steam which filled the wigwam quite disconcerted the wolves. When she had entered they had at once begun to growl more savagely, and seemed as though they would spring at her. The clouds of hot steam at once stopped their snarling, as well as their tearing at the bodies of the children, and before they could do any further injury Shakoona with one blow cut through the backbone of one, severing the spinal cord, thus rendering him powerless to move. The other one sprang at her ere she could disengage the ax for another blow. The wolf's object had been to catch her by the throat, but she had quickly thrown up her arm as a guard, and into it the cruel brute sank his great yellow fangs.

"Shakoona was in a terrible position now, but her presence of mind did not desert her, and so she quickly backed around the fire in such a way that before the wolf realized his position his hind feet were in the still red-hot embers of the fire. With a howl of pain he let go his grip on her arm and made for the door, which was of mooseskin, and which like a curtain had dropped back into place.

"In the meantime Shakoona's screams had been heard, and Indians from other wigwams speedily rushed to her help. Little did they realize, as they were coming, her sad bereavement. The first one to attempt to enter was an Indian woman. Just as she was entering the wolf with scorched feet was rushing out. The collision, as they met, knocked the woman over, and so delayed the wolf for a second or two that the next comer, who happened to be a stalwart hunter, was able to draw his tomahawk, and with one strong blow drove the keen edge of his weapon into the animal's brain. When these two Indians and others who had quickly joined them had entered the wigwam they saw a terrible sight—two children half devoured and a mother so overwhelmed with sorrow that not a tear would come from those great sad eyes. Then there was the wolf with severed spine, but still alive and looking more fiendish than ever. Very soon was the savage brute dispatched and his body thrown out of the wigwam.

"Loving hands quickly arranged and covered up what was left of the two children, and efforts were made to comfort the poor mother in her terrible sorrow. Swift runners were sent away to Kinesasis, to tell him of his great loss and to bring him home, as many feared if his wife did not soon begin to weep she would die. When Kinesasis heard the news he too was nearly heart-broken, but when he reached his wigwam and beheld Shakoona he crushed down his own sorrow to try and comfort her who had, on account of the way the great bereavement had come to her, suffered much more than he. For days and days Shakoona was as one in a dream. She was gentle as usual, but those great eyes, so sad and dry, seemed to haunt all who visited her. All said she soon would die unless she got relief. They tried many ways, but all in vain, until at length a kindly Indian woman went out and brought in the boys and girls with whom her little ones used to play. At first Shakoona seemed pained by their presence, but as they looked into those sad eyes they began weeping, and, childlike, they threw their arms around her and wept. Passively at first she received these fondlings, but soon the children's caresses broke down the barriers and the hot tears began to flow, and the woman was saved from death or insanity. But her hair turned white shortly afterward, and she has ever since been that sad little woman that you have seen her. Kinesasis has never been cruel to her, as, alas! too many of the pagan Indian husbands are to their wives."

CHAPTER XV.

The Beavers, and Something About Them—Two Hunters at Sagasta-weekee—A General Invitation to a Beaver Hunt Accepted—The Preparations—The Trip—Dog-traveling in the Woods—Saucy Wild Animals—The Wolf's Cove—The Boys' Plunge in the Snowdrift—The Rescue.

THE beaver is a very interesting animal. In the previous summer the boys had been fortunate enough to see a colony of beavers at work during a beautiful moonlight night. They had also subsequently examined the wonderful dam these industrious, ingenious creatures had made, and were much amazed and surprised not only at its size, but also at the clever way in which every part of it was constructed to meet any emergency that might occur by flood or freshet.

They also noticed that the Indians did very little hunting of the beaver, or, indeed, of any of the rich fur-bearing animals during the summer months. Now, however, that the winter had come they were all alert and active, and as soon as their fall fisheries were completed they began making preparations for the winter harvest of furs. On their success in a great measure depended the happiness and comfort of themselves and their families. They lived too far north to cultivate the land with any degree of success, and hence it was only by the sale of their furs that they were able to buy the essential necessaries for their simple lives.

The fur is only considered **prime in the winter**

months. That killed in summer is thin and poor, and for it the hunters receive but a low price. But when the cold weather sets in the fur becomes thick and valuable. Then the hunters leave their homes and go to the distant hunting grounds, often hundreds of miles away. Many are their hardships and privations. They take but little food with them, and so have to depend on what they can hunt or shoot. In some regions where the fur-bearing animals are fairly numerous those that are good for food are very few. The result sometimes is that Indians doing well in getting the rich furs of the black and silver foxes, otters, minks, and martens, and some other fur-bearing animals, are nearly starving most of the time. On the other hand, those who succeed in capturing abundance of beavers, wild cats, muskrats, and bears, live very well, as all of these animals are eaten by the natives, although their furs do not bring as high a price as the others.

The discovery of a large beaver house is a great piece of good luck to an Indian hunter. Sometimes, when the house is a small one, a hunter will with his ax only put his mark of ownership on a tree near by, then leave it undisturbed. Scores of hunters may happen to come along, but when they see that mark they never think of trying to get those beavers. It may be that the owner will mark it the second year, and again leave it for the beaver to multiply the third time. Each year the beavers are undisturbed they take down and enlarge their house, until, if thus left for years, and the dam keeps good and the water supply sufficient, they will continue extending their habitation until it is as large as a good-sized haystack.

There came one day to Sagasta-weekee, on a visit, a couple of clever Indian hunters who were great friends of Mr. Ross. Among other things they told him was that two nights away they had a large beaver house which they had preserved for three years, and that they were soon going to take out the beavers. This was just the news Mr. Ross wanted to hear, as he had often talked with the boys about these wonderful animals, and was anxious that they should see how the cleverness of the hunters outmatched all the skill and sagacity of the beavers.

Then, as it was about a hundred miles away, it would be a capital winter's trip and give them some idea of the Indian hunter's life. They would have to camp out in the wintry forest, and would thus find the difference between sleeping in the summer, with the temperature up to eighty, and sleeping in the wintry cold, with the spirit thermometer perhaps indicating fifty below zero.

When the boys heard of the promised trip they were wild with excitement. As much preparation had to be made, the day selected to start was about a week after the visit of the two Indians. It was indeed a busy week. Each of the three boys was to take his dog-train. They would be expected to take on their own sleds their beds, clothing, and part of the supplies. Snowshoes were made for them, and every day they diligently practiced this new method of locomotion. They had many amusing tumbles. Sometimes, where the snowdrifts were deep, when they attempted to pass over they somehow or other would get the snowshoes so tangled up that over they would go on their heads. The more they struggled the deeper they sank in the light, fleecy snow, until it seemed as though nothing was visible but a pair of snowshoes wildly wabbling about. Then the experienced Indian who always accompanied them would come to the rescue. Gliding up gracefully on his own snowshoes to the struggling lad, he would reach down and, seizing him under the arms, would quickly lift him up and once more place him on his feet amidst the laughter of the others. Thus they practiced and fell, tried again and again, until the knack was accomplished and they could get along very nicely.

In the meantime diligent preparations were being made indoors for this excursion to the home of the beavers. Abundance of fat food was cooked. Dogshoes were manufactured, as well as large moccasins for the travelers.

In due time the start was made. It was to the boys a most unique and novel affair. First ran the guide, a stalwart Indian, who could easily keep ahead of the fastest train. It is the duty of the guide, by running on in front, to indicate the best route. He must never make a track where it is not safe for the dogs with the heavy sleds to follow. If he finds a great fallen tree in the way it is his duty, not to jump over the trunk and push on, but to circle around it where the party following can easily advance. In rocky places he must ever have in mind the loaded sleds following, and walk or run where there is an available trail. He must never go between two trees growing so closely together that there will be any difficulty for the widest sled following to pass between them. He is supposed to know the strength or weakness of the weakest train or runner, and so must decide on each resting as well as camping place. In his footsteps all are to implicitly follow, and so his position is one of great responsibility. As a natural result, he is supposed to receive much higher pay than the ordinary dog-driver, who has not much care beyond that of his own dog-train.

This being the first trip made in this direction this season, there was not the least vestige of a road or trail. Tornado blasts had swept through the forests which abounded most of the way. The result was that fallen trees were very numerous. Some of them were so tangled together that it was at times easier to cut through than make the long detour to get around them. Knowing this, the guide carried with him an ax instead of a gun.

An old, experienced, powerful train of dogs went first. The sagacious leader never swerved from the tracks of the guide. No matter how winding or difficult the trail, he never wandered from it. Sometimes he could see the guide straight ahead, while the path seemed to veer at right angles. While the sight of the guide ahead might stimulate him to greater effort and speed, still he knew his duty was to keep in the well-defined track. A straight cut to the guide might run him into a dangerous gully or over a steep precipice. So, knowing his duty, perhaps taught it by bitter experience—and dogs have good memories—he tried his best in his doglike way to do his duty.

Mr. Ross's train followed next. They were jet-black in color, and were large, magnificent dogs. They were so trained that they as readily responded to his calls as a good horse does to the pulling of the reins.

Then following came the boys with their three trains. Frank, having the largest dogs, had the lead. Sam came next, and then Alec with the lightest but by far the fleetest train in the whole party. Behind was another sled of Mr. Ross's with more supplies, and then, bringing up the rear, was a sled belonging to the two Indians who owned the beaver house. While one of them drove the train the other, on account of the many fallen trees in the way that had to be cut out, was on ahead with Memotas, the guide.

As they thus set off they made quite a display. The boys were simply wild with the excitement of the hour. They looked very picturesque in their handsome outfits. Their deerskin suits, over the warmest of flannel underclothing, were very beautiful, as they were made under Mrs. Ross's direction by the most clever Indian women. They were beautifully adorned with bead and silkwork and trimmed with fur. Their overcoats, as before stated, were made of the heavy white blankets of the Hudson Bay Company. These blankets are very warm and firm, as they are especially made for that cold country. The caps and mittens were of the finest fur.

Their moccasins were extra large, to allow for the additional wrapping of duffel required over the warm woolen hose. They also had warm leggings of strouds, beautifully fringed and fastened with strong garters artistically worked with porcupine quills. A warm, well-lined hood or capote was attached to each overcoat. This the boys found of very great service and comfort, especially when their unexperienced sleigh dogs were unable to keep the heads of their sleds, at times, from striking against some snow-laden tree with such force that the snow in great quantities came tumbling about them. But for these capotes much of the snow would have found its way into their faces and down under the collars of their coats.

To be like the rest of the party, the lads were each the possessor of a fine dog-whip. Of course, they were not so long and heavy as those ordinarily used, but they could when well handled make a pistollike crack, and for this purpose only were they used.

The first few miles of the route were on the ice over places well known to all, as in their frequent outings they had gone in this direction. It was well known to Alec, for it was along this very way that he had skated so rapidly after leaving the river, with the howling wolves behind him.

On and on they pushed to the extreme end of the lake, for they wished to avail themselves of as much of the ice route as possible, as it is so much easier traveling on the ice than in the forest, where there is no trail.

When the sleds reached the spot where they were

to enter the forest they found that the guide and his Indian comrade had cut down some dry trees and made up a splendid fire. No sooner had the trains arrived than some of the sleds were hastily untied, the deerskin wrappings which were on all were opened, and a couple of large kettles were speedily filled with the clear, light snow and placed on the roaring fire. So light and feathery is the snow that the kettles have to be filled and refilled a good many times ere sufficient is put in to make them full of water. Then the provision bags were opened, and abundance of food was taken out for all.

One of the Indians who was skillful at this kind of work was detailed as special cook and general waiter for Mr. Ross and the boys. Very quickly he had ready the dinner of the good things Mrs. Ross had prepared for them. The boys were surprised at the quantity of the fat food that was placed before them, and were almost ashamed of the vigor and capacity of their appetites. Nature, true to her instincts, puts in the craving for the kind of food most essential for people in different parts of the world.

About an hour was allowed for the dinner halt, and then the journey was resumed. There were the usual mishaps that necessarily belonged to this mode of travel. Sleds were occasionally upset, and if at the time anyone happened to be riding he was buried in the snow, from which he emerged none the worse for the plunge, but generally amidst the laughter of those more fortunate. Several times a fox or some other animal ran across the trail, and then it required some effort and sternness to control the dogs and prevent them from starting off after these animals, which are their natural foes. The older dogs had learned somewhat by experience the folly of trying while thus harnessed to heavy sleds to capture wild foxes, and so merely confined their efforts to loud barkings and a little more vigorous tugging at their traces. The younger and less disciplined trains, however, with less discretion and more zeal, at once dashed away from the beaten trail made by the trains ahead of them, and recklessly plunged into the forest after the game.

"Who would imagine," said Frank, "that dogs so heavily loaded could thus fairly fly over the snow-covered logs and rocks and among the trees at such a rate?"

They learned then, and in many an experience afterward, of the latent strength there is in an apparently wearied dog. Only give him the stimulus to develop it, and it is simply surprising to all who witness it.

Alec's fleet train was the most excited and intractable. Bruce could not stand the sight of a saucy fox or a snarling wild cat passing across the trail, only a few hundred feet ahead of him, with any degree of equanimity. After him he must and would go, in spite of Alec's hardest efforts to keep him in the trail. Bruce, with the other three dogs, about as eager as himself, would often leave the track and with a spurt get off several hundred yards in the woods before he could be stopped. Sometimes their stopping would be rather abrupt. Generally the trees were so close together that it was not long ere the head of the sled came in violent collision with a great one. This, of course, stopped them most effectually. At other times, while Bruce, the leader, decided to take one side of a small tree, the dog next to him took the other side. This divergency of views on the part of the dogs also quickly put an end to their advance.

Alec, in his determined efforts to arrest their progress at these times, did not always escape unscathed. When in a bad forest where the snow was deep he often would stumble and fall, and before he could regain his feet had acted the part of a snowplow as he was rapidly dragged along. He received some painful bruises, but he pluckily kept to his work, and so had his dogs in fairly good submission before many such trips were made.

A laughable but fortunately not dangerous adventure happened to the boys and their trains at a place called by the Indians the Wolf's Cove, on account of the many wolves that formerly infested the place. There it was necessary to cross a very deep valley, or ravine. The hillsides were very steep and slippery under the heavy snowfall. As the dogsleds have no brakes upon them, the only way of arresting their speedy motion when going down a steep hill is for the driver to hold back the sled by the strong rope which is always attached to the rear end and is called the tail rope.

If the hill is steep or slippery, and the load heavy, this is a difficult operation and requires much care. Owing to the way in which the dogs are attached to the sleds, the drivers are utterly powerless to render any assistance in arresting the progress of the sled.

When the sleds reached the ravine there was a short halt ere the first descent was made.

The old, experienced Indian drivers were of the opinion that the boys were not strong or heavy enough on their moccasined feet to hold back their sleds, and suggested that, after they themselves had gone down with the loads, they return and take charge of the trains of the boys. This help, kindly offered, was rejected by the lads, who, having managed fairly well thus far, except where the passing game bothered them, were anxious to try this new experiment.

Mr. Ross at first was also a little dubious about it, but youthful enthusiasm and love of new adventures conquered. While the first sleds were descending the boys and the rest of the party not immediately occupied watched the operation with a good deal of interest.

"Faith," said Sam, "it's as easy as sliding down the banisters."

"The hill seems greased for the occasion," said Frank, as he noticed the ease and rapidity with which the sleds slid down in spite of the grip and strong holdback of the heavy, experienced Indian drivers.

"Plenty of snow to tumble into," said Alec, who could not forget the way he had plowed through it when his dogs ran away with him as they attempted to catch the wild cat.

Fortunately or unfortunately for the boys, there

had been a good deal of wind in this part of the country since the last snowfall, and so now there was a large drift of perhaps twenty feet that had been blown into the bottom of the first steep hill. The guides with some help had in the route through this deep snow gone backward and forward a few times on their heavy snowshoes, and had packed down a trail sufficiently hard for the dogs and sleds. All the heavy sleds with their drivers went on ahead of the boys. Thus they, coming last, had the advantage of the packing of the snow.

Sam, jolly and reckless, was the first of the boys to make the descent, while the others followed closely behind, Frank being next to him, and Alec bringing up the rear.

For a time Sam succeeded very well in imitating the experienced drivers. He kept his feet well and firmly planted on the snowy surface, and held back his sled in fine style. The other boys also succeeded in starting well on the trail. They had not gone very far, however, before a small gray wolf, that had been hidden in one of the denlike recesses in the rocks, now thoroughly alarmed by the dingling of so many bells and the sounds of so many voices, suddenly sprang from his retreat, which was in the cliffs on the other side beyond the guide. Plunging into the deep snow, he made the most desperate efforts to escape by retreating up the distant hillside in front of the whole party. Fierce fires had raged through these woods a year so so before, nearly destroying the whole of the timber. The result was that the country was now here quite open, and objects as large as a wolf could be seen for a long distance. From their higher position the boys and their dogs could much more distinctly see the wolf on the opposite hillside than could the rest of the party, who, having safely made the descent, were now on the beginning of the rise on the other side, awaiting the coming of the boys. They did not have long to wait. The sight of that wolf, so clearly seen in the bright sunshine of that wintry day on the snowy hillside, was too much for their brief discipline. Spitfire could not stand it. With a howl he was off, and well seconded were his efforts by the dogs he was leading. Sam was instantly jerked off his feet, but he pluckily held on to the tail rope of his sled. Well was it for him that his pants were made of mooseskin, for they had a good testing of their qualities now, as rapidly on them he was now tobogganing down that steep, slippery hillside.

Behind him came the other dog-trains. Of them the boys had also lost control. Such was the steepness of the hill that soon the momentum obtained by the sleds caused them to go faster than the dogs could run. Here was the real danger. When Frank and Alec saw how it was faring with Sam, and were also quick to observe that with that wolf so plainly visible it would be utterly impossible for them on a downhill, slippery grade to control their now excited dogs, they, boylike, took the risks, and at once threw themselves upon their sleds and hung on to the deerskin thongs with which the loads were securely tied.

"Hurrah for somewhere!" shouted Alec.

"Clear the track!" was Frank's hurried shout to Sam, whom he saw still in the trail, down which he was now furiously coming.

The guide, on his snowshoes, in tramping out the trail had near the bottom made a little turn to the left in order to escape the deepest snowdrift which the wind had there piled up. The foremost trains, with their powerful, experienced drivers, had been able to make this detour all right, and now had stopped only a little way ahead.

By the time the trains of the boys had reached this part of the descent they were in a most thoroughly mixed-up condition. Boys, dogs, and sleds were literally so tangled up that they were to the rest of the party an indistinguishable mass as down they came, and at the bend in the road, instead of being able to turn, they all flew into the heavy drift of snow which was straight before them, and almost disappeared. There was quick work for the onlookers now to do. At first they had been almost convulsed with laughter, as they saw the mixed-up assortment coming down in such a way. Then, when the whole flew by and buried itself so thoroughly in the deep drift of light, fleecy snow, there was instantly a good deal of anxiety for the boys.

As they began the work of rescue the sight before them was unique. There is a hand working desperately, and here is a foot waving in the air. There is a dog's head emerging as the animal makes a desperate struggle to get out, and there is the curly tail of another coming into view. Only such a land could show such a sight. Alec, the last to plunge in, was the first rescued, although he had been completely buried out of sight, as had been the others. Frank was the next pulled out, feet foremost. Sam was the last rescued. His tobogganing slide had been abruptly ended by his being entangled in the harness of Frank's train coming on behind him. Then it seemed to him as though the head of the oncoming sled, like the cowcatcher on an engine, had picked him and the dogs up, and in an instant more, he said, he was sent flying as from a catapult into the drift, the instant the sled left the track. So far ahead was he thus shot that the sleds stopped before they reached him, and so, although he was deeply buried, he was not run over.

Not one of the boys had a scratch or a bruise. The only discomfort was that, in spite of big mittens and capotes, so much snow had found its way where it was, to say the least, not very welcome. But it was light and feathery, and was soon dusted off or shaken out, and then the work was to get out and disentangle the dogs. This was no easy matter. Some of them, in the wild rush down the hill, when struck by the sleds had rolled over and over in such a way that their traces looked more like ropes than anything else. Others of them were now in such uncomfortable positions that they were howling most piteously for help, while others that had happened to be thrown together, and perhaps each thinking that the others were to blame for this mix-up, were as vigorously fighting as their entanglement in their harnesses and sleds would allow.

After the rescue of the lads the Indians unfastened one of their most powerful dog-trains from one of the other sleds and hitched it to the rear of these buried ones, from which they had, with the snow-shoes as shovels, so thrown the snow that they could be reached. With a good deal of effort and a great deal of fun they were pulled out one by one. The dogs of each train were naturally indignant at thus being unceremoniously dragged backward. As each sled and train were thus hauled out and straightened in the trail, and the harness untangled, the amount of damage could be ascertained. With the exception of a few loose articles that were buried somewhere in the drift there was no loss. It is true that some of the dogs seemed a little sore and stiff for a few days, but beyond that there was nothing serious. Snow is a capital substance in which to tumble if there is plenty of it.

This adventure, which was often talked about and caused many a hearty laugh, delayed the party about a couple of hours. As the hill up which they were now to go was about as steep as the one down which they had so quickly come, it was decided to fasten two trains of dogs to each sled. This, while making the work easier on the dogs, caused considerable delay. The result was that when the whole party had reached the top Memotas decided that it would be best there to camp.

CHAPTER XVI.

Still on the Way to the Beaver House—The Winter Camp in the Woods—Work for All—Feeding the Dogs—Our Boys Guarding Their Own Trains—The Evening Meal—Bitter Cold —Milk in Lumps of Ice—Evening Prayers—The Wintry Camp Bed—Tucked In—Mysterious Sounds in the Forest—Smothering Sensations—Sam's Nightmare—Breakfast—Tricky Dogs—Methods of Capture—Carioles and Sleds Reloaded—Trains Harnessed—Journey Resumed.

A WINTER camp in the North Land, and the temperature anywhere from thirty to sixty below zero!

Cold? Yes, we think so, and so did Frank, Alec, and Sam, as now they were passing through their first experience.

As was stated in our last chapter, to the guide was always assigned the responsibility of selecting the camping place. The place here chosen by Memotas was considered a very good one. First, because there was abundance of dead, dry trees to serve as fuel. These had been killed a year or so before by a great forest fire that had run through that region of country. Second, there was a fine, dense balsam grove that had escaped the fire. In one part of it there was sufficient space for the camp. Then, in addition, by cutting down some of the smaller of these evergreen trees, their branches, finely broken up, would help to make the bed more comfortable.

These are the essentials for a good camp: plenty of fuel and a sheltered spot. It is not always easy to find good camping places, so the guide is generally on the lookout for such localities. The result is his quick eye and good memory generally enable him to select all the camps that will be required on a return journey.

When all the sleds were at the spot selected the first thing done was to unharness the dogs, the faithful animals that had so well done their work. It seemed at first strange to the boys that the dogs could be treated so differently from what horses would have been when the day's work was done. Indeed, everything was novel and startling.

A day's journey was ended, and they were about to take a night's rest. But how different from traveling elsewhere. Here was no pleasant hotel or country tavern in which they could find lodgings. Here were no hospitable settlers to invite these strangers in to be their guests. They were preparing to stop out here in the woods all night, where there was neither hotel nor private dwelling place nearer than the home they had left now so many miles behind.

No wonder Sam said, as he pulled a piece of ice as big as a pepper caster off the fur edge of his cap, that had there formed from his breath:

"This beats all the lodging houses I ever heard of. Faith, and where is the landlord?"

Alec's practical reply was: "Well, there will be no bill to pay in the morning, anyway."

"Pay or no pay," said Sam, "I would like to know where we are going to sleep in such a place as this?"

"And where are we going to eat?" said Frank.

"Wait a little while," said Mr. Ross, "and you will see a change that will astonish you. In the meantime each of you take an ax and see which of you can first cut down one of those trees. The exercise will do you good, and then remember," he said with a laugh, "we have no deadheads on this trip."

Eagerly the boys rushed off to the sleds for their axes, and, putting on their snowshoes—for the snow was too deep for comfortable work without them—they were soon busily engaged at what was Gladstone's favorite exercise. In the meantime the men were hard at work in preparing the camp. The snow was between three and four feet deep at the place selected. Using their snowshoes as shovels, they vigorously attacked the snow and threw it up on two sides and in the rear, making a snow wall about five feet high on three sides. The two opposite walls were about twelve feet apart, while the rear wall was perhaps ten feet back from the front space where the snow was cleared away. Here a great log heap was soon piled up. Dry splinters and chips were placed under, and an Indian with his flint and steel soon had it ignited. In a little while a glorious fire was blazing, lighting up the whole surroundings. The sun had gone down in splendor and the stars one by one had quickly come out, and now the whole heavens were aglow with them. On the space between the snowbanks a heavy layer of the green balsam boughs were evenly spread. On these the robes and blankets from each sled were arranged by busy hands, while others attended to various other duties. Some took large kettles and filled and refilled them up with snow, and kept them on the blazing fire until they were nearly full of water. Meat was cooked in some, while tea was made in others.

The dog-drivers looked after their own dogs. From the sleds sufficient fish were taken to give to each dog two good whitefish. These were the daily rations of the dogs. The invariable rule is when traveling to give them but one meal a day, and that is given at the evening camp. So severe is the frost that these fish are frozen as hard as rocks, and so the drivers have to knock them off the sticks where in tens they were strung when caught. Then they are placed against a log that is rolled as near to the fire as it can be without burning. Against this log the fish are stood up next to the fire, and well thawed out, ere they are given to the dogs. Getting but one meal a day, they are naturally very eager for it, and so it is no wonder if some of them get up an occasional quarrel. Neither is it surprising if some of the stronger and more greedy strive to steal some portion of the supper from those not so active or quick in eating as themselves. One of the best times to study dog nature is when they are being fed.

The boys, having each cut down a good, large tree, hugely enjoyed the feeding of the thawed-out fish to their own dogs. They were greatly amused at the efforts of the greedy ones to rob others. They had their whips in hand, and while they each took good care not to strike his own dogs, they rather enjoyed giving a crack to some cunning old rascals from some of the older trains, that having in all probability imposed on the youngsters all summer imagined they could with impunity keep it up here.

"You would, would you, you thieving beast!" said Sam, as with hearty good will he brought his whip vigorously down on a powerful old dog that was making a cunning attempt to rob Spitfire of about half a fish.

With a howl of rage the baffled fellow quickly sprang back into the gloom.

Frank and Alec also had to be equally alert, to see that their dogs were not robbed by others.

Mr. Ross and the Indians were much amused and pleased to see the zeal and promptness with which the boys guarded the rights of their trains. They said that this was always the way with old dogs; that they would try most persistently for a few nights, in the beginning of winter, to rob the younger animals. A few good thrashings generally cured them of it; and sometimes, to the surprise of some of these old fellows, a youngster would develop such spirit and strength that he would turn on the would-be robber and give him a thrashing himself. Then there would be no trouble from that old fellow afterward.

"I wonder where the dogs will sleep," said Frank.

"Wait a little while and you will see," was the reply from Memotas, the guide.

Sure enough, it was evident that they knew how to look out for themselves. The older ones, after being certain that all the fish had been distributed, would lift up their heads and sniff the breeze. No matter how slight it was they could easily detect it. Then they would travel about the camp in the snow until they found a sheltered spot, free from the wind. Here they would turn round and round until they had made a hole in the snow, away down near the ground. Then down in it they would curl themselves into as small a bundle as possible, with their tails over their noses, and there they would shiver or sleep through the night, as the cold would permit.

The younger dogs seemed at first very uncertain as to their movements. Some of them followed the actions of the old dogs, but others that had but little of the Eskimo blood in them clung to the fire and the company of their masters. For these Mr. Ross had a driver bring from one of the sleds two or three extra buffalo skins, which he thoughtfully had brought along. These were spread out near the fire, at a spot from which the snow was partially cleared.

"Now tell your dogs to sleep there," said Mr. Ross.

The boys quickly did so, and it was not long before those that had not gone off and dug nests in the snow for themselves were closely cuddled together on the comfortable robes.

In the meantime supper was being prepared by others. Meat and fish in generous quantities were cooked in the kettles. Bread and flat cakes, well supplied with grease or fat, were being thawed out, and a large quantity of good black tea was prepared.

A large deerskin robe was carefully spread out

before the fire, and over this a plain tablecloth was laid. Then the dishes, which were all indestructible, were placed in position, and the fat meat, strong tea, and hot rolls or buns were vigorously attacked by Mr. Ross and the boys. While they were thus enjoying their meal the rest of the party, not far off, were similarly engaged.

There were several things about this camping out in the woods that much surprised the boys. One was that the numerous sparks from the fire had such long fiery tails. Another was that the frost so quickly froze up the large pieces of meat, that often had to be thawed out two or three times at each meal. Another was that the ice often formed on their cups of tea, which had been taken boiling hot out of the kettle only a few minutes before. Then they were startled by sharp reports, like pistol or musket shots, that they kept hearing from places in the dark forest all around them, as though some lurking savages were taking snap shots at them. Two especially were so near and so real that Sam jumped up so suddenly that he spilled his tea over the tablecloth.

"Faith, indeed," he exclaimed, "I don't want to be potted out here by any wild huntsmen, or Northern desperado, or red Indian."

The other boys were also much startled, but Mr. Ross quieted their fears by telling them that these sounds were caused by the bursting in the trees, as the result of the freezing sap. Water in freezing always expands, and as there is sufficient sap in some trees, when it freezes, it bursts them. It must expand, and tremendous is its power, as even the burst rocks will show.

"It is a good thing that the ice remains on the top of the water," said Frank. "As it freezes it expands, and thus, being lighter than the water, it comes to the top."

"What a mess we would be in," said Sam, "if as the ice froze in chunks it sank to the bottom and kept at it all winter. Sure then, before spring, in such a land as this, the lakes and rivers would all be one solid mass of ice, and then what would become of the fish and us?"

"A sensible remark, Sam, and characteristically put," said Mr. Ross. "If the ice were heavier than the water, and continued sinking, the colder regions would continually be encroaching on the warmer, to such a degree that in time the earth's habitable portions would be very much diminished."

"Why is it," said Alec, "that the milk which we are carrying in chunks, wrapped up in paper bags, when put into our cups of tea, does not melt as soon as do the lumps of white sugar of the same size?"

"Closely examine a lump of frozen milk, and also a lump of sugar, and you will easily see the reason," said Mr. Ross. "When milk is firmly frozen it is very solid indeed—so solid that even hot water can only melt it on its surface. With a lump of sugar it is very different, as on account of its porousness the water at once forces its way through it, and thus is able to quickly dissolve it."

Thus in pleasant chat the hour passed away in spite of the bitter cold. They were all securely wrapped up, only portions of their faces being visible. They regretted that they could not handle their knives and forks with their heavy mittens on their hands, but were obliged to exchange them for well-lined gloves while they ate. After all had eaten their hearty supper, and were now gathered near the fire, one of the Indians, who, like the rest of his countrymen in this party, was an earnest, devout Christian, struck up in a strong, melodious voice the Evening Hymn, translated into his own language.

Quickly the others joined in, while Mr. Ross and the boys sang in unison the English words. After the hymn was sung, and ended up with Ken's beautiful doxology, "Praise God from whom all blessings flow," another Indian devoutly prayed in his own language, after which the service ended by all repeating together the Lord's Prayer in English.

The boys were very much pleased and delighted with this evening service of praise and prayer. Their weird surroundings added to its impressiveness. Then the fact that they were out in the cold forest, with no roof above them but the starry heavens and no walls around them but snowbanks, and the temperature so many degrees below zero, made the petition in the beautiful hymn sung very appropriate:

> Keep me, O keep me, King of kings,
> Beneath thine own almighty wings!

After prayers the men made a thorough examination of the sleds and harness, to see that everything was in good condition, as they intended, if all was well, to start on the journey long hours before daylight.

Then the beds were made. This operation very much interested the boys. The first thing the Indians did was to put everybody out of the camp; then they scattered fresh green balsam boughs, finely broken up, over the whole spot, from which the snow had nearly all been cleared. Then, on the side where Mr. Ross and the boys were to sleep, the Indian bedmakers first spread out a deerskin wrapper, which during the day was used to hold all the various articles constituting a sleigh load, the whole then being securely lashed on by deerskin straps. It was made by sewing several large, well-dressed deerskins together. This large wrapper being made smooth and even, there was next spread out on it a couple of splendid buffalo skins. Then on the top of these the warm, thick blankets known as four-point Hudson Bay Company's blankets were placed.

While the bed was being thus prepared Mr. Ross and the three boys were busily employed in preparing themselves to occupy it. It can be readily understood that there was no such thing as "undressing" for bed in such a cold bedroom.

"Unloose your collars and shirt bands," was all the directions given, as far as disrobing was concerned.

The heavy traveling moccasins used during the day were exchanged either for long fur boots that came up to the hips, or for much larger and softer moccasins than those used during the day.

It generally added to the comfort if a few of the

tightest buttons on some of the inner garments were unloosed. Then the heavy blanket coats, which had been well dried of all the perspiration absorbed during the day and well warmed, were put on. The heavy fur caps, with the big fur ears, were well drawn down, while over all the warm capotes, as hoods, were pulled up on the head and down in front to the nose. Great fur mittens made of beaver and otter fur were then drawn on the hands, and the night suit was complete.

Mr. Ross took the outside place. Then Sam, Alec, and Frank cuddled down in the order named. There they lay with their feet as near to the fire as it was safe, so as not to burn the blankets or robes. Then the Indians quickly threw some heavy blankets and fur robes over them and began at their feet to tuck them in. Indians are very clever and handy at all such work, their movements are all so gentle and skillful. They would make the best nurses in the world. No woman is quieter, quicker, or more prompt just to do the right thing in the right way than an Indian attendant with a little training. It seems to come to them more natural than to any other people. So here they so daintily and yet so thoroughly tucked in the "master," as they called Mr. Ross, and his three young guests.

The boys enjoyed the operation hugely until they reached their heads. Then, as the Indians began to tuck in both blankets and fur robes under their heads, completely covering them up, it was a new experience, and one not very pleasant to contemplate. Mr. Ross, who was an old traveler in this land,

and one who had slept out hundreds of nights in this way, was not at all discommoded by the tucking in. But it was too much for the boys. They stood it as long as they could, and then almost simultaneously they threw up their arms and pulled down the heavy coverings from their faces.

"O dear!" said Sam. "Let me freeze to death, but for dear old Ireland's sake don't smother me. If ye must send word to my mother that I have been frozen to death or eaten by bears she will believe you, and survive, but let it never be told that the Irish lad perished in this country under fur robes and blankets."

This pathetic lament of Sam's brought forth roars of laughter from all who could understand it.

"What have you to say, Alec?" said Mr. Ross.

"Well, the fact is," he replied, "I was feeling about as Sam has expressed it, only I put it in a different way. My thoughts were: 'It is queer that I should have escaped from the wolves to be suffocated in this land for the want of fresh air!'"

"What say you, Frank. We may as well hear from all."

His answer was: "Well, as I lay there on that contracted place, and the half-smothery sensation began to make life miserable, I remembered some of the lessons we were taught at school about requiring so many cubic feet of fresh air, and I began to wonder if such laws were obsolete out here."

With a little more freedom the boys were again tucked in, and it was not long before they were sound asleep.

Memotas, the guide, rolled himself up in a woven rabbit skin robe, which was made out of a hundred and twenty skins, sixty being the warp and sixty the woof. His place was next to Frank. Then the other Indians, in their blankets, when they had finished their smoking, laid down wherever there was room. These hardy natives do not wear half of the clothing by day that white people do, neither do they require such warm beds at night.

The only disturbance in the night was caused by Sam. He set up a great howling, which caused the guide to spring up in a hurry to see what was the matter. In the morning, when Sam was questioned as to his troubles in the night, he said he was dreaming that he was sliding down one of the Rocky Mountains with an elephant after him, and just as he reached the bottom the elephant tumbled on him, and there he lay yelling for help, until at length some one came and drove the elephant away.

This was too much for even the sedate, clever Memotas, and as Mr. Ross noticed his hearty laugh, as a thing so unusual, he said:

"Come, Memotas, you must surely know something about this."

"Yes," he answered, "I saw the elephant. It was Spitfire, his dog. I heard Alec moaning gently at first, and so I uncovered my head, for I wake very easily, and there was his dog. He was coming up from his feet, for the fire was burning low. He would take one or two steps and then stop and smell. I saw he was trying to find his master, so I did not disturb him. Soon he came up so far that he could lie down on Sam's chest, on the outside on the robes. Then Sam, he began howling, and so he had what you white people call the nightmare, but this time it was the nightdog." And Memotas softly laughed again, and others joined with him at Sam's expense.

At Mr. Ross's request a large quantity of fuel had been cut the previous evening, so that the fire was not allowed to go entirely out during the whole night. The trees most common for fuel in all the North country are the dry spruce and balsam. The guides, looking for the camp, love to find a group of them where they are from fifty to seventy-five feet high. All required are chopped down and then cut into lengths of from ten to fifteen feet. They are easily handled by the stalwart men, and make a bright fire. Generally the fire is allowed to go out after all have retired to rest. However, if the wolves are howling around, the fire is well looked after all night, as these vicious brutes are very much afraid of a bright flame.

The stars were shining brightly, and there was no sign of light in the eastern sky, when all were up and busy making preparations for the day's journey. What most perplexed the boys was that there was no preparation made for washing hands or faces. Towels and soap were not considered essentials on such a journey. Each had in his pocket a comb and a toothbrush, and with these and a cup of melted snow he had to be content.

Frank, young Englishman that he was, dearly loved his tub, or bath, and so it seemed about the hardest deprivation thus far presented that he could neither wash his hands nor face.

"Too cold for that," said the guide. "A missionary once tried it, although we warned him against it. He was three months healing up his chapped and bleeding hands." Then the guide added, as a little consolation, "If you like you can give yourself a dry rub with a piece of deerskin."

The breakfast was similar to the supper of the previous evening. Indeed, there was about the same bill of fare for every meal. It was strong, hearty food, and everyone was ready to do ample justice to it.

After breakfast came prayers. A few verses from the good Book were read by Memotas, and then prayers were offered. Twice every day do these godly Indians thus worship God. They are the converts of self-sacrificing missionaries who, coming into these lands, amid the privations and hardships incident to such lonely, solitary places, here patiently toiled and labored to win these natives from their degrading, superstitious, abominable old religion to a knowledge of the one living and true God. They have not toiled in vain, as the true, noble, consistent lives of hundreds of their converts now bear witness.

The catching and harnessing of the dogs is a matter of pleasure or trouble, just as the dogs have been trained. Dogs kindly treated and taught to obey give no trouble, but with many, where their training was defective, there is constant annoyance and worry. The boys had treated their dogs so kindly that the cheery call was all that was needed. So with all the trains of Mr. Ross's except one. These were what might be called a scratch train. They had been bought singly from different parties. When in harness they were the equal of any, but the trouble was to get them into their harness. One was a pure white animal. At the first sound or movement in the camp he would sometimes quickly sneak away from where he had nested all night and then lie down quietly in the snow. So white and still was he that it was impossible for the keenest eye to detect him in the early morning starlight. No calling would bring him. He just lay there perfectly still, and buried enough to be even with the snow around him. When he had one of these skulking tricks on him the quickest way to find him was for several Indians to begin tramping in ever-widening circles around the camp until they ran on him. He would never run away, but his cunning trick was really more provoking than if he did. He was at length broken of it by being thoroughly blackened. Then, of course, he could be easily seen. This so grieved and humiliated him that he never tried the trick again, even after his beautiful white coat was cleaned for him, much to his great joy.

Some dogs, as soon as they hear the bells jingling in the morning as their drivers come for them, will skulk off into dark places in the forests. There it is often difficult to find them. Then again some are so wild that a rope at least sixty feet in length is tied to their necks in the evening as they are unharnessed. By tramping around them in the morning the driver at length gets hold of the rope and draws in the culprit.

A missionary who traveled some thousands of miles every winter with dogs had about the most satisfactory way of summarily dealing with skulkers. He had in his own team a powerful St. Bernard, so trained that all he had to do was to show him the collar of the missing dog and then send him after the truant. Hamilton gave one smell at the collar and then was off. If that dog was anywhere within two miles he was driven into the camp in a hurry. If a stubborn, obstinate dog objected to march in before him, he gave him a shaking that never had to be repeated. Dogs have good memories for various things.

The loading the sleds was not as easy a matter as some might imagine. This the boys found out when they tried to attend to the work themselves. As stated somewhere else, the sleds are only sixteen inches wide and ten feet long. They are made of two oak boards lying on the flat and well fastened together by crossbars. The front end is planed thin and steamed, and is then curled up more or less gracefully, according to the taste and skill of the maker. They have no runners on them. They just glide along on the smooth flat under surface that by wear becomes like polished glass. Along each side numerous loops are securely fastened. When the empty sled is to be loaded the first thing is to spread out over it one of these large deerskin wrappers, the sled being under the exact middle. Then the various articles constituting the load, blankets, robes, provisions, kettles, guns, dog fish, and everything else, are carefully piled up, the heaviest at the bottom, to make the upsets as few as possible. Then the great deerskin leather is carefully and tightly folded over from both sides, and the whole is securely lashed on by the strong deerskin ropes, which are passed from side to side through the strong loops on the sled. An experienced driver will so well tie on a great load of the most miscellaneous articles that it will not give an inch, or be in the slightest degree disarranged, no matter how many times it may upset or roll over or tumble down hillsides either end first or sideways. So the boys, after finding that their best handiwork in this line often came to grief in bad places, were glad to avail themselves of the assistance of a clever Indian, and there was no more trouble.

One careful look all around to see that nothing has been forgotten, and the cheery "Marche!" is heard. Away rushes the guide, and another day's journey is begun.

CHAPTER XVII.

Still on the Way to the Beavers—The Blizzard in the Camp—Sleeping and Eating under Difficulties—Vicious Little Beaver Dogs—The Beaver House—Preparations for Their Capture—The Beavers' Kitchens—Discovered by the Little Dogs—How Destroyed—The Method of Capture—Man's Experience versus Animal Instinct—The Rich Harvest of Beavers.

STILL on the way for the beavers!

We are surely a long time getting there, but every mile of the journey is interesting and full of novelty. We left the blazing camp fire at a little this side of the Wolf's Cove. The stars were shining brightly in the heavens. Even the morning star, now so brilliant, had not as the harbinger of the great sun yet made its appearance.

As a help to brighten up the trail for a short distance it is generally customary to pile on the fire, before starting, all of the wood remaining. This makes things look cheerful, and assists in the last investigation of the camp that nothing, not even a half-buried ax, is left behind.

At first the progress is not very rapid. It is fearfully cold. The dogs seem a little stiff, and some of them act as though they would much prefer to remain near that cozy camp fire. But there is no time for regrets or delays.

"Marche! Marche!" is the cry, and as the whips, wielded by dexterous hands, give out their emphatic cracks the coldness and stiffness soon wear off, and after the first mile or two the progress is very much improved as dogs and men warm up to their work.

We need not dwell much longer on the journey. Enough has been given to enable every bright boy and clever girl who reads these pages to see how it is that travelers get along in a land where only the canoe in summer and the dog-train in winter afford them any possibilities for locomotion. Here are no locomotives, but lots of locomotion, and the most of it is done on foot, as often it is quite enough for the dogs to drag the heavy loads through the deep snow and in the long, tangled forests, without carrying an additional man or boy. So it is walk, or run, or more generally trot, as the case may be, as the dogs are able to get on or the trail will permit.

Another long day with its glorious sunrise, and then, after the weary hours of travel and the several stops to eat, the sunset in cold splendor comes, and with it Memotas calls for the halt. Then another night in the woods, very similar to the one fully described, is passed, with the exception that during the hours of troubled slumber the fierce winds arose, and the light, dry snow in the three piled-up snowbanks of the camp was rudely seized hold of by rough old Boreas and driven hither and thither in his own rough way. Most of the snow seemed to find its way back to the place from which the snowshoes some hours before had thrown it, and now well it is for our young lads that they are so completely covered up in their bed, for the snow is now upon them to the depth of a couple of feet. Fortunately, the snow is like an extra blanket which Dame Nature has thrown upon them to add to their comfort. When the storm was beginning, and they began to move as some erratic snowflakes were so twisted around that they reached their faces, the guide, who well knew what a wretched night of discomfort would be theirs if they now, in the blinding storm, uncovered their heads, shouted to them with a good deal of sternness, "Do not uncover your heads; lie still and sleep." This after a little effort they were able to do. The fun, or rather discomfort, came in the morning, when the cry to get up was heard. Suddenly they sprang up, but in spite of all their quickness some of the snow went into their faces, and down their necks, and—well, it was far from agreeable.

The outlook was dismal enough. The storm still continued raging. There was, in addition to the wind playing all sorts of pranks with what had already fallen, now a heavy snowfall besides. It seemed to penetrate everywhere. It forced its way into their eyes and noses and pockets, and tried to get under their caps and capotes. The fire was completely extinguished. In fact, where the bright, blazing fire was so cheerily throwing out its heat and warmth when they were tucked in by the faithful Indian, now a great snowdrift occupied the very spot.

The experienced travelers in these lands, even under such conditions and worse, do not lose heart. Quickly they went to work. Strong axes soon felled more dry trees and cut them into logs. Others, with snowshoes as shovels, soon cleared away the snow-drift from the fireplace. A skillful firemaker soon had the dry kindling and chips under the logs in a blaze, and now the wind only fanned the flames to a greater brightness.

As the downfall of snow continues very heavy some tough poles are cut down and one end of them so fastened in the snow that they are firmly held. They are so slanted toward the fire, with the wind in the rear, that when roofed over with the big deerskin and a couple dropped each side it is astonishing how comfortably sheltered a few persons thus can be. The active Indians shook the dry snow off from some robes, and placing them as a floor Mr. Ross and the boys were soon under a storm-tight roof and gazing into the great fire just before them, that gave them both warmth and cheer. A hot breakfast was enjoyed as soon as the Indians could cook it.

Some of the Indians improvised a similar lean-to for themselves, while others stood out in the gale around the fire perfectly unconcerned. To them the heavy storm was as little heeded as the songs of the robins in springtime, or the summer zephyrs among the trees.

Owing to the delay of a half day on account of this disagreeable storm, the party did not reach the vicinity of the beaver house until toward evening. So it was resolved to find a good place for the camp, as the Indian hunters who owned this house said they would not take the beavers until the third day in the afternoon, and then they would take all they decided to in a short time. This was, of course, all a mystery to the boys, and so they were obliged to have patience and witness the contest between animal instinct and cunning and man's reason, observation, and ingenuity.

The spot selected for the camp was not far from the beaver house, which stood in its symmetrical proportions well covered with snow, and looked like a great haystack in some farmer's yard at home.

The boys had observed on the sled of these Indians who owned the beaver house a little wickerlike basket well lined with rabbit skin. One day when peering into it two fierce little dogs snapped at them most viciously, and seemed very much annoyed at their intrusion. In the evening at the camp fire they asked Mr. Ross about them, and were surprised to hear that they are what are called beaver dogs. He said they were valuable, for with their help the Indians would get the beaver in a very novel way, which they would see commenced to-morrow. Mr. Ross cautioned the boys not to put their naked hands near the vicious brutes, as they were very fierce and especially disliked white people.

The camp was a well-sheltered, comfortable one for such a place, and as the storm had completely passed away, the evening, although very cold, was a fairly enjoyable one. The routine at this camp was similar to the first. The only excitement the boys had was when one of the Indians came in from exploring the beaver house and dam and told them that a large wolverine was seen walking on the dam the beavers had made, and then round and round the beaver house.

"Beaver plenty safe there," he added, in his broken English. "Wall four feet thick. Frost make all like stone. Only one door, and that under the thick ice and water. Wolverine no catch beaver in that house." Then he added: "Beaver there for Injun to take. White boys see how him do it quick, two days more. Plenty work first, then plenty beaver."

This picturesque talk to the boys was very interesting, and so they were all eager to see, as Sam said, "the curtain go up and the show begin."

As nothing could be done the next day before daylight, there was no particular hurry in getting up. After giving orders to the men who were left in charge at the camp to see that the dogs there remained, and that everything was kept in the best of order, and dinner ready at a certain hour, Mr. Ross and the boys, like the rest, strapped on their snowshoes and away they tramped. The Indian hunters had the little dogs with them. These they carefully carried and kept covered up when not at work. The boys were first taken to the top of a hill, from which the whole pond, dam, and beaver house could be distinctly seen. Then Mr. Ross explained that, while the beaver generally dwelt in their house during the winter, they had in addition what the Indians called kitchens. These were cunningly hid along the shore at the edge of the ice. All were now out of sight and under the snow. They were ingeniously made, in such a way that the beaver by frequently visiting them and breaking away the ice, as it formed on the inside, could thus keep them open. They were really breathing places for the beaver in case they should be attacked in their houses and driven out.

Inexperienced hunters often try to get the beaver

by chopping, digging, or even blasting with gunpowder a hole into the beaver house. If the pond is well supplied with kitchens, or breathing places, the beavers need only laugh at such hunters, for just as soon as they become alarmed by these outside noises they plunge into the water, which is always open in the warm house, and dive out under the outer edge and away they go under the thick ice to the kitchens, which are so cunningly hid away. There they quietly remain and breathe the air which is necessary, as it comes through the light snow and through the rushes and reeds from which they keep the ice. When the noise is over and the beavers think that their enemies have gone, they go back to the house. If the invaders have much destroyed the house, the beavers desert it entirely and live in these kitchens until the spring freshets come and melt and carry away the ice.

Sometimes a large colony of beavers with a big house will have twenty kitchens. If one is discovered they swim to another. We must remember that the beaver, although an amphibious animal and able to remain quite a time under water, requires fresh air, and so must go where he can get it, or he will die. The length of time that a beaver can live under the ice without air is a matter of dispute, even among the experienced hunters themselves. They all, however, agree in saying that, when beavers find all of their retreats cut off, as a last resort they come up to the ice and breathe out the air in their lungs against the ice, and then, when it is good, they breathe it in again. But the trouble is that they lose some air bubbles each time, and so they soon become exhausted and die.

In the meantime, while these interesting explanations were being made to the boys the Indians had commenced their operations. They had cut down a couple of small green birch trees which were eight or ten inches in diameter. Then they cut off lengths of about eight feet each. On these they vigorously set to work with their axes, and so cut or trimmed these down, except a foot or fifteen inches at one end, so that when finished they were like gigantic pounders.

With these made and thrown over their shoulders they took their way to the pond, only carrying in addition the two little dogs. When the pond was reached the little dogs were set down in the snow near the edge. At first they only moaned and shivered and begged to be again taken up by their masters. These, however, had no intention of doing anything of the kind.

"Umisk! Umisk!" they excitedly cried, and soon this Indian word for "beaver" began to have its effect upon the dogs. Pricking up their ears, they began running about, until at length, with a couple of yelps of triumph, they were off. They hurried away as fast as their little legs could carry them through the light snow to a spot near the shore. Here they began making the snow fly as rapidly as was possible with their fore paws. One of the Indians assisted them by utilizing his snowshoe as a shovel, and, sure enough, there at the very edge of the ice they found a mass of rushes and grass most cunningly arranged, with a little space in the center where it was open water. This was a beaver's kitchen that had been so cunningly discovered by the keen scent of the little dogs.

As soon as it had been discovered the Indians quickly picked up the little dogs and stowed the shivering creatures in warm bags on their backs. Now the boys were able to see the use to which these great big pounders, hewn out of the young birch trees, were put. With both of them the men began vigorously pounding down the coarse grass and rushes, and left the place so exposed that in a few hours it would be so solidly frozen over that not a particle of air could enter.

Leaving this kitchen now completely destroyed, they began skirting the shore for a little distance up farther from the beaver house. Once more they lifted the little dogs out of the warm bags and placed the shivering animals on the ice. Then again the cry rang out, "Umisk! Umisk!" The result was as before. Like as an electric shock these words acted upon these queer little dogs, and at once they seemed to forget all about the cold and most vigorously set to work, and in a very few minutes had discovered another kitchen. This one was destroyed in the same manner as was the first.

Thus on and on they cautiously prospected and worked. At one place where they had gone, but a short distance from the last kitchen destroyed, suddenly one of the little dogs obstinately turned back and rushed to a spot where even the most experienced Indian had not the slightest suspicion of anything being until the keen instinct of the dog discovered it. Following up the little fellow to the spot where he was now barking most furiously, the men had not dug long in the snow before they found the most cunningly hid away kitchen on the whole pond. So large was it, and so well arranged as the breathing place of a large number of beavers, that the hunters declared that if they had let that single one escape them they would have completely failed when they made their attack upon the beaver house. This sharpness on the part of the little dog made the men the more careful, and so it was noon ere the end of the pond was reached and about half of this work was completed.

Dinner was ready for all when they returned to the camp. The boys were hungry and the cold had helped to sharpen their appetites.

"How is it?" said Sam, "that I find myself picking out the fattest part of the meat and hardly caring to eat anything else?"

"That is," said Mr. Ross, "because you are in first-class health. And Nature, true to her instincts, is giving you and the rest of us the craving for just the kind of food that is now best adapted to our requirements. Fat food has more heat in it than any other kind, and so that which you here crave is that which is really the most suitable. Living as we now are day and night out in the open air in this sharp cold weather, we require much more heat to keep us up to our normal temperature than if we were inside of the warm walls of Sagasta-weekee."

When dinner was ended the party returned to the

pond, and the work of discovering and destroying the remaining beavers' kitchens went on all the afternoon. The following night the two Indian hunters, upon whom so much depended, did not take any sleep, but with their heavy pounders kept on the alert against the efforts of the clever beavers. When they returned to the camp for a hasty breakfast in the morning they reported that they had had a very busy night, as the beavers seemed to have become possessed with the idea that an attack was soon to be made upon them in their house. The result was they were very active all night, and persistent in their efforts to break through the new ice as it formed, and thus, if possible, keep some of their kitchens available in case of need. Some were so bold that if the Indians had been so inclined they could easily have speared them, as they so bravely charged the new ice with their heads and broke it up. They said that at that largest kitchen, which they so nearly overlooked, the beavers made their most persistent attacks. At times as many as a half dozen would together strike bravely at the ice. However, they thought that they had now succeeded in getting every place frozen air-tight and they could safely begin the work of attack upon the house, so that they would be ready by to-morrow to begin the capture of the beaver.

Axes and ice chisels were the powerful tools required to-day. Beginning at the shore on each side of the beaver house, the Indians cut two channels in the ice about a foot wide and so converging that they met about six feet in front of the house. Then the ice was cut out about ten feet further into the pond directly in front of the house. The capital letter Y will give a correct idea of the cuttings thus made. The upper two lines are the ones from the shore on each side of the beaver house; the lower and wider part of the letter represents the channel cut in front. This was perhaps ten feet long and about two feet in width.

The next step was by careful measurement with a long pole to find the depth of the water in these channels thus free of ice. When this was done everybody able to handle an ax was soon busily at work cutting down small trees into poles not less than four inches in diameter and so long that when well driven in the mud the tops would still be considerably above the ice. None but straight, strong ones were of any use. Then, beginning close to the shore, the Indians, using, of course, the shorter poles where the water was shallow, began driving them in the mud through the channels cut in the ice. They worked very carefully, for the beaver when aroused is a strong as well as a cunning animal, and the hunter who would not fail must be prepared for every emergency. The poles were driven in the two upper sides until the approaching columns of them came within about two feet of each other at the front. From this point the Indians turned and began driving the poles in the mud in two lines, parallel to each other, running out into the pond. This left a channel, allowing for the diameter of the poles, of, say, from twelve to fifteen inches wide and ten feet long.

Carefully examining and testing over and over

again the grip of each pole which had been driven into the mud at the bottom of the pond, the men were at length well satisfied with their work and said: "Very good. Injun have much fine beaver this time. We will have beavers' tails for supper tomorrow night."

So anxious were those Indian hunters that even during the second night they slept but little, and several times slipped away from the camp and walked around from kitchen to kitchen to see that in every place the ice was firm and unbroken. In the morning, when all were at breakfast, they reported that as the cold had become so intense they felt confident of success and anticipated the capture of a large number of beaver. For days they had been working up to this consummation. Experienced men grimly and remorselessly had pitted their long years of experience against the instincts and cunning of a colony of beavers, and as it always is, in the end, man must conquer.

"What are you going to do next?" is the question of the boys. All the answer, however, they receive is to be patient and they will soon see for themselves. Their interest, however, is increased when to all is uttered the command, "Get all the guns ready, and load them heavily with powder." With several extra charges they are all soon on their way to the beaver house. When there they find that the water in the channel cut in the front yesterday has ice on it fully six inches in thickness. This will give some idea of the severity of the cold, but nobody seems to notice it in the excitement of the hour. Very quickly is this ice broken up and thrown out on the frozen surface of the pond.

One of the Indians has in his hand a long, stiff rod about the size of a bamboo fish pole. This will play an important part in the capture of the beaver, as we shall see later on. The next part of the program is of great interest to the boys. Everybody now goes to the land side of the beaver house, and at once there begins the greatest din and racket it is possible for the whole party to make. The guns are all fired off, and loaded and fired again and again. The men with their great pounders most vigorously beat against the solid walls on the land side, as though they would burst in upon the now terrified inhabitants. This attack and noise continued until it is supposed that all of the frightened animals have fled away from the house, which they must have imagined was about being knocked to pieces about their ears. The result is the house is deserted, and the now frightened beaver are away out somewhere in the pond, swimming under the ice.

As soon as the Indians feel confident that all have forsaken the house they hurry out on the pond in the front. Here in the open water, in the space between the poles which were so solidly driven, the long slender pole is pushed down firmly through the water into the mud at the bottom of the pond. One of the Indians now quickly pulls off his shirt sleeve, as well as that of his coat, and throws himself down on the ice close to the open channel which has been described. His comrade quickly throws a warm blanket over him to at least partly protect him from the intense cold. Then, arming himself with a heavy ax, this second Indian quietly steps back a pace or two.

"Hush! Everybody keep still or sit down on the ice, and do not utter a word. Do not move your feet on the ice; do not even breathe heavily, for beavers have wonderful powers of hearing."

Promptly had everyone obeyed Mr. Ross, who had uttered these commands. He had placed the boys where they could easily see the wonderful way in which these experienced hunters would quickly gather up their beaver harvest after all their effort and toil.

But where are the beavers? They are in all probability out under the ice, swimming about from one kitchen to another, vainly trying to find one in which they can get their lungs full of fresh air. If the men and those saucy little dogs have been successful in closing up all of these resorts, vain are the beavers' efforts. For a long time these wonderful creatures are able to keep alive under water, but there is a limit to this ability, and then it becomes a matter of life or death to them. Thus it now was with these beavers. They had been frightened from their home, and had hoped to be able to obtain fresh air at places carefully prepared for just such emergencies. But, alas! these have failed them, and now there is nothing else to do but to make the effort to get back to their home as soon as possible. This they now find is no easy matter. A strange barricade of stakes is in the way, and there is only one opening, and even that is a very narrow one. But they are now in such sad straits for fresh air that they must try that one place and get to their home or perish.

Meanwhile the boys, sitting so still and quiet on the ice, began to think that it was getting very monotonous, especially Sam, who found it to be extremely difficult to have to hold his tongue so long. But look! The top of that long slender twig is being roughly shaken, and quick as a flash down goes the naked arm of the alert Indian, and as rapidly does it come up again, and in the strong grasp of his hand is a fine, large beaver. With a sudden swinging movement he sends it sprawling out on the ice, where his comrade is waiting to dispatch it with his ax.

Now the boys see the important part played by that little stick. See, it moves again, and once more the long, naked arm is thrust down and another great beaver is thrown out on the ice. This one, like his predecessor, is quickly dispatched. For a time all is still again. The beavers crowding behind these two that have been so readily captured have been frightened by their sudden movements, so unnatural, and so they hesitated to follow. But others are closely following behind, and all are suffering acutely now for the want of fresh air, and thus it is only a minute or two before the moving stick tells the story that another beaver is making the attempt to reach a spot where he can get some fresh air. Vain indeed are his efforts, for no sooner does he touch that fatal stick than down goes that strong, muscular hand and arm and he is thrown out on the ice, to be killed in the same manner as were his fellows.

See what a splendid black beaver that is! But, O

dear! he has lost him. Yes, he has. That is too bad, and he brought him up far enough for his head to be out of the water, and so he once more filled up his lungs, and as he tumbled in he fell beyond the stick. So that one is lost for this year.

But there is no time for mourning over the loss of one, even if he was a beauty. They crowd up quickly now, and the Indians are busy. They keep cool and alert, for the harvest is increasing.

The condition of the beavers is now so desperate that recklessly they are crowding on, and although the man is pulling them out as rapidly as possible it is evident that numbers, especially of the smaller ones, are slipping by and thus are lost for that year. In order to secure a greater number the second Indian gives his ax to Mr. Ross and goes to the help of his comrade.

No need of quiet now. The remaining beavers must get by that stick or perish, and as they make the attempt, while some are captured, many others escape. Thus it goes on until the last one has either been secured by the Indians or has eluded them. Let us hope that he escaped to live another year.

"Count the spoils, boys," shouts Mr. Ross. No second command is needed. They collect them together and find that there are forty-seven of them, and not a small one among them. In addition, there were plenty that escaped to restock the house, and in two years it will in all probability be as rich a beaver harvest field as it has been to-day.

CHAPTER XVIII.

Wise Economy of Indian Hunters—Game Never all Killed—Beavers' Tails—The Boys Interested in Them—Preparations for the Return Trip—Loads Packed—Wolverines—Their Cunning Theft of Five Beavers—Dogs and Men on Their Trail—Surviving Beavers Already at Work—The Return of the Hunters—Captured Wolverines—Journey Resumed—The Camp—The Cry of "Wolves!"

ALLOWING a number of the beavers to escape was the almost universal custom of those northern Indian hunters. They never killed all the game of any kind. Thus where they alone hunted the forests continued to yield their yearly supplies. But when the white trapper enters with his steel traps and poisons he kills all before him, if possible, even if he does not secure one half of it. The result is that great regions once rich in valuable fur-bearing animals are now as completely denuded of them as are the prairies of the once countless herds of buffalo. Pathetic is the picture of the last of the buffalo!

The call, loud and clear, was sent by the far-reaching voice of one of the hunters to the watchers at the camp, and speedily in answer came a couple of trains of dogs. These were attached to the two now well-filled sleds, and the whole party, flushed with triumph at their success, returned to the camp. They are all in good trim for their dinner, and speedily is it dispatched, for all these beavers must be skinned, if possible, before they freeze.

The Indian servants of Mr. Ross aid the hunters,

and so the work is rapidly done. As the flesh of the beaver is very much prized as an article of food, the carcasses were carefully prepared. The tails were left attached to the bodies with the exception of a half dozen, which were left out for the evening meal. These tails very much interested and amused the boys, not only on account of their odd appearance, but because of the many queer tales they had heard about them. The tail of the beaver serves as a rudder to its owner when he is swimming. It aids him in various ways when he is building his cozy house and marvelously constructed dam. Next to his powerful teeth it is his best weapon of defense, as with it he can strike a very heavy blow. Thus it was no wonder that the boys were interested in these half dozen tails on which they expected to dine that evening.

The process of preparation was very simple. The tails were from twelve to fifteen inches long and from six to eight inches in width, and about an inch thick. They were oval-shaped, somewhat resembling in appearance a mason's trowel. They were covered with close-fitting, fishlike scales. The first thing necessary in preparing them for the table is to hold them so close to a hot fire that the scales will speedily blister off. The next thing is to boil them for a long time, especially if they are the tails of old beavers. Then it is best to allow them to get thoroughly cold, as they taste very much better then than when eaten hot. In carving them the correct method is to cut the meat in long strips from the powerful central bone. These are then to be served up and eaten with a little salt. Beavers' tails thus prepared make a very dainty dish. Indeed, it is one of the great delicacies of the country, prized alike by both Indians and travelers. The other two great delicacies of the country are the moose's nose and the bear's paws.

"That looks queer to me," said Sam, "that the delicacies of a country should be the beaver's tail, the bear's paws, and the moose's nose. If such is the case, you see that when here eating even the delicacies of the land you are reduced to extremities!"

"A very good one, Sam," shouted the boys. "Old Ireland forever!"

The beavers' tails, although never tasted before by the boys, were very much enjoyed by them. They racked their brains and memories to try and think of some article of food that had a taste somewhat similar, but had to give it up. So they had to agree with Alec that if you wished to know just how beavers' tails tasted—well, you must eat one.

As the evening promised to be a calm and beautiful one, Mr. Ross said that they had better start not long after midnight. They could travel on the back trail until they reached the camp where the storm had struck them without much difficulty; after which in all probability they would have to make a fresh trail. A blizzard storm in that land quickly obliterates a trail, and thus the return journey is often made without a single evidence of any other trip ever having been made in that region of country. Their great success in capturing so many beavers meant a large additional weight on their sleds. However, against that was the fact that their vigorous appetites had very considerably reduced the weight of their outfit, and in addition their dogs had, since they left home, devoured about a thousandweight of fish. Forty-seven beavers weigh a good deal when they have to be drawn many scores of miles on dog-sleds, and so, in spite of the lightened loads, it was no easy matter to arrange them on the sleds.

That they might be ready to make the desired start in good time it was thought best that Mr. Ross and the boys should go to bed in their camp outfit as has been described, while the men should load up the sleds as far as possible, just leaving sufficient room in the deerskin wrappings for the packing away of the bedding and the other essentials required at the midnight meal. This meant that the Indians would have at least two hours' less sleep than the whites. This would be no unusual occurrence. As a general thing the Indians sleep very little when traveling, in summer or winter. This is especially the case when they are employed as canoemen or dog-drivers. They are so alert and watchful and anxious that everything should go right, that often white men have traveled for weeks together with several of these red men in their employ without ever having once seen one of them asleep. They seldom think of lying down until long after their employers have gone to sleep, and then they are up long before them in the mornings. And yet how few there are who have given these most vigilant and faithful of comrades or servants their due meed of praise!

To the music of the few quiet, whispered words of the men, as they actively attended to the work of packing up the sleds, Mr. Ross and the boys quickly fell into dreamless slumber. When the men had finished packing and fastening up the loads they dragged them out in line on the homeward trail, leaving sufficient space between the sleds for the dogs when they should be harnessed to them. The result was that the whole line of sleds, when thus stretched out, extended quite a distance from the camp.

Loud were the shoutings and many were the indignant utterances which quickly aroused Mr. Ross and his young bedfellows from their slumbers.

"What is the matter?" demanded Mr. Ross.

"Wolverines!" was the quick response.

Great indeed was the excitement, and at first the boys could hardly realize how the mention of that one word could cause such commotion. Even Mr. Ross was about as much excited as anyone else. While guns were being loaded, and other preparations were being made for a speedy hunt, the cause of all the excitement was soon told. It was that in spite of the presence of so many persons and dogs the wolverines had crept up to the sleds and had stolen away five of the best beavers, and in addition had so badly scented with their horrid odor more than a dozen others that they were absolutely worthless.

"How was it possible that none of the dogs detected them?" asked Mr. Ross. "They are generally sleeping in various places around the camp. I am sure I cannot understand how those brutes, cunning as they are, could play such a trick upon us."

In response to this one of the men explained that

after they had finished arranging their loads they went out and brought into the camp all of the dogs, so as to have no trouble in finding them when they would be required. They stated also that during the brief time they tried to get a little sleep some of the dogs were very restless, and they had to speak sternly to them to induce them to be quiet. Then he added:

"The dogs most uneasy were those of Sam's train. Several times they growled, and were very uneasy. Spitfire was the worst, and acted like a dog ready for a fight."

The stupid drivers, instead of calling the hunters, who were very sleepy from the fact that they had had hardly any sleep for several nights past, sternly threatened the dogs, and thus succeeded in quieting them down. After a time some disagreeably tainted air reached the sensitive nostrils of one of the Indian hunters. He did not require a second sniff to tell him what it indicated. With a bound he was up. Suddenly rousing his comrade, they rushed out into the gloom of the forest. Unfortunately for them, the fire was about out, and so at first it was impossible to see how great had been their loss from these stealthy, cunning animals. It was when they had rushed back to the camp, and were rousing up the other men and rebuilding the fire, that the commotion was made which had so suddenly called up Mr. Ross and the boys. A casual glance had enabled them to see, as we have mentioned, something of the nature of their loss. On a closer investigation it was found that the damage was even much greater.

What was to be done? This was the question now

discussed, and quickly was a decision arrived at. It was to organize a party and have them get on the trail of the wolverines and follow them up until they were reached. It was decided that those dogs which manifested any great eagerness to pick up and follow on the trail should be the ones encouraged to push on as rapidly as possible, while the hunters with their guns should follow as speedily as it could be done in the dense, gloomy forest.

Spitfire and the rest of Sam's train were the first when taken to the place to immediately pick up the scent, and, as soon as they were encouraged by Sam to do so, away they dashed in the gloom. Bruce and his comrades were equally as eager, and as Alec's cheery voice rang out his dogs quickly responded, and away they sped on the hot trail of the audacious, cunning thieves. The two hunters and a couple of Mr. Ross's best men, with their guns well loaded and with their snowshoes on their feet, as rapidly as was possible strode after them.

Mr. Ross and the boys waited until the last sounds of the dogs were lost in the distance, and then, by the light of the now brilliant camp fire, made a more careful inspection of the sleds, and so were able to see the full extent of the depredations made by these most cunning of all animals in those regions. There they not only saw the full extent of their destructiveness, but under the guidance of the Indian now keeping watch over the sleds they were able, by following back on their tracks, to see how five wolverines had outwitted the whole of them, dogs included.

When they returned to the warmth and cheer of

the camp fire they found that old Memotas and others had prepared for them a good warm breakfast. While it was being partaken of Frank turned to Memotas and said:

"How is it that you, who are so great a hunter, are not off in the woods with those other men?"

With a grim, sarcastic smile he replied: "Better some one stay in camp for fear wolverines come in on other side and steal what is left."

This answer was at first quite a riddle to the boys. But the fact was he was so thoroughly disgusted at the remissness of those whose duty had been to have watched that night that he felt that a great disgrace had come to them all. The idea of allowing five wolverines to thus steal such a march upon them was too much for even the patient, kind-hearted Memotas.

"Why," said he, "it will be the story at every camp fire this winter—yes, and for long years to come. We all know that wolverines are cunning animals, but when the fact is known that there were so many of us in the camp at the time that five beavers were stolen from our sleds—why, great will be their ridicule and contempt for us."

It was indeed a long time since Memotas had made such a long speech of this kind, and so when he stopped there was an awkward silence. Even Mr. Ross had nothing to say. It was very evident, however, that he felt that there had been very great carelessness on the part of somebody, and perhaps he chided himself that he had not interested himself in the matter. However, he had his hopes that in spite of the cunning of the wolverines the men would succeed in killing some of them, and as one wolverine skin is worth four beaver skins, if they were successful there would at least be some satisfaction in that.

As it was still a long time until daylight the boys were persuaded to lie down in their bed, and Memotas carefully tucked them in. Refreshing sleep speedily came to them again, and when they awoke it was to hear Mr. Ross giving some final instructions to three dog-drivers who were just about to start on the trail made at midnight by the wolverines, barking dogs and angry, indignant hunters. Wrapped securely upon their sleds was a liberal supply of food, with kettles, axes, and other things that might be required.

As they started the eastern sky almost suddenly became illuminated with the brightness of the coming day. So beautiful was the morning that the boys longed to go with the departing trains. It was thought best, however, owing to the uncertainty and probable hardships that might have to be encountered, not to run the risk. To pleasantly and profitably pass the time it was suggested that some of them go out on a tour of investigation on the trail of the wolverines, and see in what direction they came and how it was that they had so well succeeded in their movements. Dear old Memotas, disconsolate as he was, was persuaded to go along and explain the various movements of these clever animals to the boys. This he could well do, as he had hunted them for many years and knew much about them, although he always declared that there were some of them that could outwit any Indian.

They all first went to the spot where stood the sleds from which the beavers had been stolen. Then, with Memotas leading, they followed back on the tracks, and soon they found as they went on that the cautious animals had completely crept around the camp ere they had begun their depredations. Continuing on their trail, still going back, they found that the wolverines had come directly from the spot on the dam where the beavers had been captured, as has been described.

While so near the beaver house Memotas said to the boys that it might be interesting to try and find out if the surviving beavers had as yet gone to work again. That anything could be found out seemed impossible to the boys, but the experienced eye of the old Indian saw evidences of their industry very close at hand. Of course the intense cold had again frozen up the water where from it the ice had been cut and thrown out. This newly formed ice, of course, firmly held up the row of strong stakes which with so much trouble and care the men had driven so solidly in the ground. Drawing his hunting ax from his belt, Memotas struck the projecting ends of the stakes a few smart blows, just sufficient to loosen them from the new ice. Then said Memotas to the boys:

"Try and see which of you is strong enough to pull any of them up."

Eagerly they each seized hold of one, and, expecting that the other end was still securely stuck in the mud, they pulled with such vigor that the three of them nearly fell over on their backs. To their astonishment they found by the appearance of the short sticks in their hands that the beavers had cut them off just below the ice.

After some further interesting investigation they returned to the camp, for very naturally they were all anxious to get some word from the hunters and the dogs. Fortunately they had not long to wait, for very soon after their return the expected ones dashed into their midst. On their sleds they had three dead wolverines. The dogs had returned panting and tired. They were all in good shape except Bruce and another one of Alec's train. These, in battle with the wolverines, had each received a couple of severe flesh wounds, but they seemed to think nothing of them, and in a short time they completely healed up. Everybody was, of course, anxious to hear their story, and so one of the hunters was asked to be the spokesman for the whole, and here is about what he said:

"You all know how we started. You boys set your dogs on the tracks, and away they went and we after, as fast as we could follow. The dogs could travel much faster than we could, and so it was not long before they were out of hearing. The wolverines must have got a good start, as it was a long time before we found any trace of them. But we pushed on as fast as it was possible for us to do in the darkness. Sometimes the northern lights shone out, and then we made very much better time. By and by we came to a half-eaten beaver that had been dropped by one of the thieves. This told us that the dogs must be driving them very close, for a wolverine will make a big fight before he will give up what he has secured. Still on we hurried, and it was not long after this before we heard the dogs again. Then we found another of the skinned beavers, and now the barkings of the dogs told us that the fight was on in good earnest.

"We had been so much hindered by the dense woods, that was the reason we were so far behind, but now, as we came out from a bad piece of the forest, right there before us was a sight to please us for our anger at the loss of the beaver. The dogs had driven one wolverine up into the branches of a large tree, while others were barking furiously at two others which they had chased up among some steep rocks. It was at this time, just as we reached them, that some of the dogs got cut and wounded. They seemed to be so glad to see us coming to their help that they made a furious attack upon the two that were upon the rocks, and some of them were taught that wolverines have sharp teeth and know well how to use them.

"We speedily shot these three animals, and then began at once to look for the tracks of the other two. After some time we found them, and in following them up we soon saw that they had reached the great cliffs, among which are their dens. We could not then hope for much more success. So we returned to the spot where we had left the three dead ones, and were just about beginning to skin them when the sleds arrived, and it was thought best, after we had had something to eat from the supplies Mr. Ross was so good as to send us, for us all to return, and here we are."

This was the story, and it showed quick, sharp, thorough work on the part of both men and dogs. This long delay had caused quite a break in their plans. Mr. Ross, however, decided that just as soon as the wolverines could be skinned, and dinner prepared and eaten, the home journey must be resumed. Some of the party would have preferred to have remained until the next day before starting, but Memotas sarcastically remarked that they had better go on for fear some more wolverines might come and carry away the rest of the beavers! It is a remarkable fact, and one interesting to study, that the Indians are much more bitter and sarcastic on each other for any act of carelessness in capturing or securing their game than for any other defect or folly.

The homeward journey was soon resumed, and after traveling about twenty miles the winter camp was prepared. Fortunate was it for them that they were able to find a favorable place in the very midst of a large quantity of dry trees. So warm and invigorating was the work of cutting down these tall dry trees that not only did the boys, but several of the men, as they said, for the fun of it, slash away until an unusually large number had thus been made ready for the fire.

The owners of the beavers were not to be caught napping again, and so they erected a kind of a staging near to the camp, on which the valuable loads of meat and furs were safely placed. Memotas had to have another drive or two at them, and so he ironically congratulated them on their late precautions. Sam said it looked like the old proverb of locking your stable after the horse was stolen. Alec's more charitable remark was, "It is best to be made wise by the loss and then strive to save the rest."

Yes, indeed, it was a wise precaution, for even now, while the men were thus hard at work and others were thus discussing their actions, far back on the trail hungry and cruel enemies have caught the rich scent of the beaver, and with long, louping strides are rapidly drawing near. Supper and prayers were over, and the men had nicely tucked in the boys in their warm bed. Before lying down themselves they had as usual lit their pipes and were having a quiet chat over the usual incidents of the day. With a sudden start they were all on their feet in an instant, for coming down on the wind, in the direction in which they had so recently traveled, they heard a sound so blood-curdling and so ominous that it has chilled the very heart and caused the cheeks to blanch of many a stout-hearted traveler, the howlings of a pack of wolves!

CHAPTER XIX.

The Coming Battle with the Wolves—Thorough Preparations—The Cry of the Wolves for Reinforcements—The First Attack and Repulse—Wounded Wolves Devoured—Memotas's Comments—The Second Attack—The Powder Explosions—Final Victory—Dogs Reluctant to Attack Wolves—Explanations—Mr. Ross's Story of the Bears Stealing His Pigs—Dogs More Confident in Attacking Bears.

THE Indians very quickly aroused Mr. Ross, who at once realized the danger that menaced them. The Indians, prompt to act in such emergencies, had already begun their preparations to meet the oncoming foes. They had seized their axes, and were already hard at work cutting down more trees, that there might be an additional supply of wood with which the fire could be kept brilliantly burning. Some of the men were busily engaged in getting the guns and ammunition ready and in making other arrangements that would aid to success in the approaching battle.

To Mr. Ross the Indians left the work of calling up the boys and informing them of the coming danger. This he speedily did, and great was their surprise when informed of the fact that in all probability they were in for a fierce battle with an unknown number of savage wolves.

To judge by their howlings the wolves were still a long distance from the camp. The hearing of the Indians is very acute, and when the temperature is down so low that the mercury is frozen sounds are heard very much more distinctly, and from a greater distance, than under ordinary atmospheric conditions. Thus there was fortunately a little time for preparation ere they would have to meet the fierce assault.

The boys were each urged to quickly put the harness on their own dogs and bring them into the camp, which was rapidly being enlarged. The old dogs, that had a wholesome dread of wolves, were, it was thought, wise enough to look after themselves. Before even Mr. Ross and the boys had heard the wolves the old dogs had detected falling on their ears the melancholy sound, and trembling with fear they came crowding into the camp, and to the feet of their different drivers.

Trees were fallen all around, under the vigorous blows of the choppers, and were being cut into lengths that could be carried in. Three or four men would seize hold of these great dry logs and speedily bring them into the position which they well knew would be to the best advantage. The sleds were rearranged, and so placed that logs could be piled on them. The harnesses were all hung high, and everything made as secure as possible. Wolves are afraid of fire, and so now it was that on this fire the Indians were going mainly to depend. Already the men had thrown a number of fresh logs on the fire, as well as extended it out in crescent shape to the right and left. Behind the camp they cut down a number of the trees, so placing them that they made a natural barricade as they crashed into each other. It was not at all wolf-proof, but it would prevent a rush attack, and those bold enough to try to venture through could be easily seen and shot.

About five hundred yards from the camp the trail made quite an ascent ere the camp was reached. Up to the moment when the wolves reached the top of this ascent they had traveled altogether by the strong scent of the castoreum which is found in the body of the beaver, and which had most thoroughly perfumed the whole party, dogs, men, and outfit. As the brilliant fire now for the first moment was seen by them their howlings suddenly ceased, and it was evident that they were very much perplexed.

"Bothered are you?" chuckled Memotas, as he carefully examined his gun. "Wanted beaver, did you, and prepared to take it raw, and now it looks as though, if you get it, you will have to take it hot? Well, come on for it, if you dare."

These sarcastic words were helpful to the boys, who had worked splendidly under Mr. Ross's guidance. There was no doubt about it that the boys were excited. Alec, whose fearful race against such monsters came visibly before him, was agitated, yet he bravely did everything desired of him, and felt that he was in for another triumph. It is no sign of cowardice to be conscious of the danger to be faced. The bravest of the brave are those who realize the greatness of the task before them and then unflinchingly face it, to conquer or to die.

Unfortunately, on this trip the boys had not brought with them their guns. However, before starting Mr. Ross had seen that one apiece for each of his men, including Memotas, with abundance of ammunition, was placed upon the sleds. The hunters fortunately had an extra gun with them, and this was handed to Mr. Ross.

"I wonder what conspiracy they are hatching now," said Memotas, as the wolves continued so strangely silent.

"Nothing that bodes any good to us," replied Mr. Ross. He had been in critical positions like this before, and now as the scent of battle once more was on him he handled his gun with pleasure and rejoiced in the excitement of the hour. He would have been glad if the boys had been safe at Sagastaweekee, for as yet it was utterly impossible to form any estimate of their as yet unseen foes' numbers, or to judge of the fierceness of the attack which they would shortly make.

For about half an hour this strange, unnatural stillness continued, and then there broke upon their ears a horrid din that seemed to come from every point in the compass around them. Although the sound was some distance off, yet so blood-curdling was it that the boys were startled, and Alec pulled his fur cap down over his ears in a vain endeavor to shut out the horrid sounds. The dogs seemed at first to try and answer this noisy challenge, but soon their courage sadly oozed out, and they tremblingly huddled together in the camp, or close to their masters' feet.

To the boys' amazement, the Indians unconcernedly put down their guns, and taking up their pipes began to smoke. Turning to the boys, Mr. Ross said:

"You had all better lie down and sleep, for we are not going to be troubled with the wolves for a good while."

"Why, dare we do that," said Frank, "when the wolves are now all around us?"

"Yes," said Mr. Ross, "that last cry we heard was from different points around us, but it was not the challenge of immediate attack, but a call sent out for reinforcements. Every wolf within ten miles of us heard that far-reaching cry, and is galloping in this direction."

"That means," said Sam, "that every wolf within four hundred miles of us is mustering for the fight?"

"Precisely," said Alec, "if you square the circle."

It was rather trying for the boys to be asked to lie down and go to sleep under such circumstances, yet they promptly obeyed the request of those they knew would only give them the best of advice. Strange as it may appear to some, our brave boys were soon sound asleep, and when about an hour after they were called up again they found themselves refreshed and doubly nerved for the coming conflict.

The subdued howlings of the wolves were again distinctly heard, and it was the opinion of the Indians that they were holding a big council to decide on the plan of their attack. Knowing so well their methods, it was the opinion of them all that the heaviest assault would be on the leeward side, as there the wind carried the strong scent from the castoreum and the meat. To impede them in their rush if they should try that method of attack, a couple of Indians with their axes ventured out in that direction and cut down a number of trees, which they caused to fall in such a way that the wolves, when approaching, would be delayed by them, and thus render it easier for them to be shot. While these men were thus chopping, in that advanced position of danger, others with loaded guns stood not far behind as their defenders. However, they were not disturbed except by one skulking fellow, that was doubtless acting as a scout. When he saw that he was discovered he quickly retreated back in the gloom of the forest.

The increasing din and the more confident yelps told the men, who, living in the forest, had become familiar with the various sounds and calls of the wild beasts, that reinforcements were coming in, and that the attack would soon be made.

The camp could muster ten guns. Six of these were doubled-barreled, but they were all muzzle-loaders. When the boys were aroused the second time they were each given small-sized axes as their weapons of defense, in case the battle should reach the camp, which, however, was not anticipated. In addition they were expected to keep the dogs together and soothe and quiet them as much as possible.

Noticing some peculiar rolls of birch bark well back from the fire, on which Memotas was keeping a careful eye, Sam inquired what they were, and was interested to learn that they were a kind of improvised hand grenade, made by Memotas, to be used if the wolves should strive to come too close. They each contained two or more pounds of powder, and if they did but little execution they would at least add to the noise and excitement.

At the request of all the men Mr. Ross was appointed as captain, whose word was to be obeyed by all. That he might be able to wisely direct the men to the points where the attack seemed to be most directed, a scaffold of logs was hurriedly erected on the windward side of the camp. So abundant was the supply of wood that the fire was kept burning so brightly that Mr. Ross, from his elevated position, could see quite a distance into the forest in every direction.

As was anticipated, the attack was made on the leeward side with a rush, and with howlings that were blood-curdling the savage beasts in a pack rushed forward as though confident of success and an easy victory. The newly fallen trees bothered them but for a moment as on they rushed. As they emerged from them the men began firing at them from the point in front of the camp to which they had advanced. As the first volley from the ten guns rang out a number of wolves fell dead, while others, badly wounded, with howls of pain quickly retreated. Mr. Ross could see that they met with no sympathy, for, wounded as they were, they had to fight for their lives against some of their comrades that, having tasted the blood of their wounds, were anxious to devour them.

In the meantime the men with the double-barreled guns kept picking off the more venturesome of the wolves, while the men with the other guns rapidly loaded them. Thus they kept loading and firing until the disheartened survivors drew back beyond the range of the light into the darkness of the forest. For a time all that was heard were the yelpings and snarlings of the wounded and their assailants. These discordant cries seemed to amuse Memotas very much.

"Ha, ha!" said he, "you came for beaver, did you? —with perhaps a man or boy or two thrown in; and now you are content to eat your brother wolf's flesh! You are easily contented, anyway."

"Wait, Memotas," said another Indian; "those wolves are not through with us yet, and it is likely that we will have a bigger attack from them than what we already have had."

Quietly calling one of the Indians, who was possessed of marvelous powers of vision, up on the scaffolding where he was, Mr. Ross called his attention to the stealthy movements of the wolves. Keen as were the powers of vision possessed by Mr. Ross, those of this Indian were much superior, and so he at once was able to detect the wolves skulking back to a point far in the rear of the camp. Their object was to make an attack from that direction. To meet this new movement, Mr. Ross withdrew most of the men from the front and placed them where they would be able to render most effective service. About a hundred feet or more behind the camp stood a very tall, dead balsam tree. Seizing a large ax, and calling another Indian to do likewise, Memotas rushed out with his comrade and speedily cut down that tree, causing it to fall directly from the camp. Then taking his queer-looking rolls of gunpowder in his arms, and slipping his snowshoes on his feet, he hurried back to the place where the top of the tree now lay upon the ground. This was at the place along which the wolves would probably come when they again made their attack. Here Memotas carefully arranged his powder-loaded rolls of birch bark, and connected the fuses of each with a heavy sprinkling of gunpowder, which reached to the trunk of the tree. Then pulling the cork out of a horn full of powder, which had been slung on his back, he laid a train on the trunk the whole length of the tree. Coming into the camp, as he relit his pipe, he coolly said to the boys, "I think I will give them some singed wolf meat as a change after a while."

As was anticipated, at this point a number of wolves gathered to make the attack. They cunningly kept themselves as much in the shadows of the trees as possible, and so were the more difficult to hit. However, they never got very near the camp until the firing for a time had to be nearly suspended owing to the guns becoming too hot from rapid use. This was Memotas's opportunity. Seeing a number of wolves, emboldened by the apparent ceasing of the firing, coming on with a rush toward the spot where he had placed his birch rolls of powder, he boldly seized a flaming brand from the fire and rushed out to the spot where he had stood when he had cut down the tree. As from his position he could not very well see the oncoming wolves, he waited for Mr. Ross to give him notice when to fire his little train of gunpowder. The instant the word was given he touched the firebrand to the powder, and at once rushed back to join the other Indians, who with their guns were again ready for their foes. Some of the wolves, more eager than their comrades, had already passed by the mine laid for them, and so were a little startled by the spluttering little stream of fire that passed them as it made its way along the trunk of that tree. Carefully and well had Memotas done his work, for soon there was a series of explosions mingled with yelpings of pain and terror, and a number of frightened hairless and wounded wolves turned into the forest and were seen no more. A forward rush of the men, firing heavily as they advanced, completed the work, and that strange battle was over.

There was but little rest or sleep for any of the party in the camp during the brief remainder of the night. The fires were kept brightly burning, and in turns the men with guns loaded kept vigilant watch against their treacherous foes. As an extra precaution a gun was occasionally fired, so that any skulking wolf remaining in the neighborhood might know that the inhabitants of the camp were on their guard and ready to renew the fight if it were necessary.

As soon as it was broad daylight, escorted by some of the Indians fully armed, Mr. Ross and the boys went out on a tour around what might be called the battle field. They were surprised at not finding more dead wolves than they did. They were, however, simply disgusted at the many evidences of the rank cannibalism of those that had escaped the bullets. They had without any pity or remorse most rapidly devoured the dead and wounded, with the exception of those that had been singed by Memotas's improvised fireworks. So successful had been this explosion, and so accurate the aim of the men, that several wolves of different kinds were found within a radius of half a mile. Some had been killed instantly, and so lay just where they fell. Others, mortally wounded, had managed to crawl away quite a distance ere they died. But of all those that in any way had been singed or burnt by the fire not one had been torn or mangled by the survivors. However, such had been the effects of the fire upon them that their skins were valueless as fur, and so they were left undisturbed where they had fallen.

A good breakfast was ready for them all when they returned to the camp. Soon after it was over the sleds were again loaded, the dogs harnessed, and the journey once more resumed.

It had been a memorable night for the boys. They had remained cool and collected, but alert and watchful. The conduct of the dogs rather humiliated and disappointed them. Why some of them should act so cowardly and so tremble at the howlings of the wolves was to them a mystery and an annoyance. They, however, stoutly declared that their own young trains growled and even barked back their defiance when the howlings of the wolves were most severe. At the resting place where they stopped for dinner they had quite a discussion on the subject. Sam confessed that he had been eager to let the dogs loose and then urge them on to the attack. At this candid confession Mr. Ross was much amused, and said that when a boy, long ago, traveling with his father and some Indians, one night in a camp where they were bothered by the howlings of some wolves he, against their advice, urged his own splendid train of young dogs to the attack. Only three of them managed to get back to the camp, and they were in such a wounded, torn condition that they were worth but little for weeks. The fourth one had been devoured by the wolves.

"As one result," added Mr. Ross, "I had to walk or run on snowshoes the rest of the long journey home, and as it was over a hundred miles I often wished I had not been so eager to set my dogs on a number of great northern wolves."

"What do you think would have happened," said Alec, "if Sam had set the three trains we boys are driving on to those wolves that attacked us last night?"

"I think," said Mr. Ross, with a bit of a twinkle in his eye, "that there would have been seen along here somewhere three tired, down-hearted boys trudging along on snowshoes and mourning the loss of twelve splendid dogs."

"Well," said Frank, "I am glad we did not get up a wolf fight, for this is jollier than trudging along all day on snowshoes."

With a laugh he threw himself on his dog-sled, and then with a cheer he was first off on the trail of the guide. Quickly the rest followed, and the journey was resumed.

When the journey was ended, and in after days as various incidents of this eventful trip were being discussed, the boys were loth to have to believe that it was running a big risk to allow sleigh dogs to attack wolves.

"What about bears?" said Sam.

"There is not one quarter the risk run by dogs in attacking bears that there is when they venture to assail wolves," said Mr. Ross. "These big wolves of the North are generally in a half-starved condition. When attacked they seem to know that it is for their very life they are fighting, and so they use their long, sharp teeth and powerful jaws with the greatest ferocity imaginable. Bears, on the contrary, fight in an entirely different way. When they are assailed by dogs they very seldom if ever fasten on them with their teeth as do the more vicious wolves. Their one great effort in the conflict is to seize hold of the dogs. If they can once get them in the grip of their long, strong, muscular forearms —well, one hug is all the most powerful dog requires to use him up for that day. Fortunate is he if he is not killed by the fearful squeezing he has received. Dogs seem, by some sort of instinct, to very quickly find out where their danger is, and so, unless they are young and inexperienced, they will fight shy of getting within the reach of those strong forearms that can give such an unlovely hug."

"How do the clever, experienced dogs attack bears?" asked Alec.

"I am in hopes," said Mr. Ross, "that before many more months you will be able to see for yourselves, but as there is much uncertainty about all these things, I will try and describe a battle we had not a mile away from Sagasta-weekee a couple of years ago. We had brought some young pigs out from the Selkirk country, and had them well housed in a warm pen, around which was erected a high, strong stockade. We knew that bears were fond of pork, and were also aware of the fact that they were good climbers, but with all our experience of them we never imagined that they would attempt to scale that high stockade and try to steal our pigs. But they did, and with a certain measure of success. Without alarming the dogs, or even any of the several Indians about the place, they succeeded in climbing over that high stockade, and each bear—for there were three of them—grabbed a pig, each one weighing perhaps fifty pounds, and succeeded in getting back over the stockade and off for the woods ere the loud squealings of the frightened young porkers gave them away. Of course, we were instantly aroused by these unusual noises, and at once suspecting the cause, I gave instant orders that the dogs that were at home should be immediately let out of their kennels and put on to the trail of the bears. As soon as possible a number of us quickly followed. Fortunately for us, the morning had so advanced that there was sufficient light for us to see our way. We had no trouble in reference to the direction in which to go, as the squealings of the pigs and the excited barkings of the dogs were quite sufficient to guide us. When we reached them we beheld a sight that made the most stoical of my Indians laugh. Here we found the three bears brought to bay. Each one of them was bravely holding in one forearm, as a mother does a child, one of the stolen pigs, while with his other forepaw he was giving resounding whacks to every dog that was rash enough to come within range. My largest sleigh dogs were still out with Kinesasis at their summer home, and so the bears were more able to repel the attacks of these much smaller ones. Still there were some plucky ones among the dozen or so in this pack, and they knew how to fight bears when they had them on the run. But they were bothered to know what to do with these big fellows, sitting here with their backs against a tree and a noisy pig in one forearm while they used the other like a terrible boxer.

"From a distance we watched for a time the peculiar conflict, and perhaps would have done so longer if it had not been that we saw one of my pet dogs, a very courageous little fellow, make a too venturesome rush and get within the sweep of that great arm. Suddenly the bear dragged him in, and although the plucky fellow tried to use his teeth, it was of no use. The bear hugged him to himself with such a crushing grip that the poor dog's ribs were broken like clay pipestems. Then suddenly the dog was flung quite a distance to one side.

"We did not want to see any more valuable dogs thus treated, and so we at once pushed forward. When the alert bears saw us approaching they at once started for the distant woods. Now the advantage was all with the dogs. It was very comical to see the desperate efforts made by those bears to hold on to those pigs, and also to fight the dogs and to keep up their retreat. Experienced dogs know that the tenderest spot in a bear is the tendon of his hind leg, and so that is where they try to seize hold of him. Two clever dogs are all that are necessary to delay until the hunters come up the largest black bears in our country. It does not depend very much on the size of the dogs. Indeed, large dogs are rather at a disadvantage, as it is harder for them to get out of the range of the bear when he turns upon them. In this fight all my dogs did was to assail each bear in front and rear. While the dog in front kept up a vigorous barking as close to his nose as it was safe to venture, the dog in the rear, watching his opportunity, sprang in and gave him a severe nip in the tender spot in his hind leg. This, of course, could not be put up with, and so the bear, still holding on to his pig, quickly whirled around to repel this second assailant. The instant he did so the clever dog that had been in front, but was now in the rear, instantly sprang in and caught the bear in the same tender spot. This, of course, brought the bear back again to him, but he was too clever to hang on, and having done his work he quickly sprang out of the reach of those dreaded paws. Seeing the bear once more turned from him, the other dog again dashed in and gave him another severe bite in the same place. Thus it was that the dogs, while not daring to close with such large bears, were yet able to keep them from escaping until we came up and shot them."

"What about the pigs?" said Frank.

"They were alive, and not much the worse for their queer adventure, although for some days they seemed dull and sore," was the reply.

CHAPTER XX.

A Bear Hunt in Winter—Mustagan a Famous Indian Guide—Bears' Den—How Discovered—Boys' Perplexity—The Journey to the Den—A Cold Morning—The Telltale Column of Steam—The Attempt to Dig Down to the Bears—Total Failure—Successful Tunneling Operations—Exciting Fight in the Icy Cavern—The Battles Between the Men and Dogs and the Escaping Bears.

A BEAR hunt in winter! No wonder the boys were excited when they heard of it. Yes, that was what it was, and a very interesting one at that.

Mustagan was a famous hunter, as we have already seen. In addition to that, he was a wonderful guide, and had also been a great traveler. He had gone several times on great expeditions to the Arctic Ocean. He was with Sir John Richardson on his memorable search for Sir John Franklin. He had also gone with Dr. Rae and others on similar Arctic exploring trips. Then this Mustagan was the old Cree Indian who found the silver spoons and other remains of Sir John Franklin among the Eskimos. Their recovery gave the final definite knowledge of the tragic ending of that memorable expedition. These relics of that sad expedition, in which about a hundred and forty of the bravest of men perished, some of whom might have been saved if Paulette had been true, are now in the Greenwich Museum.

But although Mustagan had been long years thus employed he was yet in the full vigor of life, and as a hunter was unexcelled. He was, like Big Tom, particularly noted for his skill as a moose hunter, and it was when out on the tracks of a moose that he made the singular discovery that led to this bear hunt in winter. When he came over to Sagastaweekee with the news that he had some rare sport for the boys they were, of course, full of curiosity to get all the information.

During the previous summer they had all had their peculiar experiences in bear fights, but this finding of bears in winter was a revelation, as they were always taught that the bears, especially in cold countries, hibernate during the winter; that is, that they den up in some quiet retreat in the rocks, if possible, and there remain in a semi-unconscious condition for months together. They generally go in very fat, and on this fat they keep alive all winter.

"Is it true," said Sam to Mustagan, "that a bear sucks his paws like a baby does his thumb?"

"That is what is believed by the Indians," said the old man. "But," he added, with a bit of a twinkle in his eye, "I don't remember any one of us ever having sat up to watch one doing it."

"How in the world did you find out where this bear's den is which you are inviting us to see?" said Alec.

"Perhaps," said Frank, "he marked it in the fall, like other Indians mark their beavers' houses."

"No, indeed," said Mustagan. "I never thought of one being in that place until I found it by the steam."

Here was a bigger mystery than ever.

"Steam!" said Sam; "and where was the engine?"

"Down deep under the snow in a den among the rocks," was the answer given.

This did not clear up the mystery, but rather added to their curiosity.

"How far away is it?" asked Mr. Ross.

"One day's journey," said Mustagan.

So it was decided that on the following Tuesday, if the weather continued bright and fine, the start would be made very early from Sagasta-weekee.

"No use going then," said Memotas, "if the days are not bright and cold. No see any steam if no sunshine."

This was a great perplexity to the boys, and they appealed to Mr. Ross to help them out. But he wished them to have the real surprise that Mustagan had in store for them, and so he told them to wait until they could see it for themselves, when on the ground.

The weather was everything that could be desired. On Monday four trains of dogs, with a full camping outfit and plenty of supplies to last for five or six days, were prepared. The boys took their guns along with them and plenty of ammunition. They were going to have their share of shooting if there was any to be done. Mustagan, with a couple of his sons and two dog-sleds, arrived very early, and the whole party started while the stars were still shining. One of Mustagan's sons, who had been with the old man when the den was discovered, ran on ahead of the trains as guide. As the trail had been made by Mustagan and his son when they returned after the discovery of the bears, this made the traveling more rapid and agreeable.

Three or four times during the day's journey they stopped, and cutting down some dry trees made up a big roaring fire, at which they warmed themselves and cooked a hearty meal. About an hour before sundown they reached the place. As it was too late to do anything that evening in the way of bear hunting, it was decided to make the camp and have a good night's rest. This was not as easy a matter as it had been in some other places. There was not at any one spot sufficient dry wood for a good camp, especially if they should be attacked by wolves and thus require for their safety a good bright fire all night. However, the matter was arranged by making the dogs help. They were unfastened from their sleds, and while some of the men cut down the dry trees, wherever they could be found, the boys and one or two men hitched their dogs to them and dragged them to the vicinity of the camp, where they were speedily cut up into the desired lengths. There were numbers of green balsams around, and so some of these were cut down and so arranged as to be helpful in keeping off the cold winds. The frozen fish were thawed for the dogs, and then some of the men prepared the usual supper, which consisted of the fattest meat that could be obtained. Prayers were offered after the Evening Hymn had been sung, the beds of fur robes and blankets were made, and Mr. Ross and the boys were soon very thoroughly tucked in. Nothing unusual disturbed them in the night, although some of the men had an uneasy half hour, as the dismal howlings of a solitary wolf in the distance could be distinctly heard. The mournful sounds at length died away, and the men again went to sleep.

As they were retiring Mustagan told the boys that the steam would be going best just after sunrise, and so they had better all be up early and after a good warm cup of tea and something to eat be off to see it and then return to breakfast. Then he said, "After that we will find out what makes the steam."

There was only the faintest glimmer of the coming dawn when the boys were called up. My, but it was cold that morning! How the lads did shiver! Wistfully they looked back at the warm robes and blankets which the men were rapidly rolling up. Gladly would they have tumbled under them again, the cold was so terrible. It must have been at least fifty below zero. It seemed to chill them to the very marrow of their bones. Their teeth chattered. The tears in their eyes froze into ice. The breath touching their fur caps, or capotes, instantly became white and shining. Well was it for them that the fire was brightly burning ere they were called. Speedily were seats of rolls of blankets prepared for them, and here, with a big buffalo skin thrown around each one as an additional protection, they were seated as close to the fire as it was possible to get without setting their clothes or robes on fire. How warming and delicious was the tea that morning!—well sweetened, and with a lump of cream in it. Cup after cup was taken, and soon the bitter cold was forgotten.

"Very cold morning," said Mustagan. "Take good breakfast now, then another good one will be ready when we come back from seeing the steam."

With all the clothing that could well be worn consistent with rapid snowshoeing the party soon set off. Their direction from the camp was due south. As far as the boys could make out the region was full of great rocky ravines. But the snow covered everything, and it was evident that the high winds had caused enormous quantities to drift into the hollows and ravines. Mr. Ross and Mustagan were in front, while the boys and some Indians were not far behind. All at once Mustagan, who had been on the alert, called Mr. Ross's attention to an object which at first was to him more imaginary than real. Sharp as were his eyes, he was asked to look upon what to him was at present invisible and intangible. The party had all now stopped, and each one was endeavoring to see what already seemed so real to Mustagan.

"O, I see it!" shouted Alec and Sam together. "See, as the sun's rays fall upon it, it shines like a small bit of a rainbow."

"Yes," said Frank, "I see it, like a thin column of steam lit up by the morning sun."

Then it was visible to all. For as the sun arose a little higher, and its full rays fell on it, at the right angle to the spot where our party now stood, there it was, clear and distinct, a tiny spiral column of steam rising up in the clear cold air from a great snowy expanse. There was not a sign of a tree or of a den. Then Mustagan explained that there was a deep ravine full of the snow, and at the bottom of it some bears had made their winter's nest in the fall. Whether they had much of a den or not he did not know. They would find that out when they dug them out. Anyway, here they were under many feet of snow. The breathing caused the snow to melt around them and above them, until it formed an icy crystal roof. Then, as they went on breathing and breathing, by and by in a little opening it found its way through the crust and through the fine snow, until it made a small chimney all the way up to the top; and then he added, "There it comes out, as you see it now."

Carefully they all walked up to the spot. The opening was not more than an inch in diameter. It was hardly perceptible. The little bit of steam froze into the tiniest particles of ice, which were invisible except when the sun's bright rays shone on them. It was a great curiosity to the boys. "How many feet below us are the bears?" asked Sam, in tones so subdued that everybody laughed. But the fact that only a lot of light snow separated him from he knew not how many savage bears had a tendency to make him a little nervous, and hence his whispered question. Glancing over the landscape, and taking notice of the hills in the distance and the amount of country that the storm had swept over, Mustagan and Mr. Ross came to the conclusion that between twenty and thirty feet of snow were between them and the icy cave where these bears were drowsily sleeping away the long winter months. After some further investigation, and a talk about the best way of getting down to those bears, the party returned to camp for breakfast.

The snowshoe run back was a vigorous one, and enjoyed on account of the cold. The second breakfast was dispatched, and the plans talked over for getting down to the bears. If the snow should be found light and dry quite a distance down it would be impossible to dig a well-like hole down to them. If the wind had packed the snow hard as it filled up the ravine it would be an easy matter. If it were found impracticable to get to them that way, then they would have to tunnel in from below, in the valley, until they reached them. A tunnel can always be dug in deep snow, as the pressure of the mass above sufficiently hardens the snow near the ground to make it quite possible to accomplish the work. Thus they discussed various plans, and then decided to go and begin operations on what seemed the best way when they reached the spot.

Axes, ropes, a big baglike bucket for hauling up snow, snowshovels, and other things considered necessary were taken along on a couple of dog-trains to the spot where the steam was quite visible, now that it had been discovered. After some consultation it was decided to go to a cluster of trees not far off and cut down a number of them and build a kind of platform on the snow directly over the steam orifice, and then commence the work of digging down to the den below.

Soon all were busy. The men cut down the trees, and the boys claimed the honor of driving the dogs that dragged the logs to the place where they were to be used. As the snow over the bears' den was so very deep the boys had to keep on their snowshoes all the time. It was very difficult at first for the dogs to get along, but after the snowshoes had tramped out the trail a few times the snow then easily held them up.

The log platform was built, and in the large space left cleared in the center, which was about eight feet square, the work of digging was commenced. When all the snow was thrown out that could be reached with the long-handled snowshovels a rude windlass was made, and then the leather baglike bucket was brought into requisition, and the work went on as fast as it was possible to haul up the snow and have it dragged away on the dog-sleds. When the well-like hole was down about fifteen feet, and they were congratulating themselves that at least half of the work was accomplished, there was a sudden collapse. The whole thing had caved in and carried down the platform and all to a distance of eight or ten feet. Nobody was badly hurt. The two men who were in the bottom at the time, busily filling up the leather bucket, were hit with some of the falling logs and nearly buried in the avalanche of snow that seemed to them to come from every quarter above them. Those who had tumbled in were more scared than hurt. The difficulty now was to get the men out, as the sides were so light and yielding.

"Use the dogs to do it," said Frank. And quickly a strong rope was tied to an empty sled and it was let down to the first man. A strong dog-train was attached to the other end of the rope.

"Marche!" was shouted, and away went the dogs, and soon there emerged one of the men who had fallen in. Quickly was he rescued, and speedily this operation was repeated until the dogs had dragged out all therein imprisoned.

All this work had gone for nothing. Some other plan must be devised. Half a day's work gone and nothing to show for it. This was rather discouraging.

"What is to be tried next?" was asked by several.

"Dinner is next," said Mr. Ross. And so away they hurried back to camp, and there while eating their well-earned meal they talked over the next attempt, and decided to go down where the ravine ended out on a level place and there begin tunneling.

When they came back and examined the spot and measured the drift they found that in order to get low enough to reach the bears they would have to tunnel at least two hundred feet. This meant a lot of heavy work. But they were there to get those bears, and were bound to succeed. At first they dug away the snow like a deep trench, until they reached a place where it was too deep to be thrown out, and then the work of tunneling really began. To their delight, they found when they had gone some way in that the pressure of the immense mass of snow upon the lower portion had so packed it that it would not require supports, as has already been referred to.

They worked in relays with their big shovels, and cut the snow out in great pieces, which were dragged away by the dogs as fast as the sleds could be loaded.

That evening, when they stopped work, they estimated that they had cut about half the way into the bears' den. Then they returned to the camp for supper and rest, and hoped to be able to finish their work on the morrow.

That night there was a most beautiful display of the aurora borealis. Their ever-changing glories delighted and so fascinated the boys that they were loth to cover up their heads in their camp beds. These wondrous visions in the North Land exceed in weird beauty anything else that this wide world can show.

Mr. Ross was so anxious that they should get the bears to-day, so that the whole party could begin the return journey to-morrow, that he had them all up at such an early hour that they were eating breakfast by starlight. Just as the sun rose, and the Indians were calling, "Sagastao! Sagastao!" ("The sun rises!") to each other, they were already at the tunnel, anxious to resume operations. They had to be careful now to so run the tunnel that they would directly strike the bears. So while the men were digging Mr. Ross and Mustagan were constantly traveling on their snowshoes with a compass to try and help the diggers, who were rapidly pushing on their work.

The boys could hardly understand how it was that it could be so cozy and comfortable in the tunnel while outside the cold was so terrible. To their surprise, they here learned that there was warmth even in a snow tunnel. While thus digging away and dragging out the loads, all at once the dogs became very much excited, and began barking furiously. Suspecting that it was because of the scent of the bears, which passes a long distance through the snow, the guns and some axes were immediately sent for.

"Did you ever shoot a bear?" said Mustagan to Sam.

"I was chased by one once," said Sam, with a laugh. "But I fancy I got even with him before the summer ended."

"O yes," said Mustagan, with a comical grin, "I do remember now a boy coming running into the camp with a bear at his heels. That's why your hair stands up so straight ever since."

Poor Sam, whose hair had a natural tendency to stand on ends, said he thought he had heard enough of that bear story of his, and so was about blaming the old Indian for being too hard on him, when he was astonished at hearing him say:

"I want you to be the first to walk into that bears' den with me. Mr. Bear chased you once. You killed some of his relatives since then, but he has lots of brothers, and perhaps some of them are in this den, and so now is your chance to teach them a lesson for one of their relatives making your hair stand up straight. Fact is," added the old Indian, who had never seen a person with his hair standing up like Sam's, "Indian thinks you will have to keep killing bears until your hair gets over its scare and lies down flat again."

This bit of humor from Mustagan amused everybody, and Sam himself joined heartily in the laugh.

Thus they chatted until the guns and axes arrived. Then the work was vigorously pursued. The tunnel was dug in further and further, as fast as the snow could be hauled out. Every time the dogs came in with their empty sleds they were permitted to remain a few minutes to scent the bears. As they had quieted down after their first noisy actions it was decided that they were still a good way off from the bears.

As a precautionary measure Memotas went out and cut a long, slim pole, which was about twenty feet long. This he pushed in through the snow ahead of the diggers. By this plan he was able to guard against any surprise, for he had stated to Mr. Ross that as the snow was so deep the den would be found very warm, and he would not be surprised if they found the bears so wide-awake that they would have a bit of a fight with them ere they killed them. When this was heard it added much to the excitement of the whole party, and so while everyone worked with a will they were all on the alert for some sudden developments.

After Mustagan had pushed in the pole two or three times and found nothing but the ordinary snow, which was being rapidly dug away, he at length struck against something hard, which was about fifteen feet in from the end of the now long tunnel. When the dogs came in for their last loads Mustagan pulled out the pole and let the dogs put their noses to the opening. They were simply furious, and at once began most vigorously to dig into the snow around the hole. Of course, they were quickly stopped and again fastened to the sleds, which on account of the narrowness of the tunnel had to be backed in. Cautiously they worked, and soon were within only four or five feet of the obstruction, whatever it was, that prevented the pole being pushed along any further.

A consultation was now held, and it was decided to very much enlarge the end of the tunnel, so that if there was to be much of a fight there would be room enough for the men to stand up and easily move around. This enlarging the tunnel and getting out the snow consumed the best part of an hour. Fortunately, it was not very dark, although they were so far from daylight in any direction. The pure white snow seems to throw off a certain amount of light. However, it was warm work, and so the men frequently went out with the dogs in relays. Once outside they quickly cooled off and were glad to return. When the enlargement of the tunnel was about completed, and the men were again engaged in cutting out great blocks of the snow that was between them and the bears, there suddenly reached them a perfume so strong as to be almost sickening. No need of telling anyone who has ever been near a close old bears' den where they were now.

All the shovels except a couple were quickly dropped, and the weapons were seized by those who were expected to do the fighting. The arrangements were speedily made. It was difficult to say how many bears were in the den. If only two or three, there would not be much trouble in killing them, but if, as sometimes happened, a number had clubbed together, there might be as many as eight or ten, and if so there would be lots of excitement, and perhaps somebody might get hurt. So it was decided that Mr. Ross with Frank and Alec should go out to the mouth of the tunnel, and there with their weapons remain, with the dogs unharnessed, and wait for developments, while Mustagan with Sam and the others would face them in their dens. If any tried to escape through the tunnel those watching at the mouth would fire at them or run them down with the dogs.

Cautiously the intervening wall of snow was broken down and trampled under foot. Listen! There are low growlings heard, and it is evident that the bears are on the alert. These sounds show that the bears have long been hearing the noise made by the approach of the tunnelers, and are getting their courage up for a fight with the disturbers of their long repose. Mustagan had taken the precaution to bring along some torches which he had specially made. The principal materials of them were rolls of birch bark saturated in balsam gum. The gum had been boiled down and otherwise so prepared that when ignited it made a most brilliant light and yet emitted but little smoke. At length the diggers came to a wall of icy snow, which was very close and hard. This was the wall and roof of the whole den. The party attentively listened, and now the bears were easily heard. Mustagan said:

"Some of them wide-awake, others seem like sleepy boys called early. They are growling and snarling, and seem to say, 'Be quiet and let us sleep till it is time to get up.' We'll wake you so you will want to get up in a hurry," added the old man with a chuckle, as he made his final arrangements.

These were as follows: The men who had been using the shovels were ordered to exchange them for their heavy axes. With these they were to at once smash in a place large enough for Mustagan and Sam to step through. They would each have one of the brightest torches, and so the old man believed that the sleeping animals would crowd from the bewildering light to the other side of the den. So the flint and steel were struck and a light made by one of them, while the axmen now vigorously broke through the thin glassy wall.

Soon an opening sufficiently large was made, and the old Indian and Sam fearlessly stepped in, with guns and torches. As anticipated by Mustagan, the bears, frightened by the brilliant torches, at once crowded away from the dazzling flames. So he and Sam were safely in, but it did not take him long to see that they were not altogether safe in there. My, what a crowd of them! and bears of all sizes too.

"Chop away at the ice," was Mustagan's first command, as he and Sam kept slowly edging their way around. So numerous were the bears that they dare not think of letting go their splendid torches that were burning brightly.

"We are going to try and drive them out," were his next words; and then the old Indian shouted, "Look out, men, and be ready for them!"

Sam was cool and collected, for he had all confidence in Mustagan, but he could not help being startled and surprised at the number of the bears that lay there snarling and growling like a drove of pigs. The size and beauty of the winter house was also a revelation. As the winter had advanced the warmth of the bears had caused the icy walls and roof to keep slowly receding, until now here was a capacious vaultlike room of clearest crystal. As the brilliant light flashed on it, it seemed like some dream of fairyland. One look, however, at the startled, growling bears showed that the fierce occupants were anything but nymphs and fairies. Seeing their numbers, Mustagan quickly called in a couple more men, with axes and additional torches. Pointing out a very large one that seemed ready to begin battle at any moment, he said, "You, Sam, you shoot him fair between the eyes."

Sam at once obeyed. Tremendous was the effect. So confined was the place that the sound was as though a cannon had been fired. All the torches were instantly extinguished but one, and the ice cracked and fell in great pieces around them. Speedily were the torches relighted. The bears were wide-awake now. Fortunately, the biggest and fiercest was stone dead. Sam's aim had been sure, and his bullet had done its work. Mustagan was now so fiercely attacked by the next largest one that he could not bring up his gun to his shoulder, but he skillfully fired from his side and sent a bullet into the heart of his assailant. This quickly finished him. This second report was, if possible, worse than the first, and so some seconds were lost in relighting the torches.

"Drop your guns," said Mustagan, "and fight with your axes and knives."

And fight they had to, for the bears were now full of fight and each went for an opponent. Sam bravely tackled a fine two-year-old with his ax. He raised it and made a desperate blow to try and split the animal's skull open. But just as he plunged forward to strike the bear suddenly rose up and with a side blow struck the ax such a clip that it fairly flew out of Sam's hands, while the lad, unable to keep his footing, stumbled forward at the bear's hind feet. He was fortunately able to reach sideways and seize one of the flaming torches that had been thrown on the ground, and which was still fiercely burning. He was none too soon, for already the bear's strong forearms were winding round him for a hug that he would have long remembered. However, as the blazing torch was pushed into the bear's face it so suddenly singed his handsome whiskers that he had to throw up his paws to defend his face. Finding himself thus free again, Sam was quickly on his feet. Drawing his knife, he was able to look around. Two or three bears were killed and others wounded, but so carefully were they using their paws in parrying the blows of the men that they were fairly holding their own. One man had a shoulder blade broken, and another's crushed ribs were making him groan.

"Let us drive them out," said Mustagan, and already it was evident that the bears' quick instinct had enabled them to catch the scent of the fresh air through the tunnel.

"Run for your lives!" shouted Mustagan to the

two men who had been left in the tunnel, "and tell Mr. Ross and the boys to be ready at the mouth to receive them."

They lost no time in getting out, for they were about half blinded and suffocated by the smoke of the guns and could render but little service. They were soon out, and found Mr. Ross and the boys ready for the bears. All were much excited, for they had distinctly heard the two shots fired inside.

Mustagan, Sam, and the Indians had now wedged themselves so around the bears that they had them all between them and the opening into the tunnel. The cunning animals were loth to leave their winter quarters, and so they very slowly and reluctantly gave ground as Mustagan and the others, with their flaming torches, gradually forced them on ahead. It would now have been easy to have shot some of them, but Mustagan was afraid that as so much of the ice had fallen already from the roof of the den a few more such reports might find them all buried under the great mass above them. So he decided to drive the bears out into the open air, where the fight could be renewed.

At the great opening in the crystal wall the bears made a determined stand. There were still seven or eight of them unwounded. There they raised themselves upon their hind feet against the opening, and seemed to say, "We will not be thus driven out of our house." Beyond this point it seemed impossible to drive them. The torches would not burn much longer, and something desperate had to be done. Mustagan, while fearful of the effects of a powder explosion on the roof, yet resolved to try one. Skillfully throwing some powder in handfuls at the feet of the bears, he said to Sam and to the men:

"Get back as far as possible, before I fire this train of powder. Pull your caps over your eyes, and put your heads to the ground."

Then he plunged one of the torches into the little train of gunpowder that reached from him to the bears. Away flew the little stream of fire across the den, and then there was a commotion. The powder went off in sheets and tongues. The bears went off also. They did not stand on ceremony now. They could not stand such a fiery house, and so they wanted to get out of it as quickly as possible. With growls and snarls away they hurried, while Mustagan and Sam and the rest, with the expiring torches and noisy yells, followed quickly after, keeping them on the move. Mr. Ross and the others heard them coming. They had wisely retired a little from the mouth of the tunnel, so as to let the bears get well out before they should catch sight of these new assailants. At the mouth of the tunnel, as they caught the cold air, so different from the comfortable quarters they had left, there was a decided desire on the part of the bears to retrace their steps, but that horrid din and those blazing torches were just behind, and so they made a break for the distant forest, which was quite visible across the snowy waste.

"Fire now!" was the cry. And the guns of Mr. Ross, Alec, and Frank rang out, and a couple of bears tumbled over, one of which quickly regained his feet and was off after his comrades. Unfortunately, the man holding the six dogs that had been unharnessed could no longer restrain them, and so they were off after the bears. This was a great annoyance to the men who had guns and were now emerging from the tunnel. They dare not now fire at the bears, for fear of hurting the dogs. The snow on the open plain was not more than a foot deep, and so the bears, as well as the dogs, could make very good speed. Some time was lost ere the men and boys could get their snowshoes on and take up the chase. It was a great fight. Some foolish dog would close in on a bear and would get a hug that sent him howling back. Others were wiser and went in pairs. When they overtook a bear they immediately separated, one rushing to the front, while the other remained behind. Thus they keep at him and, as a general thing, so thoroughly engage his attention that the hunter can come up and shoot him at his leisure. In this way Frank and Alec were each able to get a shot at a couple of bears, which they easily killed without any great risk to themselves.

A single dog has hardly any chance with a large bear, as one of Frank's train found to his cost. Pluckily he rushed in and made a gallant effort to seize the bear by the throat, but the powerful forearms gave him a hug so terrible that he was so crushed that he had to be shot to be put out of misery. His ribs were found broken like clay pipestems. Poor Frank dropped a few honest tears over Swag's grave, which was only a hole in the deep snow. This death was the first break in any of the boys' teams, and although another fine dog took poor

Swag's place, it was long before the boys ceased talking about him and his sad end.

Some of the fleeter bears succeeded in reaching the trees, but they made there in the bitter cold but a sorry fight, and were soon all killed.

For the first time almost for hours, now that the last bear was killed, one and all began to feel the terrible cold, and no wonder. Such had been the excitement of the last few hours that they had not noticed that it was long past the dinner hour, and when eating is neglected in such a temperature much suffering will quickly follow. So the cry was, "Back to the camp!" No second order was necessary, and great was the delight of the boys to find that some one more level-headed and less excited had long since returned and had a bountiful dinner awaiting everyone.

It was too late to return home that day, and so a swift runner was sent back for additional sleds, while the men, under Mustagan's guidance, with the dogs available—and they were not many—dragged the bears to the camp, and there during the evening and night carefully skinned them and cut up the meat.

Mr. Ross and the boys, who were thoroughly tired, wrapped themselves well up in their robes and rested in the camp, feeling that they had had enough excitement for that day. This unique experience of bear-hunting in the depth of winter was often talked about in after years. Many skeptics scoffed at it as a dream, but they who were in it knew better.

Frank never forgot poor Swag's sad end, and for long days he mourned the loss of his faithful dog.

CHAPTER XXI.

The First Signs of Spring—The Eagle Moon—Expressive Indian Names for Some of the Months—Chats Among the Boys About the Phenomena of the North Land—Power of the Frost—Cunning of Animals—Cleverness of the Guides—Invitation to a Muskrat Hunt—Gladly Accepted—Habits of These Little Animals—Methods of Capture—Their Many Foes—The Queer Battle Between Wild Cats and Wolverines.

THUS rapidly and pleasantly passed the winter months at Sagasta-weekee. Cold they were, and at times the blizzards had howled around, but as a general thing the days had been full of sunshine and the nights of wondrous beauty. Wretched days of fogs and mists and damps were almost unknown. The air at all times was full of ozone, and knew no taint of fever or malaria. There was a luxury in living where the skies were nearly always bright and the air was always absolutely pure.

For long months the Frost King had reigned supreme, but now there were indications that his grip was lessening and that his power was coming to an end. In sunny, sheltered spots the snow began to soften and then to disappear. Then tiny little rivulets in the warmest hours of the day began to make sweet music, gathering strength and courage and hurrying on to play hide and seek as they dashed under the great icy coverings of the still frozen lakes. Strong south winds blew frequently, and under their magic influences the great snowdrifts rapidly lessened and then disappeared. From underneath the still hard, dry snow some mysterious melting influence was at work, and the great masses sank down and soon all flitted away under the wondrous but unseen influences of the coming spring.

"I saw a great golden eagle," said Alec, as one day he came in from a short hunting trip with Big Tom.

"Did you see it first?" said Sam.

"No, indeed," replied Alec; "Big Tom's eyes were more alert, and so he first saw it and then pointed it out to me as it was flying in graceful circles far up in the blue heavens."

"The Indians will be all saying that spring indeed has come," said Mr. Ross. "As the appearance of the eagle is, as I think I told you, the beginning of spring, Mikisewpesim, the eagle moon, is the first spring month."

"Is it not," said Frank, "a very uncertain way of marking the seasons?"

"The variation is not as great as a person would at first imagine," was Mr. Ross's reply. "We talk about an early spring or a late spring, and March with us is sometimes like April. Then some other years it is just the reverse. So the Indians' methods of marking the months by the arrival of the birds, or other events in nature, is not generally much out of the way."

"What birds follow the eagles?" asked Sam.

"The wild geese." replied Mr Ross, "and as they do not come until the great marshes, which are their early feeding grounds, are partially bared of snow, they are about a month behind the eagles."

"Then is there a goose month also?" asked Alec.

"Yes, indeed," replied Mr. Ross, "and it is a very important one to the Indians, and I anticipate that we, too, will have our share of excitement in it. It is called Niskepesim, from 'niska,' goose, or 'niskuk,' geese, and 'pesim,' month. The Niskepesim, goose moon, which corresponds with our April, is followed by Unekepesim, frog moon, as then those denizens of the swamps and ponds begin their croakings. In our North Land frog moon corresponds with May. Then comes Wawepesim, egg moon, as in June the birds are nesting and hatching out their young. So it is with all the other months, each has some equally expressive name."

"I am sure we are thankful for all this information," said Frank.

"It is a pleasure to get information, even if it sometimes has to be acquired under difficulties, and it is equally pleasing to impart it to those who will make use of it," was Mr. Ross's reply.

"I am sure," said Sam, "we will have a deal to talk about when we return home next summer. The only thing that is bothering me is that lots will say that it is only a pack of lies that I am trying to cram down their throats."

"Well, then," replied Frank, "we will not be the only returned travelers whose veracity will be questioned. Don't you remember, Sam, about the first ambassadors to England from a tropical country in the south of Asia, that when they returned home they were rash enough to say that in England sometimes in winter the water became hard enough to walk on. Then the king was so mad at them for telling such monstrous lies that he immediately handed them over to the executioner and had them shortened by the length of their heads."

"I wonder what he would have done with me," said Sam, "after I had enlightened him on some of the facts of this country, for that mere trifle of a statement about ice forming on a river in England was a mighty small incident in comparison with what I have here discovered."

"What would you tell him," asked Alec, "supposing the old rascal were still alive, and should ask you to visit him and then set your tongue a-wagging?"

"Sure," replied Sam, without any hesitancy, "if his Satanic majesty—I beg his pardon, that Siamese king—wanted any more water information, I would say to him, 'Sire, your majesty, once, in a fit of indignation at the doing of a stable man, called Pasche, I seized a bucket of water, just drawn, and up with it to throw over the fellow, and, wonderful to relate, it just hit him in chunks of ice as dry as marble.'"

"Well, we know that is true," said Alec; "but supposing the old fellow still left your head on your shoulders, what next would you tell him?"

"If the old questioner still wanted anything more about liquid matter, I would just inform him that we carry the milk of our cows wrapped up in old newspapers, and that it keeps that way for months, as solid and tidy and handy as a brickbat in the end of a stocking."

"If he could stand that and let you survive, what next?" said Frank.

"I fancy I would confound his intellect by telling him that the breath-laden air of the church, one bitterly cold Sunday, where some hundreds of Indians worshiped, so froze up that the whole of it fell to the floor in beautiful snow so plentifully that in one place, near a cold window, it was over a foot deep."

"Supposing he survived that, or rather let you survive, what next would you cram him with?" said Frank.

Sam, glib of tongue and ever ready, at once answered:

"Well, if that son of the sun, or whatever his Oriental title may be, wanted any more information about our liquids, I would enlighten him with the information that here, as a pastime or scientific experiment, we take quicksilver or mercury and cast it into bullets that become as hard and solid as lead, and then shoot them through stable doors."

"Anything more?" said Mr. Ross, who had been an amused listener, and had been much pleased with Sam's ready answers, which showed how well he was gathering up the facts of the country to use them in other lands in years to come.

"Well, yes," said Sam, "I would tell his bibulous majesty, if he were in the habit of imbibing moisture of a fiery kind, that on one of our long journeys with our dogs I had with me on my sled, for purposes that need not concern his majesty, a bottle of the strongest wine. One day, when no eyes were on me, for good and honest purposes I made a visit to the aforesaid bottle, and to my horror and grief I found the bottle burst into a hundred pieces. Feeling carefully around—for it was in the dark when I had made this visit—I discovered that the wine itself was frozen into a solid mass exactly the shape of the bottle. I carefully wrapped it up in a handkerchief, and thus carried it along. Suffice to say, none of it was lost."

"Well," said Frank, "if just about water, milk, mercury, and wine we will be able to tell such things, shall we not have lots of fun when we talk of our dogs and their doings, and of many other things that at first seemed so marvelous to us, but are now everyday occurrences and have in a measure lost their force and novelty?"

"I fancy," said Alec, "that some of the things we can also tell them about the cunning and cleverness of the wild animals we have been hunting, or seeing the Indians hunt, will open their eyes."

"After all," said Frank, "the cleverness of the Indian guides in finding their way through the pathless forests, day or night, where there was not the least vestige of a trail, sometimes for hundreds of miles, and often when blizzard storms howled around them for days together, was to me as wonderful and unaccountable as anything I have witnessed."

"Yes," said Mr. Ross, "that is indeed wonderful. I have been studying it all my life, and I am just as much puzzled to-day as I was at first with these first-class guides. They are not all thus gifted, but there are some who never blunder, or even hesitate, under the most difficult circumstances. The sky may be leaden with clouds all day, and an ordinary person get so bewildered that he does not know north from south, or east from west, but the guide never hesitates for an instant, but on and on with unerring accuracy he pushes day after day, or even night after night."

"That is wonderful indeed," replied Alec, "but the cleverness with which the wolves tried to get ahead of me by cutting across the necks of land in the river, and their other deviltries, are what I will never forget."

Here this most interesting conversation was ended by the arrival of Paulette and Mustagan, with the word that the melting snow had exposed the houses of the muskrats, and that they were off on a hunting excursion to a great pondlike swamp where these animals were known to be very numerous. At once it was decided that a party would be made up to join them at a designated spot in the forest on the edge of this great swamp. The distance was between twenty and thirty miles, and as the greater part of the route would be on the ice, it was decided not to start until the chill of the evening had hardened the snow, which now nearly every day softened in the midday sun. Traveling with dog-trains in half-melted snow, or even when it is just soft enough to stick, is very heavy, laborious work. However, as soon as the sun ceases to shine upon it, at this season, it hardens up again very quickly.

Arrangements were made for a three or four days' trip, so a regular camp outfit was taken along on the dog-sleds. In addition to their guns the boys were each supplied with a long, lancelike barbed spear for effective use when securing the muskrats. Two or three Indians were taken along by Mr. Ross, who remarked to the boys, when he decided to accompany them himself, that perhaps this was the last hunting trip of the season with the dogs, with perhaps the exception of the one to the goose hunt, which would not be long distant.

The whole party left Sagasta-weekee about sundown, and as it was a crisp, cold, beautiful moonlight night, everybody enjoyed the trip exceedingly. The boys, however, could not help remarking the great change in the temperature from midday. Then the sun was so hot that the snow was melting at a marvelous rate; now everything was as hard and firm as though it were still January. Through the portages and over the frozen ice expanses they hurried, and some time before midnight they reached a splendid camp already prepared for them by Paulette and Mustagan. A great roaring fire looked very attractive to all, even to the boys, as they had become quite accustomed to these wintry resting places when the heavy day's work was done. Kettles were quickly filled and a late supper was eaten, and then all lay down to sleep. Nothing disturbed their rest except the distant mournful screeches of the wild cats and some other wild animals, that were already, now that spring was coming, like themselves, on the lookout for muskrats.

In the morning, after an early breakfast, the whole party set off for the great pondlike morass that extended for miles. Numerous tracks of wild animals were seen, and Mustagan pointed out to the boys not only those of some wild cats, but also a number of those made by the great feet of the wolverines, as these latter animals are as fond of muskrats as are any other. When the edge of the shore was reached the boys were surprised to see how rapidly the snow had disappeared from the surface of this lakelike pond. On it they noticed a large number of what seemed like bundles of straw, as though a farmer in a great loaded wagon had driven over the surface and had here and there in many places pitched out large forkfuls and left them to decay.

"It looks," said Sam, "as though some farmer hereabouts had been drawing out the contents of his barnyard to enrich his fields."

"Just what I thought," said Alec.

"All those little hillocks of marsh hay and reeds are muskrat nests," explained Mr. Ross. "They were made last summer on the little mossy hillocks that everywhere abound in all of these great marshes. Being then entirely surrounded by water, they are fairly safe from the prowling wild animals that hunt them as their prey, as wolverines and wild cats dislike the water. Then in the winter they are completely covered by the deep snow, and so are as safe as beavers' kitchens. But in the early spring, when the snow melts off the ice, they are at the mercy of their foes. The ice remains solid for another month or so, and on its hard surface these water-hating enemies travel and tear open these nests and devour those that have not deep enough burrowings in which to hide themselves away. Of course, as soon as open water comes they are safe, as they are thoroughly amphibious animals."

The boys were each armed with long, lancelike spears, while the Indians had in addition to these some axes and guns. At the first nest the boys found that the wild cats and wolverines had been there before them and had cleared out every muskrat. However, as under the guidance of the Indians they pushed out further on the ice, they found many nests or little houses undisturbed. A few blows with the axes knocked the house to pieces, and then there was quick work in spearing the almost helpless animals. In the houses near the channel of the stream, or where there was deep water, very often the clever muskrats had a channel dug from their little straw houses to the water. These "runs," as they are called, serve as a line of retreat whenever their home is attacked. In other places the muskrats contented themselves with merely having a well-like place under their little houses. While some of them were deep enough to save them from the wild cats or wolverines, they were not sufficient to save them from the spears of our boys and Indians. It seemed at first cruel to thus stab the helpless animals, but their flesh was food for the natives, and their furs were sold to the traders for things essential to the Indians' comfort. So numerous were the nests in this extensive morass that there was work enough for the hunters for days. The boys, however, soon became tired of killing the poor muskrats, and so only remained at the work with the Indians for the one forenoon. After that they left their long spears at the camp, and taking a dog or two with them, and their guns, had some good sport among the partridges, which were fairly numerous.

The second morning the boys were aroused very early by a couple of the Indians who had been on the watch during the night guarding the now large pile of muskrats and skins. Paulette and Mustagan were too clever to let their game be stolen from them, as were some beavers earlier in the winter from other hunters, as we have described elsewhere.

"Get ready soon, and get your guns and come with us, and we will show you something that will please you."

It did not take them long to respond, and so they were soon on the trail with Mr. Ross, while the two old Indians noiselessly led the way. The other Indians had orders to remain in the camp and keep the dogs with them, and as quiet as possible. They had not traveled more than half a mile before the boys heard the most discordant screeches. Still they had not the slightest idea of what sort of an experience was before them. Louder and louder were these sounds, as they came directly with the wind toward them. When they reached a little depression in the trail they found that Mustagan and Paulette had stopped and were awaiting their arrival. It was now so light in the eastern sky that the boys could see as they approached that the Indians were making signs for perfect quiet. So as noiselessly as possible they, with Mr. Ross, joined them. Then they were informed that just over the brow of the steep hill before them a couple of wolverines had chased a couple of wild cats up into a large tree. The cats had each captured a muskrat, and were making off with them when the wolverines came along and tried to rob them of their prey. However, the wild cats had succeeded in getting up into this solitary large tree with their game, and although the wolverines can climb trees they did not like to do so to attack these fierce cats, as their being already above them in the tree would give them such an advantage.

Very distinctly now could be heard the growls of the wolverines, and then the defiant snarls of the cats. With their guns loaded with ball, they all began the cautious crawl up the hillside, with the Indians in the advance. Fortunately for them, the top of the hill was studded with short, stunted spruce trees. By each person keeping one of these well in front of him, they were all able to crawl up to positions where they could distinctly see the tree with the wild cats ensconced on its large branches and the wolverines at the foot of it. The tree was not an evergreen, and so every branch was distinctly visible. For a time they watched the various manœuvers of the animals. They noticed that when the wolverines were not active in their movements the wild cats kept eating bits off the muskrats. This seemed to anger the furious brutes on the ground, and so they would one after another make the attempt to get up the hard, smooth trunk. How the cats had succeeded was a mystery to the boys. Wolverines are fairly good tree climbers, but they had no show at all here, for when one of them succeeded in getting well up the almost smooth, bare trunk a fierce blow from the unencumbered paw of one of the wild cats, securely seated on the large lowest limb, which ran out almost parallel from the trunk of the tree, quickly caused him to loose his grip and fall helplessly to the ground. Then with apparent satisfaction the wild cat would take another bite or two of his muskrat. Several times, as though on purpose, the wild cats dropped small bits of meat or half-picked bones to the ground. The taste or smell of these fairly drove the wolverines furious, and so they would desperately make fresh attempts to get at their enemies, but without success.

It was fortunate for our party that the wind was blowing toward them, and also that the air was so thoroughly tainted with the musky smell of the muskrats. Under ordinary circumstances they would have been detected long ere they had reached the top of the hill. So, unsuspected, they watched the strange antics of these animals, until suddenly the reports of a couple of guns rang out, and then up sprang both Mustagan and Paulette and dashed down to the foot of the tree, loudly calling to the rest of the party to quickly follow. Following Mr. Ross, the boys speedily obeyed, and when they reached the tree they found that one wolverine was dead and the other was hobbling off, as speedily as he could, on three legs. The other had been broken by the ball of one of the Indians. The frightened wild cats had dropped what was left of the muskrats, which was not much, and had found their way much higher up in the large tree, where they vainly tried to hide themselves by stretching out on a couple of large branches. Quickly loading his gun again, Paulette hurried off after the wounded wolverine, that, in spite of his broken leg, was rapidly making for the distant dense forest. But vain were all his efforts, for behind him was an Indian who, although now well up in years, was one of the fleetest runners in the tribe. Soon the gun rang out and another wolverine was dead.

It was decided that the boys should have the work of shooting the wild cats. So close and flat did they crawl down on the big branches that the boys had to move back to a considerable distance from the tree to get a good aim. Sam and Alec were to fire first, and if either cat failed to drop, then Frank was to bring it down. Mr. Ross and Mustagan with loaded guns stood ready for any emergency, for wild cats are uncertain animals, and are not to be trifled with. They are very fierce, and will sometimes, when thus treed, if furious with hunger, or driven from their young, spring down into the midst of the hunters and fight like tigers. When the boys had secured a good position, and each knew which wild cat he was expected to kill, Mustagan gave the signal, and together the reports of their guns rang out. The cat at which Sam had fired at once dropped to the ground, stone dead. The other did not move, much to the chagrin of Alec, who could not understand how he should have missed him. Just as Frank raised his gun to fire Mustagan's quick eye saw what the boys did not, and so before Frank could fire he stopped him by saying:

"That cat is dead; do not waste another bullet on it. You only more injure his skin."

And so it was; when the body was at length obtained it was found that Alec's bullet had hit him squarely behind the fore shoulder and had gone clean through his body, of course killing him so suddenly that there was not even that muscular quiver which generally causes animals when thus killed to fall to the ground. This was what actually happened to the one that Sam shot.

Paulette soon after made his appearance dragging the wolverine. They were all delighted with the morning's work. Mr. Ross and the boys hurried back to the camp and speedily dispatched an Indian with a dog-train and empty sled for the game. While some skinned these animals, others spent the day in killing additional muskrats, and then after supper, as soon as the snow had frozen hard again and the glorious moon was well up in the heavens, the home trip was commenced. Loaded down as they were, they did not travel as fast as they had done in the outward trip, and so it was about daybreak when they reached Sagasta-weekee.

CHAPTER XXII.

Niskepesim, the Goose Moon—Excitement Among the Indians—The First Goose—Their Northern Migrations—Feeding Grounds—Methods of Hunting Them—Nests—Decoys—Our Boys Off with the Indians—The Shooting Grounds—Their Camp—Great Success—Frank's Queer Accident—Hit by a Dead Goose—Sam's Comments—Laden with Spoils.

NOT many days after the return from the muskrat hunt the weather became, for that land, decidedly warmer. This created so much excitement among the generally stoical Indians that the boys could not but observe it. So one day, when a number of them were at Sagasta-weekee, Sam asked Mustagan the cause of it. The old man answered but one word, and that was:

"Niskepesim" ("The goose moon").

"Yes," said Kinesasis, who had just come in, "it has surely come. Some passing hunters saw some wild geese near the mouth of the river, at Lake Winnipeg, and others who were out spearing muskrats said that they heard flocks of them passing over during the night."

Great indeed was the excitement everywhere at this news. It rapidly flew from Sagasta-weekee to the fort, and then on to the mission. As though by some mysterious telegraphy, it passed from one Indian settlement to another, yea, from wigwam to wigwam, until the cry everywhere was, "Niskepesim! Niskepesim!" ("The goose moon! The goose moon!")

Why there should be such commotion among these northern Indians about the arrival of the wild geese has long been a puzzle to outsiders who happen to be among them at the time. Nevertheless such is the case. The fact that this moon is really the beginning of spring, which is so welcome, after the long and dreary winter, may have something to do with this general excitement and gladness. It is really the first month that the family have a flitting out from the close, confined houses or wigwams in which they have passed the cold, dreary months. Then it brings them a welcome change of diet, which is much prized after the long six months' dining twenty-one times a week on frozen whitefish, with only the variation of a little venison, muskrat, or beaver.

At Sagasta-weekee the excitement was as great as anywhere else. Mr. Ross had to exert a good deal of authority to keep some of his men at work after they had seen a great flock of these splendid gray geese fly over their heads. Over at the mission Mr. Hurlburt had failed completely in holding his men. He had been for some time urging them to clear up and put under cultivation what ground they had around their village that was good and fertile. At a good deal of expense he had secured a fine supply of axes, hoes, spades, and other necessary implements, as well as seeds, to help them. For some days they had worked industriously and well, and there was every prospect of a large portion of the ground being prepared and planted. One day, when Mr. Hurlburt had about thirty men hard at work in the fields, what should come flying along on the south wind but a great flock of geese? They were in broken ranks, not more than fifty feet above the ground, and evidently tired and looking for a feeding place. The sight was too much for the hunting instinct of the Indians, and so every ax, hoe, and spade was instantly dropped, and away they rushed for their guns. The missionary did not see one of them again for two weeks.

The wild geese are of various varieties. The first to arrive are the great gray ones. They seem to come up from Central America, Mexico, and Southern California, where they have spent the winter months. Then follow the brants, wavey, or laughing geese, which are all smaller varieties. When on their long migrations the geese all fly very high, and generally in long lines or triangles. But when they reach the north country, where they hope to spend the summer, they fly low over the ground. They seem to be then on the lookout for feeding grounds and suitable locations for nest building. If undisturbed, they speedily break up in pairs. They arrive very hungry, and so spend some days in heavy feeding on the peculiar many-jointed grass, called goose grass, the Indian name of which is Niskeanuskwa.

At Sagasta-weekee the boys had heard so much about the goose hunt that they were full of curiosity and excitement as the time of its expected arrival drew near. White suits and white caps had already been made for them, and the guns were all freshly cleaned and oiled. Camping outfits were all ready, and the boys observed that in addition to the winter's supplies there were added large heavy oilcloths, like tarpaulins. The next morning after Kinesasis had reported the words of the passing Indians there came in another hunter, and he had with him the first goose of the season. He was delighted to be the first, as a handsome reward is given to the one who is fortunate enough to kill and bring in this kind of first fruits of the harvest of these great birds. The sight of this goose was all that was necessary to have all arrangements completed, and it was decided that on the next morning all who could go should be off to the great goose hunt.

The point selected for the camp was on the border of one of these great swampy plains, from which the greater part of the snow had been melted by the warm south wind, leaving exposed over hundreds of acres vast quantities of this jointed grass on which the geese feed with such avidity. The frost was still in the ground, and so there was no difficulty on the part of the hunters in arranging their shooting nests and decoys as they desired. The camp was made very similar to those already described. There were a few changes, however. The soft snow was all cleared away, and a deep layer of fine balsam boughs were evenly spread out over the cleared place. Then over this a couple of tarpaulins were spread, and on these the usual camp beds of robes and blankets were arranged as elsewhere described. A great log fire was built up in front, and numerous logs were cut for use when required. A number of good stiff long poles were also cut and placed where they could be quickly utilized, if needed, to erect a roof or barrier against a storm of sleet or rain which might unexpectedly come up.

While the camp was thus being prepared by some of the party, in this cozy elevated place, back among the trees, where it would not frighten the geese, others were equally hard at work making the nests out on the great open meadowlike place where the goose grass was most abundant. These nests were built up of dry grass and dead brush, and made so that they looked just as their names would indicate —like great nests. Each of them was large enough to comfortably hold two hunters, who could easily move around, and thus be able to fire in any direction. They were about four feet high, and so constructed that when the hunters inside were crouching down they were quite invisible to the passing geese. Some Indians used to pile lumps of snow here and there on the edge of the nest to help the disguise. It is a peculiarity of wild geese that white objects never frighten them. This was the reason why the hunters all wore white suits and white caps. Then a number of decoys were made. They were rather rude affairs. The bodies were hewn out of logs about the size of a goose. A couple of sticks were driven in for legs; then the heads and necks, which had been prepared beforehand out of crooked roots, were fastened in their places. They were poor affairs, but seemed quite sufficient to attract the simple geese. A number of these decoys were assigned to each nest, and the hunter had to arrange his own according to his own judgment. The direction of the wind had much to do in rightly placing them. Care had to be exercised in arranging the nests so that the occupants of one would not be in danger from the firing from another, as in the excitement of the settling down of a large flock, or in their circling completely around a nest, a person is apt to forget everything but his anxiety to shoot as many as possible.

As soon as the sleds were unloaded they were all sent back to Sagasta-weekee, as not a dog must be allowed at the camp. No geese will come where there are barking dogs. For the first day or two there was nothing but anxious watching. The southern horizon was eagerly scanned for the oncoming lines of gray geese that were so eagerly anticipated but seemed to be so late in arriving. During the second night the wind, which had been blowing from the northeast, suddenly veered round to the southwest. This was noticed at once by the old, experienced men, Mustagan, Big Tom, Memotas, and Kinesasis, who had been invited by Mr. Ross to join his party. They were convinced that this wind would bring the geese, and so, dark as it was, they proceeded to make all arrangements for the next day's shooting. They first went out and arranged all the decoys in the right position, so as to attract the geese coming with such a wind. Then they carried the guns and arranged them four apiece in each nest, with the ammunition.

Before this work had been completed the geese could be heard flying over their heads. Some of the flocks were so low that the vibrations of the air could be easily felt. When they returned to the camp, although it was still starlight, they called up Mr. Ross and the boys. Breakfast was quickly prepared, and while it was being eaten the rush and calls of the rapidly increasing flocks could be distinctly heard. Then Mustagan and Frank, each taking a white blanket with him, hurried off to the most distant nest, which was almost north from the camp. There they cozily ensconced themselves and anxiously waited for the first blush of morning. Alec and Big Tom took possession of the nest on their left, about two hundred yards away. Sam and Memotas were assigned to the nest about the same distance south of them, while Mr. Ross and Kinesasis took possession of the one about three hundred yards distant on the right. All were in white suits, and had in addition their white blankets, as a protection against the cold. While one or two men were left to take care of the camp, the others went off to different places where they thought they could get successful shots.

It was not long before the morning star showed up above the eastern horizon, and then the first dawning of the day appeared.

"Chist!" ("Listen!") said Memotas to Sam, and quickly they were on the alert. The Indian's quick ear had detected a low-flying flock, and so before they were seen in the dim morning light they were heard. On they came, little dreaming of danger now that they were so far away from civilization, and so they flew not a hundred feet above this hidden place of their enemies.

Bang! bang! went the two guns into their midst, and soon bang! bang! went the other two barrels. With loud, discordant cries, those that were uninjured veered off to right and left. Memotas then threw down his empty gun and quickly seized his loaded one, but did not attempt to fire it. Sam also quickly picked up his extra loaded one, and was about to fire at the now rapidly retreating geese. Memotas, however, stopped him, and showed him that his gun was pointed exactly in the direction in which was the nest where Alec and Big Tom were stationed. Sam was frightened at what might have been the consequences if he had fired, and gratefully thanked Memotas for his caution. Memotas, who was busily engaged in reloading the guns, only said: "Soon daylight; then you will see better."

In the meantime the others had heard the firing and were on the alert, and so when the divided flock turned to the right and left some of the geese came close to the nest of Alec and Big Tom, and the rest were not very far from that of Mr. Ross and Kinesasis. There was firing from both parties, but their success was not very much, as the darkness was still too great, and the geese were not so close to them as they had been to Sam's nest. Memotas went out and found a couple of geese which he brought into the nest. He and Sam were quite proud of having killed the first. In the meantime, with the increase of the wind there was an increase in the number of the passing flocks. And now soon they began to be distinctly visible, and the firing became quite frequent. Of course, a good many shots were lost, as it is no easy matter to hit a flying goose, large as it is. No experienced hunter thinks of firing directly at a goose that is flying by him, or even overhead. He has to calculate for at least a foot ahead for, say, each hundred feet the goose is away from him, and it takes a quick eye and good judgment to correctly estimate the distance. Sam said he liked best to fire at them when there was a string of them in line. Then by blazing away at the first he generally brought down the third or fourth.

It was now full daylight, and so it was necessary for the hunters to be much more wary and keep themselves well down in their nests and very quiet. When they were perfectly still the geese took them for lumps of snow. This was the reason why there was nothing but white in their dress. Even the belts they had tied around them were pure white. Soon the Indians began calling, to bring the geese within range. The rude decoys were placed as though they were having a glorious time feasting on the rich goose grass. The calls of the Indians were exact imitations of the geese calling to their fellows. Sometimes these cries sounded like "Honk! honk! honk!" Then they seemed to be more like "Uk! uk! uk!" Then sometimes they were like the calls that the ordinary barnyard geese make when well satisfied with food. It was interesting to the boys to notice how quickly a far-away flock caught these sounds. Marvelously acute was their hearing. Then they acted so differently. Some were very wary and shy, and at once began to endeavor, as it were, to climb up higher and higher in the sky. This, however, was a difficult task just then, as the wind was behind them. When geese, as a general thing, wish to quickly rise up high in the air, they turn and go against the wind. In some way or other it speedily seems to lift them up. Other flocks, as soon as they thought they heard some of their comrades having such a good time, came right on and were close to the decoys and nests before they were aware of their blunder. Then the firing was rapid and destructive. Some of the flocks had dropped down so low that in order to rise up again they had to circle round and go back against the wind. Then there was double sport for the hunters. Often a flock would come in on the left side, and just as it was about to light among the decoys the guns would ring out and do their deadly work. The survivors were so low down that they could not go on with any advantage, and so had to turn sharp to the right and try to get away by going back against the wind. This movement brought them now on the right side of the nest, and as they passed more of the guns were fired and more victims fell dead to the ground.

Such were the positions of the nests in reference to the wind, that Sam and Memotas had, by all odds, the best place that day. Generally after they had fired the flock broke in two, and Alec and Big Tom got part, while the other portion generally found Mr. Ross and Kinesasis. However, when a great flock pushed on unbroken it generally went directly over and very near the nest where Frank and Mustagan had their quarters. Then there was some fine shooting, as each had two double-barreled guns and Frank had become quite famous as a shot. Many of the geese dropped at once to the ground when shot. Others, although mortally wounded, only fell when quite a distance beyond, as the momentum of their rapid flight seemed to carry them on. Some fell when they were only shot through one wing. During the lull after the firing, when the boys went out from the nests to bring in the spoils, there were some additional battles to be fought ere some of the geese were conquered. Especially was this the case with those that were injured in only one wing. When these were approached they instantly stood on the defensive and struck out most viciously with the unwounded wing. Some of the boys had had some experience in this line, and so were now on their guard, and thus escaped feeling the tremendous power of a goose's wing. Others viciously used their bills and made lively work for the boys ere they were conquered. Others unwounded in their legs made off as rapidly as possible, and then there was great fun in the work of running them down. Those that could use even their wounded wing, or wings, to help them in their movements made capital time, and while most of them were captured, others succeeded in getting away altogether. Doubtless they would be picked up by alert Indian hunters, who were, or would be in a day or so, literally swarming over every place where a goose was likely to be obtained.

When noon arrived they nearly all returned to the camp, where dinner already awaited them.

Twenty-seven geese were the results of the shooting in the four nests. Other Indians came in with their bags. Some had done on the average better than this, and some not so well. As the wind remained steady in the one direction the flocks of geese were very numerous. There was hardly a period of ten minutes' time when some were not visible. Of course, the great majority of the flocks were high up in the air. On and on they flew, their eyes fixed on a point further north, perhaps a thousand miles beyond. No call from the hunters reached them, no ball even from a rifle pierced the thin air of that exalted region in which, at perhaps a rate of a hundred miles an hour, on they flew. The Indians say that the same geese come back, when possible, to their old feeding grounds year after year.

After dinner the sport was resumed. When no flocks were near the boys would jump out of their nests and by some racing and frolicking on the ice keep themselves warm, as there was much of winter still in the air. The cry of "Niskuk! niskuk!" ("Geese! geese!") would send them racing back to their respective nests, and it was often as much as they could do to reach their retreats ere the geese were upon them.

A queer accident happened to Frank. As a small flock passed over the nest in which Sam and Memotas were sitting Sam blazed away with his last barrel, just as the geese had gone by. He struck one of them and mortally wounded it, but it had vitality enough left to keep itself up until it reached the nest where Frank and Mustagan were crouched down watching another flock that was approaching from the other side. Without any warning the goose suddenly dropped dead with a whack on top of Frank, knocking him over most thoroughly and causing his gun to suddenly go off, but fortunately without hitting his Indian companion. A great gray goose weighs something, and so the whack from this dead one nearly knocked Frank senseless. The inmates of the other nests quickly came to his assistance. He was so dazed with the blow that it was decided that he and Sam, who had had about enough of goose-killing to suit them, should go to the camp for the rest of the afternoon. It was wisely thought that Sam's irrepressible fun and good nature would be the best medicine for Frank for the time being.

That evening, when the shooting was over and all were seated on their comfortable robes around the bright camp fire, there was a lot of talk about Frank's queer accident. All were thankful that the blow did no more serious harm. Mustagan said that he had shot geese flying over the ice where they had fallen with such force that they had broken clean through ice so strong that men could walk over it with safety.

"What do you think about it, Sam?" said Alec.

"Think about it, do you ask me?" replied Sam. "I have done a deal of thinking about it. I've been thinking that was the queerest weapon of offense I ever heard or dreamed of. I have heard of arrows and bullets and darts and clubs and shillalahs and tomahawks and boomerangs, and even thunderbolts, but the idea of hitting a poor, defenseless English lad with a dead goose! It beats me hollow! Sure I can hardly believe my senses. I'll be denying the whole thing to-morrow, although I saw the complete performance to-day."

The next morning Frank was fully recovered from this queer blow, and just as eager as ever to take his place in his nest with Mustagan. The wind veered around to the southeast, and so all of the decoys had to be changed. The shooting was good all day, but not equal to the previous one. The Indians were very clever in even calling some flocks back that had been fired into with deadly results. The explanation the Indians gave for the returning of these flocks was that although they still kept together in great numbers the geese had selected their mates, and the shooting of one or other of these pairs had caused the whole flock to return to look them up, in response to the cries of the bereaved survivors.

Sam said that he thought that the elegant voices of the Indians as they cried "Honk! honk!" had more to do with it than any affection in the heart or gizzard of an old goose. This remark of Sam's was at once challenged, and a number of stories were related to prove that even the despised goose was worthy of a much better record than was generally given her.

Thus, with varied success, several days were spent at the goose grounds. Two or three times the boys succeeded in each bringing down four geese with the four barrels of the two guns. This was considered very clever shooting on the part of young fellows on their first spring's hunt.

In due time the dog-trains returned from Sagasta-weekee. The last visits to the nests were made, and the closing two hours of the goose hunt were voted by all to have been the best, as the geese were so numerous that at times the guns were hot with the rapid work. The boys would have liked to remain longer, but Mr. Ross stated that they had already shot as many geese as they could eat at home or could give away, and that it would not be right to kill any more of such valuable birds. The true hunter thinks not only of present needs, but of the years to come. In times of plenty he remembers there are days and years ahead. This was a satisfactory explanation to all.

The loading up of the geese on the extra sleds was soon accomplished. A good warm supper was eaten, and then at about ten o'clock at night, when the frost had again hardened up the snow that had been so soft and slushy a few hours before, the home journey was begun, and among "the wee small hours beyond the twelve" the welcome lights in Sagasta-weekee were seen, and the happy, tired excursionists were glad to hurry off and half bury themselves in the beds and pillows filled with the downy feathers of geese killed at the spring hunts of years before.

CHAPTER XXIII.

Sudden Transition from Winter to Spring—Interesting Phenomena—Sam's Last Great Run with His Dogs—His Unique Adventure—The Open Water—His Novel Raft—Successful Crossing—Frank and Alec's Duck-shooting Trip—The Mighty Nelson—A Hunter's Paradise—Returning Under Difficulties—One More Shot at the Wild Geese—Frank and Rumors—The Fair Visitants at Sagasta-weekee.

VERY rapid indeed is the transformation from one season to another in the high latitudes. When the long, steady winter breaks it does so with a suddenness that is startling to a person who observes it for the first time. The snow disappears with a marvelous rapidity. The ice, that was like granite in hardness and several feet thick on the great lakes, becomes dark and porous, and in spots literally seems to rot away. Then along the great cracks, where it had burst by the power of the terrible frost some months before, it now opens, and soon great fields of it become floating masses on the waters. Under the action of the brilliant rays of the sun it becomes disintegrated, and falls away in crystals that are of various sizes and as long as the ice is thick. This crystallization begins early, and makes the ice very dangerous and uncertain. The Indians call this slivering of the ice candling.

Sam had a narrow escape from drowning on account of this rapid transformation of the ice. He had harnessed his dogs and gone out on the shining lake for a run. The snow had all disappeared from the land, and so the great icy expanse was all that was left for an invigorating run with the dogs. The frost had been keen in the night, and so everything was firm and hard when he left in the morning. The day was an ideal April one. The sun was full of brightness, and the south winds were full of warmth. For miles and miles Sam recklessly dashed along with his splendid dogs. He was sorry at the thought that he was so soon to forever leave them behind in that North Land. Soon some pools of water on the ice into which his dogs splashed brought him to his senses, and he turned for the home run to Sagasta-weekee, now perhaps twenty miles away.

"Rip Van Winkle," said Sam; "sure, I am that same old fellow, to judge by the change since I traveled over this icy lake."

Great indeed was the transformation which the sun and south wind had made. While there was still plenty of good ice, there were many dark, treacherous spots all around, which had so crystallized by the sun's rays that, although the ice there was still three or four feet thick, it was unsafe for dogs or boy. Fortunately, dogs become very wise in this matter, and so Spitfire carefully wended his way among these dangerous places, cautiously keeping where the ice was firm and solid. Rapid traveling was in some places impossible, for fear of running into a bit of rotten ice.

Suddenly Sam was stopped by coming to a long stretch of open water. It was a place where during one of the coldest nights the ice had suddenly burst open with a report like a great cannon. The crack then made was about twenty or thirty feet wide and some miles in length. So intense was the cold that the ice in a few hours formed again on the water which was in this great opening. But when these great breaks in the thick ice occur, toward the end of the winter, the new ice that forms is never so thick as is the rest, and so when the spring warmth comes it is the first to disappear. It was to one of these open seams that Sam had now come. In the early hours of the morning it had been covered with ice sufficiently strong to hold him, but now it was full of broken fragments that rose and fell on the water that was stirred up by the strong south wind. As far as the eye could reach north and south extended this open channel. Sam was perplexed, and hardly knew what to do. To drive across was impossible, as the seam was much wider than his cariole was long. To wait until the night frost again froze up the water was a risk, as to judge by the warm south wind then blowing, if it so continued there would be no freezing of any consequence. Thus Sam was troubled and annoyed at having allowed himself to be thus caught, especially as he and the other boys had heard Mr. Ross and the Indians refer to just such experiences. With his vexation at having thus had his trail so suddenly broken there flashed into his memory the stories of how some of the Indians, when in just such dangerous places, had escaped by making great rafts of the ice and on them floating across the open water. No sooner had this thought come to Sam than he fairly shouted out:

"This is my plan. Now I will have a story to tell that will sound well in dear, darling Dublin."

It was well for him that an ax and ice chisel, which he had been using in cutting a hole in the ice the day before, were still lying in his cariole. With these in his possession there came a feeling of elation in his heart, and he fairly shouted with delight at the position in which he found himself. With great zeal he set to work, and having placed his dogs in what he imagined was a safe position, he first carefully marked out around them a line to indicate where he was to chop. Industriously he set to work. But, O dear!—well, it was hard work. Soon off came his outer coat, then he threw down his mittens, and his fur cap followed next. Bravely he toiled, until his hands were about blistered and his back sore. To his great disgust he found out that not one tenth part of the task was accomplished, and yet he was about tired out. He had selected the firmest ice he could find, in order that his raft might be perfectly safe. While this was a wise thing to do, and would have been all right if there had been sufficient strength available to cut it out, it was a mistake on the part of Sam, and so he realized when he had toiled until weary. But he was not disheartened, and so resolved to try and find a place where the sun's rays could be utilized. Straightening out his dogs, he drove along the ice for a mile or so before he reached a place that seemed to suit him. When he had found what he thought would do he set to work at once, for the day was now advancing.

The spot selected was a solid-looking piece of ice not much longer or wider each way than his dogs and cariole. It projected somewhat into the water, and on the icy side were several dark places where the ice was rotten, on account of its crystallization by the sun's rays. Here Sam with renewed vigor set to work. He made rapid progress, and found that all he had to do was to cut the firm ice that lay between these different dark spots where the ice had lost all of its cohesive power. Sam found ere he had finished that his dogs were getting strangely nervous, and to keep them from rushing off he had to turn the train around and tie them to the cariole. While doing this he discovered the cause of their fear, and was also thankful that he was with them in the middle of his now floating raft. The strong wind blowing directly up the channel, narrow though it was, had so agitated the water that there was a good deal of force in it, and so now, even before Sam had completely severed the ice from the main body, the water had begun to cause it to slightly move. Dogs are more sensitive than human beings, and so they had noticed it before Sam had, and while he was trying to quiet them the whole thing broke loose and began slowly to move north.

As this novel raft broke loose it was quite unsteady for a few minutes, and Sam saw with disgust his ax slide into the water and disappear. However, he still had the ice chisel, with its strong handle, which was about eight feet in length. At first he had all he could do to quiet his excited dogs. They acted as though they would plunge into the water in spite of all his efforts. Some soothing words, and also some vigorous kicks, quieted those of different temperaments, and they settled down at last and seemed to say: "Well, if our master can stand this, surely we ought to be able to." Not until Sam felt that he had his dogs well under control did he make any effort to get his novel raft across the channel. But when they all lay still and quiet he took up his ice chisel and was ready for work. He vigorously pushed against the icy shore from which he had broken loose, but his strength did not at first seem to make much impression, as the wind was somewhat against him, and so his raft at times ground roughly against the side from which he had broken away. However, he was slowly working north, and he was not discouraged. Sam was always an observant lad. When on shipboard he had been interested in watching the sailors shift the sails to catch the changing winds. So now an idea came to him, and he resolved to see what could be done with an improvised sail, even if it were only made out of a large buffalo robe. Lashing one side of the robe to the pole of his ice chisel, he then firmly fastened one end of it to the head of his cariole. Cutting two holes in the outer corners of the robe, he there tied a couple of strong deerskin strings. Then, taking his place in his cariole, he pulled his sail up against the wind and awaited the result.

He was not very sure just how to manage to get across the channel, but he had no anxiety about getting further off, as that was an impossibility, as he was now jammed up against the ice. So he pulled in his sail and then let it out, until at length he found the right angle for the brisk wind to cause him to gradually draw away from the side he had been on. When in the middle of the channel so pleased was he with his novel craft that he let out his sail, and for a time sped along north between the two icy shores. Then, observing an indenture in the ice to the east sufficiently large to serve for a harbor for his queer vessel, he steered for it and safely ran in, but struck the icy landing place with such a crash that his raft was split in the middle under him. However, all he had to do was to hang on to his cariole and straighten out his dogs by the calls they well understood. In an instant they sprang ashore, and easily dragged Sam and the cariole after them. Facing toward the distant home, the dogs required no special urging, and so rapidly, yet carefully watching against the treacherous places, they hurried on, and about sundown home was reached.

Mr. and Mrs. Ross had begun to feel anxious about him, and so were not only relieved by his return, but very much amused by the characteristic account he gave of his adventure on the ice raft.

In the meantime, although it was not quite dark, there was no word as yet from Frank and Alec, who with some Indians had gone off early in the morning on a duck-shooting excursion.

Following the geese, the hunting of which has been so fully described in a previous chapter, came the ducks in great flocks. They could be seen in great multitudes during every hour of the day, and the whistling sounds that accompany their rapid flights could be heard every hour of the night. They seemed to be of about every known variety, from the great gray ducks down to the smallest teals. The Indians were after them incessantly, and killed great numbers of them. They resorted to no such elaborate preparations in hunting them as they did at the goose huntings, but shot them at the various points along which they seemed to crowd, and in the many pieces of open water on the marshy shores, where they tried to find some favorite food. The boys were out almost every day, either with Mr. Ross or some trusted Indians, and had some capital sport.

The morning that Sam had prepared to have a good long final run with his dogs Frank and Alec had gone to what was called the Old Fort, where the mighty Nelson, gathering in Lake Winnipeg the waters of many rivers, begins in its full strength its fierce, rapid, onward career, that ends only when it reaches the Hudson Bay. This has been for generations a favorite shooting ground of the Indians, and here for the day the two lads and their Indian attendants came. They had made the journey very early in the morning, and so their dogs had had no trouble with the ice, which in the night frost had quickly become firm and hard. In the friendly shelter of some trees they had secured their dog-trains. Here building a fire, their Indian cook had a second breakfast soon ready for them. While eating it they could hear the cries of many wild birds, that the now strong south wind was bringing over them. Flocks of wild geese, principally the waveys, a very much smaller variety than the great gray geese, were quite numerous, as well as an occasional one of the larger kinds. Swans flew by in straight lines with such rapidity that many a shot was lost in trying to shoot them. Pelicans were also there in great numbers, and the boys were intensely interested in their awkward, and at times comical, movements. As they are not good for food, only one or two were shot, as curiosities. Cranes stalked along on their long, slender legs in the marshy places, while snipe and many similar birds ran rapidly along the sandy shores. The ducks were everywhere, and so the shooting was everything that our enthusiastic hunters could desire.

The Indians, toward noon, began to get uneasy about the return trip, on account of the effects of the sun's rays and the south winds on the ice. They suggested an early start, but so fascinated had the boys become in the shooting that they kept putting it off from hour to hour. However, the return trip was at length begun, and then the boys saw the wisdom of the Indians' suggestion for an earlier start, and heartily wished they had agreed to it. Playgreen Lake, which in the morning seemed still one great mass of glittering ice, now appeared half broken up. Wherever the ice had burst in the winter, and there frozen up again, now there were long channels of open water. Suspicious-looking pools of water were on the ice in many places, and so the outlook for the return trip was anything but pleasant. Frank's train was the first to come to grief. His heavy dogs in passing over a dark-looking patch of ice broke through, and were with much difficulty pulled out. What amazed him and Alec was that the ice was still over two feet thick where the accident occurred, but under the effects of the rays of the sun it had simply disintegrated into long icy crystals that had no cohesiveness, and so when they were trodden upon they afforded little more support than so much water.

The dripping dogs were no sooner hauled out, and once more started, than the appearance of a flock of geese, in one of the open stretches of water, was too great a temptation to be resisted. The trains were halted, and Frank and Alec took their guns and crept round to an icy hillock from which they would be able to get a capital shot. In a few minutes the guns rang out their reports, and up rose the great flocks of geese, as well as many ducks and other birds. Frank and Alec had both been successful, and so speedily they dashed over the ice to attempt to secure their geese, which seemed to be only badly wounded. As the Indians, who were in charge of the dogs, saw them thus recklessly dashing straight for the open water they instantly started the dog-trains toward them. They were none too soon, for the boys, apparently seeing only their splendid game struggling in the narrow channel, noticed not the dangerous black spots on the ice. Poor Frank, who was a little in advance, almost suddenly disappeared. Down he went, and that so quickly that he had not time even to throw from him his gun, which speedily sank.

He had all he could do to save himself as he sank in the icy crystals that sounded around him like the smashing of scores of panes of glass. Alec, alarmed at Frank's sad plight, madly rushed to his rescue, but ere he had gone a dozen yards he too found himself, as he afterward expressed it, like a person dropping into a well. Fortunately, he was holding his gun crossways to his body, and as the hole of rotten ice into which he so speedily dropped was but a small one the gun struck solid ice each side, and as he had held on securely to it he did not fall in as completely as did poor Frank. His plight was, however, a very awkward one, as the hole was so small and the firm, jagged ice so gripped him that unaided he would have had some difficulty in extricating himself.

Well was it that the Indians had been on the alert, and so it was but a few minutes ere they were on the spot and at once set about the work of rescue. Alec was the first reached and was speedily pulled out, although it required some effort to do so on account of his being so wedged in so small a hole with the sharp, jagged ice. His ribs were sore for many days. In the meantime Frank's position was much more dangerous. The speed with which he was running, when he so suddenly tumbled in, caused him to go completely under the ice. He was, however, a good swimmer, and had presence of mind enough to know that for his own safety he must come up in the same place where he had gone down, as all around was solid ice. He was sorry to have to drop his gun, but there was no hope for it if life was to be saved. He found the sensation of trying to swim up through a mass of ice crystals that seemed to be two or three feet long, and no larger in size than pencils, a unique experience. As he bravely struggled through them they broke in thousands of pieces, some of them cutting his face like glass. When he was able to get his head above them he found that only a few strokes were necessary to take him to the strong ice, as this bad spot, in which he had fallen, was not more than twenty feet across. Getting out of such a hole on the slippery ice is no easy matter, and so, as he could see that help was near, after a few efforts he was content to wait until strong arms came to his assistance and rescue.

Speedily were some of the outer garments of the boys pulled off, and as much of the water as could be rubbed off from those remaining on them. Two of the Indians pulled off their dry coats, and with these on the boys were well wrapped up in their carioles, out of which many ducks were thrown, and then at once, with the swiftest and yet most cautious Indian on ahead as a guide for the safe places, the rapid race to Sagasta-weekee began. It was no easy matter for the Indian in front when darkness began to hide the dangerous places. More than once the rotten, treacherous ice gave way under him, and only by a sudden throwing of himself forward did he escape going through into the water.

The distant lights in the windows of Sagasta-weekee, well called the house full of sunshine, were indeed welcome sights. Mr. and Mrs. Ross and Sam had been long on the lookout for them, and were shocked and frightened at the sad plight of the two boys. Frank and Alec, however, tried to make light of it, but neither had the slightest objection to offer to the hot baths at once prepared, and then their suppers, taken that night in bed. They were both badly shaken up. Frank felt worse in his mind, because he had lost such a valuable gun, while Alec's ribs were the spots that were for some days his tenderest places.

All sorts of rumors went out in reference to the accident. The story had so enlarged that when it reached the mission house it was that the boys had been rescued in a dying condition and were still very low, and so there was great sorrow over there, even so much that it was said that two sweet young ladies refused to be comforted. When Mrs. Ross heard this her motherly heart was touched, and so, as the wind had changed and the cold north wind had again made the ice safe for experienced Indian drivers, two carioles were dispatched to the mission for the aforesaid young ladies to come and spend a week or two at Sagasta-weekee. The missionary, with his dog-train in charge of an experienced driver, also came over at the same time as did his daughters. Ere they arrived the boys were up and dressed in moccasins and dressing gowns, and so were able to receive their very welcome visitors. Mr. Hurlburt only remained to a very early tea, and then after an earnest prayer, in which there was a great deal of thanksgiving for their deliverance, he, with Martin Papanekis, the driver, returned to his home.

Of that happy week that followed we confess our inability to write. That it was a very delightful one was evident to all. The only sorrow that tinged its brightness and bliss was the fact that soon the ice would be all gone, the boats would be arriving, and then the home trip of these three boys would begin.

CHAPTER XXIV.

The **Arrival of the Spring Packet**—Welcome Letters—Arrangements for the Home-flitting—Sam's Raillery—Rachel and Winnie at Sagasta-weekee—Happy Hours—Canoeing Excursions—The Cyclone—Young Excursionists Exposed to Its Awful Power—The Narrow Escape—The Refuge of the Rock—Napoleon, the Tame Bear, in Possession—Gun Signals—The Happy Rescue.

THE arrival of the spring packet was, and still is, an interesting event to the dwellers in those remote northern regions. Not a letter or paper had reached Sagasta-weekee since the Christmas packet, and now it was June. And so when the first boats of the Hudson Bay Company arrived from Red River and Fort Garry, with supplies and great bundles of letters and periodicals, there was great excitement. A swift canoe was in readiness at the fort, and so it was not long ere the large number directed to Sagasta-weekee were hurried over to the expectant ones. They were quickly assorted, and then each person with his own rushed off to fairly devour the contents.

"Faith," said Sam, as he eagerly seized his bundle, "the sight of my blessed mother's handwriting puts sand in my eyes and a lump in my throat. Blessings on the darling! May she live a thousand years!"

Frank and Alec were equally as much interested, but they controlled their feelings and left to the more demonstrative Sam these joyous ebullitions, that were as natural as it was for him to breathe.

After Mr. Ross had perused a number of his letters he quietly signalled to Mrs. Ross, and immediately they both left the room. He had received a letter from Liverpool which informed him that a very serious disease had begun to undermine the constitution of Frank's father, and while no immediate fatal results were expected, it was thought best that Frank should return by the speediest route possible. In Frank's own letters from home all that had been mentioned in reference to the matter was that "father was not quite up to his usual health, and they would all be glad to have him return as speedily as possible." Neither Mr. nor Mrs. Ross said anything to the boys in reference to the matter of their return until after the evening meal, when they were all in the cozy study discussing the various events that had been occurring in the outside world during the last six months, and of which they had all been in profound ignorance until that day.

Each boy had read his letters to the others, and together they had been delighted with all the news received, except that concerning Frank's father. Then, for the first time, the matter of the return home was seriously discussed. So happy had been the months since their arrival, nearly a year before, that even the discussion of the return trip had been kept in the background as much as possible. But now they were face to face with it, and sharp and quick must be their decision if they would avail themselves of the first opportunity for their departure. This would be by the return of these Hudson Bay Company's boats to Red River. In them they could travel as far as to Fort Garry. From that point they would take the overland trail on the great plains to St. Paul, and there, boarding the flat-bottomed steamers on the Mississippi, would once more begin traveling in a civilized manner.

This plan was the one on which they finally settled. It would be much more expeditious than the long waiting for the sailing ship at York Factory, and then returning by the Hudson Bay and North Atlantic route. This decided, the next question was how to make the best of the ten days that would elapse ere the journey would begin.

"I'll wager my dog-whip against a pair of moccasins," said Sam, "that I know where a good part of the time will be spent if a couple of young gentlemen friends of mine can have their own way."

"All right," quickly responded Mrs. Ross, "for although I consider a wager, at best, is but a fool's argument, and so you may keep your whip, I will accept your challenge and say that I know that here at Sagasta-weekee is the spot where the two young gentlemen you have in your mind will prefer to spend the time until the home journey is commenced."

The sudden extinguishment of Sam's pet phrases of "I'll wager" and "I'll bet" by the gentle Mrs. Ross was much relished by Frank and Alec, who well knew that they were the young gentlemen to whom he referred, and on whom he was about to turn his raillery. Generous, good-natured Sam was quick to acknowledge the error of his ways, in the use of those expressions from the betting world that had, he hardly knew how, found their way into his vocabulary. Still, as he gracefully apologized to Mrs. Ross there was a half-comical, half-perplexed look in his face, and so, as he never could keep even his thoughts to himself, amidst the laughter of all he blurted out:

"Sure I was thinking of the young ladies over the way there at the mission, and that it would be in their sweet smiles my two chums would wish to be basking."

"We have been thinking of them also," said Mrs. Ross, "and before this, I imagine, the canoe has reached the mission, with a cordial invitation for both of them to come over, with as many others of the family as can leave, and spend the time with us until the boats start for Red River."

"Hurrah!" shouted Frank and Alec in chorus, and ere they seemed aware of what they were doing, in the exuberance of their boyish delight, they had hold of Mrs. Ross and were gyrating with her around the room, to the great amusement of all, especially of Roderick and Wenonah, who speedily joined in the sport.

This being settled, the next thing was to talk over the preparations essential for the return trip. So many and varied were the trophies of the chase, as well as Indian curios that each of the boys wished to take back to the home land, that orders were at once given to the carpenters for the requisite number of large casettes. This is the name given in that region to water-tight boxes made out of the spruce lumber of the country. Indian women also were engaged to prepare the requisite traveling outfits for both the water and prairie routes. Then they all settled down to a loving talk over the happy months of the past and the outlook of the future. Speaking for the three boys, Frank said:

"We can never sufficiently thank Mr. and Mrs. Ross for this memorable year. It has been an education to us all that will, we are sure, be helpful to us in years to come. We shall not only, in the many trophies of these happy and sometimes exciting days, have before us in our different homes the tangible reminders of our glorious sports and adventures, but engraved in our memories will be the many remembrances of the unfailing love and indulgent sympathy you have ever shown toward us. We are all very grateful to you both, and, while naturally pleased at the prospect of soon being with our loved ones across the sea, we are very sorry that we shall soon have to say good-bye."

This touching and nicely worded speech of Frank's was too much for tender-hearted Wenonah and Roderick, and so they burst out into weeping and hurriedly left the room. Sam seemed to be suddenly attacked with a bad cold and blew his nose vigorously, and for once had nothing to say. Alec, more able to control himself, added a few kindly, grateful words to these so well put by Frank.

Mr. and Mrs. Ross were deeply stirred, and in reply stated the happiness that had come to them in having had within their home three young gentlemen who had ever been a source of pleasure and inspiration to them. Kindly were the words of counsel given them for their guidance in the harder battles of life before them—to be manly, self-reliant, and ever honest and true. "Remember this," added Mr. Ross, "upright, honest boys will make the true men the world needs."

The memory of that evening long lingered with them, and in after years, in some fierce moral conflicts, in which they each had to wear a face as of flint against temptation, the words of wisdom there heard enabled them to triumph against the fiercest attacks. "A word in season, how good it is!"

Early the next morning the boys were up, and after breakfast and prayers they began assorting their various collections gathered, for skillful Indian hands to carefully pack up for the long, rough journey that lay between them and their distant homes. A month or so before this they had parted with their dogs. Kinesasis had taken them all out to the distant island, where in idleness they could spend the few brilliant summer months, ere another winter would call them back to their work again. The boys had found it hard to part with the faithful animals. Alec especially, who had, in his Scottish nature, formed a great attachment to his gallant four that had found a warm place in his heart by the way they had secured for him his victory in that memorable race, was almost disconsolate. Two or three times had he secured a couple of Indians and a good canoe, and had gone over to the island for a romp with them.

The friends from the mission arrived in the afternoon, and were cordially welcomed. They had accepted Mrs. Ross's invitation in the spirit in which it had been so genuinely given. In such a land there is but little of the artificial and conventional. Friendship is true and genuine, and loving words have but one meaning. Frank and Alec greeted Rachel and Winnie in Oo-che-me-ke-se-gou fashion. They did not know whether to be pleased or sorry when they saw tears in the bright eyes of these young ladies, when the news was told them of the speedy departure of the three young gentlemen to their distant homes across the sea. Alec said he was rather proud of seeing the tears in Winnie's eyes, as it made him more than ever think that she did really think something of him, and he would try by hard and steady effort in the coming years to prove himself worthy of her love. Frank, more open and impulsive, when he saw the tears in the eyes of his beloved Rachel, could not restrain his own, and was visibly affected. Sam, who had been an interested spectator of the arrival and the various greetings, must of course make a few remarks.

"Look at Alec there," said he. "The self-opinionated young Scotchman! He thinks so much of himself that he is pleased to see a sweet young lady shedding some tears for him."

This was rather severe on the part of Sam, but he could not bear to see anyone in tears, and so he was a little extra-critical just now. His keen eyes had also narrowly watched Frank, and as he saw the tears in his eyes and noticed his visible emotion, even fun-loving Sam was touched, and he impulsively exclaimed:

"Frank, my darling, I love you for your great big heart. But my feelings are all mixed, for why should a young gentleman, who has just kissed his sweetheart, be after weeping and giving redness of eyes to the rest of us?"

Then, with a merry laugh, he roused himself out of these dumps, as he called them, and exclaimed: "Frank, my boy, here is a conundrum for you: Of which of the venerable men of the past does your conduct remind me?"

Various guesses were made, but none were considered satisfactory, and so Sam was called upon to solve his own riddle. His answer was clever and characteristic. "Well," said he, "when reading the blessed book my mother gave me I found a portion which said, 'And Jacob kissed Rachel, and lifted up his voice, and wept.' Why he should have shed any tears at such an interesting transaction bothered me. But now I think I get a glimmering idea in reference to it, since I have seen the events of to-day."

"Sam, Sam," said Mrs. Ross, who had heard this quaint reference to the old patriarch, "why do you thus bring in such names in your pleasantries?"

"I don't know," replied the irrepressible Sam, "unless it is that it is in my blood; for one of the last things I heard my mother say, ere I left home, was that, to judge by the thinness of the milk furnished by the farmer who supplied us, he much reminded her of Pharaoh's daughter, as he took a *profit* out of the water!"

"Chestnuts," said Alec. "I have heard that before."

It was new to the majority, and the droll way in which Sam gave it put everybody in a good humor, and a very happy, delightful time was spent by them all.

Rapidly sped on the few days that intervened between the arrival of the packet and the return trip of the boats to Red River. These Hudson Bay Company's boats had come loaded with furs caught the previous winter, which would be sent down to York Factory with vast quantities from other parts of the great country, and from that fort shipped to England. Then, loaded with goods for the next winter's trade, the boats would return to the different posts from which they had come. With the exception of canoes, they afforded the only means of travel in the summer time in those regions.

Mr. Ross had gone over to the fort at Norway House, and had obtained from the gentlemen there in charge permission to send Frank, Alec, and Sam in these boats as far as Fort Garry. He also decided to accompany them that far in their journey, and see that everything was secured necessary for their long trip across the prairies to St. Paul.

As the weather had now become very pleasant for canoeing, several very delightful outings were arranged by Mr. and Mrs. Ross for the young folks. The boys had become expert canoeists, and in the long gloamings of the lengthened days in June, in those high north lands, they had many memorable excursions.

As the Indian women and maidens are all experts in handling the paddle, so it becomes a point of honor among the ladies, young and old, in the Hudson Bay fort and mission to be able to, at least in a measure, imitate the dusky, bronzed maidens of the wigwams. Mr. Hurlburt had wisely trained his daughters in this accomplishment. Living as they did, where there were really no walks except the trails that immediately led into the primeval forests, where lurking wild beasts were at times so bold that they came up close to the dwellings of the villagers, it was really dangerous to go far from home. Canoeing thus became the great summer recreation and amusement. And for the upper part of the body there is no better exercise. The result was that Rachel and Winnie were both skillful and fearless canoeists, and very much enjoyed this, which has well been called "the poetry of motion."

Mr. Ross prided himself on his beautiful, graceful canoes for the summer time, about as much as he loved his dogs in the long winter months. The Indians, knowing his love for their graceful canoes, had presented him with some great beauties, on which they had exercised all their ingenuity and skill in construction, and their artistic taste in ornamentation. These were all now in much demand, and merry and happy indeed was the whole party, as perhaps in six or eight canoes they started from the little land-locked harbor of Sagasta-weekee. Frank and Rachel were company enough for one of the prettiest canoes, while the same could be said of Alec and Winnie in another not less handsome.

To the last, Sam's joy was to have with him the little children, Wenonah and Roderick. To him was assigned a large, safe canoe, and a couple of trusty Indians to aid in the paddling. The rest of the party went out more or less frequently, as it best suited them. So much had to be done to complete the arrangements for the journey that often the young folks went out alone on their joyous trips.

One afternoon Mr. Ross was a little troubled, and at first seemed inclined to ask all to give up their excursions on the water for that day and amuse themselves at home. His trusty barometer, that had stood so steady for fine settled weather for days, was now acting in a most erratic manner. A change of some kind was evident, and so Sam and the children did not venture out. Still, as the sky was cloudless and the blue waters of the island-studded lake looked so peaceful and quiet, he did not prevent Frank and Alec, with the young ladies, from venturing out, but gave them some words of caution and then let the happy canoeists embark, and saw them strike out in unison as away they glided over the little sun-kissed waves. For a little while the music of their laughter and song fell on the ears of those who had gone to see them off. When they had disappeared among the beautiful fir-clad islands the spectators returned to the house, and were soon busy in their various duties.

Crash! Boom! What is that?

Too well was it known by Mr. Ross and those who had lived in that land. It was a dreadful thunderbolt, the precursor of the fierce cyclone, the sudden storm that is coming upon them at the rate of something near a hundred miles an hour. Worst of all, four young people are out in it, in a couple of frail canoes, and who can tell what may happen to them when in its full fury it bursts upon them?

And how fares it with the young folks about whom there is now naturally so much anxiety at Sagastaweekee? With laughter and song we saw them dash away, as under their skillful strokes their light canoes, like sea birds, glided along over the peaceful waters. Now, drenched and half dazed by the blinding glare of the terrific storm, they are battling for life in a very maëlstrom of waters. Suddenly had the storm struck them. They had remarked the strange actions and the frightened cries of the birds, that all seemed hurrying in one direction. Then they had observed the dead calm that had settled down on everything. Even the aspen leaves on the trees, on the islands along which they glided, for once were ominously still. Every wavelet on the waters hushed itself asleep, and the whole surface of the lake was as a sea of polished glass.

Rachel was the first to take alarm from this deadly calm, and she exclaimed:

"This is unnatural, and means danger. Let us return at once."

Quickly they turned their canoes, and now only a few yards apart they began the race before the coming storm, although as yet it had not revealed itself. The first intimation they had of its approach was the rapidly rising wind, which fortunately arose directly behind them. It was at first different from any ordinary breeze. It seemed to come along like a thing of life, now catching up a handful of water and scattering it like sand, then bounding up in wanton sport, and then once more trailing on the waters and making it ripple in lines or lanes, as in mad sport it now more rapidly hurried along.

Then, as they looked back over their shoulders to the northwest, they saw coming up the cyclonic cloud. It was dark as midnight, ragged at its edges, and above it was a rim of sky so green and so unnatural that our brave young people for a moment almost recoiled with terror at the sight.

"Paddle for that island!" shouted Rachel. "No canoe can live in such a storm as will soon be on us."

Hardly had she uttered these words ere there shot out a thunderbolt so vivid that they were all nearly blinded by its intense brightness. It seemed to fill the whole heavens around them with its dazzling whiteness, and then as suddenly it was gone.

"One, two, three, four," began Rachel, who, although paddling with wondrous effectiveness, was calm and collected.

"O, don't stop to count," called Winnie, who was like the rest desperately yet cautiously using her paddle. "It would be better to pray than do that."

"We'll do that shortly, but paddle for dear life now, and don't interrupt the count. Where was I? Ten, eleven, twelve—" and at eighteen there came the crash of the thunder of that lightning flash that had so nearly blinded them. It was as though a thousand great cannon had simultaneously been fired.

"Hurrah!" shouted the brave girl the instant it died away. "We have two minutes and a half yet ere the cyclone reaches us. In two minutes we must reach the other side of that high rocky point, and in the remaining half minute we must get on the lee side of the great sheltering rocks. Courage all, and let every stroke tell!"

And there was need for courage, for already the white caps were around them, and behind them the waters hissed and shrieked like demons let loose and howling for their victims. The heavens were rapidly being overwhelmed with the blackness of darkness. But here is the point! Skillfully the two girls, who were in the stern of the canoes, steered them sharply around, and the strong strokes of Frank and Alec did the rest, and they were in the shelter of the rock. But it would only be safe for an instant.

"Now all spring for your lives!" again cried Rachel; "and let everything go, Frank, but your gun and some cartridges."

"Can we not save the canoes?" shouted Alec.

"No, no!" cried Rachel. "It is our lives here only that we must think about, for the sake of those who even now, perhaps, are mourning us as dead."

The shelter of the rocks was within a few flying bounds, and they were safe. It was an enormous rock that towered up some scores of feet, and on the lee side, where our young folks had found shelter, hung over for perhaps twenty feet. Fortunate indeed were they to have reached such a refuge.

A few seconds later, when, with backs against the mighty rock, they were in a measure recovering from the violent exertion of that fearful struggle, Winnie cried out, "O, where are the canoes?"

Not a vestige of them was ever after seen. They had been caught up in that cyclone that came thundering on so close behind that in the brief seconds in which the young people had run from them to the rock they had been picked up and whirled into oblivion.

"It is well," said Alec, "I did not stop to try and save the one I was in. But why, Rachel, did you ask Frank to bring along his gun and ammunition?"

"You will soon see," said the brave, thoughtful girl, "that they will be worth more to us and our anxious friends than the canoes."

In the meantime, the storm in passing the point had spread out over the whole place, and the rain, which was now descending in torrents, began to be very uncomfortable. A rim of light was still in the distance, and with the now almost incessant flashings of the lightning it was possible to grope around for a dry and more sheltered spot under the great rock. Alec, who had volunteered to go out and try to find a drier place, and who was now groping along in one direction as the lightning lit up his path, was heard to suddenly let out a cry of alarm and then almost immediately after burst into a hearty peal of laughter.

"What in the world have you found in such a place to cause you to act like this?" said Frank, who was really annoyed at the merriment of Alec after such a narrow escape.

"Come here and you will see," was the only reply they could secure from Alec, who was acting in a manner so strange and unaccountable.

So, waiting for the lightning flashes to enable

them to pick their way over the rough stones under the sheltered place, they cautiously moved toward him. As they came within a few feet and were now in the gloom, waiting for another flash to light up the way, Alec said:

"Don't be frightened at what you will see. It is only old Napoleon, and he is as frightened as he can be, and seems glad to have me with him."

The sight that met them as the next vivid flash blazed out was indeed enough to try older and stronger nerves, for there was Alec with his back against the dry rock and one of his arms around the neck of an enormous bear.

"Don't be alarmed," shouted Alec. "It is old Napoleon, and he is more frightened by the cyclone than any of us."

"How do you know it is Napoleon?" asked Winnie, who was noted for her extreme cautiousness.

"Know him? Why, of course I know him, and he was as pleased as an affectionate dog to see me. And see, here are the two brass rings I put in his little round ears last winter at the fort, some time before Christmas."

This was convincing proof that their comrade was a tame, harmless bear, and so without any more alarm they all crowded into what proved to be a dry and safe retreat from the fearful storm that still raged outside.

"Bears know a thing or two," said Alec, "and so old Nap in selecting this spot was quite confident that it could stand a cyclone."

Meantime the storm continued to rage with awful

fury, but sheltered by the rocks they were safe from its ravages. All they could do was to patiently wait until its fury was spent. So they sang some sweet hymns, and the girls gave some reminiscences of previous storms and adventures.

As soon as the storm began to abate Rachel said: "I think, Frank, it is time you began to use your gun."

"What, would you have him shoot this affectionate old bear?" asked Alec.

A merry laugh burst from the lips of both of the girls, and Winnie asked him if he had any idea of the reason why Rachel so urged Frank to save his gun and ammunition, even if everything else should be lost.

"Not the slightest idea," was his answer.

"Well," replied Rachel, "as the fury of the storm is about spent, it is time to be beginning to explain the mystery. And so now suppose you take the gun and go out on the beach and fire three times in quick succession."

Frank and Alec at once comprehended the riddle, and laughed at their own stupidity. The firing of the gun would bring their rescuers speedily to them.

Unfortunately for these young people, their retreat was too distant from Sagasta-weekee for the report of their gun to reach that place. However, just as soon as Mr. Ross saw the storm approaching he summoned every available man, and had boats in readiness to begin the search as soon as it was possible to risk the angry waves which a cyclone of this description stirs up. For at least three hours they had to wait ere they could make a start. Then in the still angry waters they shoved out their boats, and in different directions started on the search.

In the meantime let us again go back to the young people in their strange place of refuge. Noting the increasing brightness, as the black clouds were now rapidly rolling away, Rachel suggested that three more shots be fired. In a few minutes more they were repeated, and soon after, as the rain had now nearly ceased, the whole party came out from their gloomy cave retreat. On every side were evidences of the terrific power of the cyclone. Great trees had been torn up by the roots, while others had been snapped off, leaving the stumps standing from twenty to fifty feet high.

Apart from the sad evidences of the storm, everything was soon simply delightful. In those high latitudes the June evenings are very long. Here was now one of wondrous beauty. The angry waves were quickly dying away into pleasant ripples. The sun was setting behind some lovely clouds of gold and crimson, and the air, purified by the cyclone, seemed exhilarating in the extreme.

"Keep up your firing, Frank," said Rachel, "for doubtless there are boats out long ere this, looking for what is left of us."

"Listen!" said Winnie, who, being wonderfully gifted in hearing, had been the first to detect an answering gun. "One, two, three, four. Fire again!" she cried. "They have heard, but are uncertain as to the direction."

Again the three reports of the gun sounded in

quick succession, and soon there was the answer of two guns, which meant, "We hear you now and will soon be with you."

To Mr. Ross's great relief and satisfaction, it was the boat, manned by four oarsmen, of which he himself had charge that was the first to hear the firing of Frank's gun. Some of his Indian crew had detected reports before he had, but nothing would satisfy him until the welcome sound fell on his own ears.

"Pull, men!" he fairly shouted, "and let us see how many of those loved ones have survived that storm. If any of them are drowned, you need not take me home."

Not a man in that boat, white or Indian, needed any urging. Such was the love they all had for those young people that gladly would any one of them have risked his own life for theirs.

Around the next point, now not far away, again rang out the three reports, and soon a most welcome sight greeted the eyes of Mr. Ross and his crew. For there, distinctly visible on the shore, were four happy young people waving their welcomes.

"Thank God!" reverently said Mr. Ross. "They are all safe." And, strong man that he was, he wept like a child. Other eyes than his were moist also. With an effort he checked his deep emotion, and was so able to control himself that ere the shore was reached he was calm and collected.

When within hailing distance hearty words of congratulation rapidly passed back and forward. Such was the nature of the shore that a good place where they could step into the boat from the shore was not easily found, and so the men at the oars rowed up on the sandy beach as far as they could, and then running out three oars made a walk that answered very well.

Good Mr. Ross was so wild with delight at the fact of the preservation of these young folks, whom he loved so well, that he was the first to rush out and try and gather them all in his arms.

In the excitement of the rescue Napoleon, the tame bear, had been quite forgotten, but now he acted as though he had been doing his share of thinking, and had come to the conclusion that if his liberty was to be associated with cyclones, he had had enough of it; and so, just as Mr. Ross and the young people were about to go on board the boat, he deliberately came marching out of the cave and, carefully balancing himself, walked up on the oars and took a comfortable position in the boat.

His unexpected appearance very much startled the men, and there was a general scramble for guns. Alec, quick to see his danger, rushed up, and taking a position beside Napoleon forbade any shooting, and speedily made some very necessary explanations, much to the relief and amusement of all.

It did not take long to return to Sagasta-weekee, and great indeed were the rejoicings there.

Soon the other search boats returned, and the anxieties of all were thus speedily relieved. After the recital of the story of their narrow escape an impressive thanksgiving service was held, and every heart was full of gratitude for their deliverance.

CHAPTER XXV.

Homeward Bound—Farewell to Sagasta-weekee—Old Norway House—Sam's Clever Surmisings—A Glad Surprise for Frank and Alec—Sam's Well-deserved Ducking—A Glorious Evening—The Early Call—Just One More Sweet "Good-bye"—"All Aboard!"—On Great Lake Winnipeg—Sam's Successful Shot at a Bear—Red River—First Glimpse of the Prairies—Fort Garry—The Bells of St. Boniface—The Long Trip Across the Plains—The Exciting Buffalo Hunt—Saint Paul's—Still On by Lakes and Rivers—Montreal—On Board Ship—The Ocean Voyage—Liverpool—Home at Last.

THE start was made from Sagasta-weekee in time for the boats to go that afternoon as far as to the old Norway House fort, where the mighty Nelson River begins its career. Here for scores of years it has been the custom for the boats to camp for at least one night and make their final preparations for the long trip of the whole length of Lake Winnipeg to the mouth of the Red River.

To the great delight of the boys, some extra boats were sent in with the Red River brigade, and so they had Big Tom as their guide, Martin Papanekis as their cook, and Soquatum as bowman.

These boats are each propelled by eight sturdy oarsmen. The work of rowing all day at these heavy oars is very laborious, and so there is great delight when the wind is favorable and a mast can be placed in position and a great square sail hauled up into the favoring breeze. Then the voyage is a joyous holiday. What is most dreaded is a long, continuous head wind, against which they can neither sail nor use the oars with good effect.

Early in the forenoon on the day of starting the young gentlemen said farewell to their good friends of the mission, Mr. and Mrs. Hurlburt and the sweet young ladies, Rachel and Winnie. It is almost needless to add that both Frank and Alec declared themselves as the most devoted of lovers, and vowed that in a few years they would return and claim them as their brides. We must leave time to tell the results of these youthful loves, which had begun under such happy and romantic auspices.

To the surprise of the young gentlemen, Mrs. Ross and the children left Sagasta-weekee at the same time as did Mr. Hurlburt and his family, and so were not there to see them off when they left a few hours later.

So thoroughly and well had the packing been done that not much time was lost after the arrival of the boats before everything was on board. The kindly farewells to all were said, and they were off. Sam could not help shouting back to Pasche, as he stood on a rock with a sorrowful face:

"Don't set any more traps for moose bulls, Pasche!"

"No, mon garçon, I have had enough of that work," he shouted, amid the laughter of the other servants.

With waving of handkerchiefs and shouts of "Bon voyage" and "Good-bye," Sagasta-weekee was left behind. There were tears in the eyes of the lads who had spent within its comfortable walls such an eventful year. They had grown much, not only physically, but there had been development mentally and morally that would tell for good in the oncoming years. To have been under the guidance of such a couple as Mr. and Mr. Ross in such a formative period of their young lives was of incalculable value. Happy are the boys who have such guardians; happier still if their own parents are of this splendid class.

As the wind sprang up from the north the mast, which had been securely tied to the outside of the boat, was quickly placed in position, and the sail was soon doing its work. Mr. Ross and the lads had comfortable seats arranged for them in the stern of the boat. Just behind them stood Big Tom, skillfully using a great oar as a rudder. Wild ducks and a few geese flew by, but there was now no time for shooting. On they sped, and it was easy to observe from the quiet yet frequent consultations in the Indian language that passed between Mr. Ross and Big Tom that there was something more than the sail in the wind. Sam, who had picked up quite a knowledge of Indian, was the first to suspect what was before them, and so he blurted out:

"Faith, I believe Oo-che-me-ke-se-gou is going to be repeated."

"What do you mean?" asked Frank.

"Mean, is it, you ask? Why, I mean that I fancy some other hands than Martin's will pour the tea for us to-night."

"Do stop talking riddles, Sam," said Alec, "and tell us what your palaver is all about."

"Well," replied the incorrigible tease, "I fancy

that, if you young gentlemen are getting sick of having pledged yourselves to eternal loyalty, or, in other words, plighted your troths either to others, as the book says, you will both have a chance to tell the fair damsels to their faces ere the sun goes down."

"Sam!" they both shouted, "what do you mean?"

This explosion on their part caused Mr. Ross to turn from his consultation with Big Tom. In response rather to his looks than anything he uttered Sam said:

"I have been trying to get it into the thick heads of these two boys that there is an agreeable conspiracy on foot for their mutual consolation and edification, but for the life of me I believe they are as much in the dark as when I began."

"Chist!" ("Look!") cried Big Tom. "Akota wigwam!" ("There is the tent!")

These words of Big Tom caused everything else to be forgotten, and so even Mr. Ross, who was vastly amused that Sam had been so observant, did not make any reply to the lad's remarks.

Rapidly they sped along, and now soon to all was visible a large tent and a number of persons on the distant sandy beach. Sam keenly watched his comrades, and saw their cheeks flush and their eyes get moist as they caught the sight of white handkerchiefs waving from the hands of those to whom they had become so deeply attached.

"It is too good to be true," said Frank, as he gripped Alec with one hand, while with the other he was waving his handkerchief wildly in response to those of the loved ones on the shore.

Onward sped the boat, and soon all were recognized. Here they found all who had left early in the morning—Mrs. Ross and the children and all the mission friends. What a delightful surprise, and how happy they all were that it had been such a success! Poor Sam, the only one to see through it, was the only one to come to grief. He had not patience enough to wait until three or four of the big oars were lashed together to serve as a rude gangway on which to walk safely to the shore, but seeing the ease with which some of the agile Indians ran out on a single oar, in spite of the rocking of the boat, he boldly tried to do the same, and ere he knew where he was he was down in the water and nearly drowned by a retreating wave under the boat. Quickly was he rescued, but he was completely drenched to the skin. He was somewhat bruised, but was not long the worse for the accident. But as he was quickly hurried off to the shelter of the tent and dry clothes secured for him he admitted that he deserved the ducking, as he had purposely hurried ashore to make a few remarks when the young lovers should meet again.

And so Frank had the joy of again meeting his Rachel and Alec his sweet Winnie, and a delightful visit they had with them while Sam was having his bruised body well rubbed in sturgeon oil by a stalwart Indian. This is the Indian's drastic remedy for such a mishap, and a good one it is. Very delightfully passed that long June evening. It was full eleven o'clock ere the gorgeous colors all died away in the west and the stars one by one came out in their quiet beauty and decked as with diamonds that peerless northern sky. After a time the auroras flashed and blazed in quiet beauty. To-night they seemed not as warriors bent on carnage, but as troops of lovers tripping in joyous unison to some sweet strains of music unheard by mortal ears.

Amid such surroundings sat and talked this happy group. It was, they well knew, their last evening together, and so amid its joyousness there was a tinge of sorrow and regret. As the evening darkened into night they had all gathered near the great brilliant camp fire, which is always welcome and agreeable even in June nights, no matter how warm has been the day.

After the delightful events and incidents of the past had been referred to and discussed by all, the conversation turned to the many dangers that had come to some of them, and their narrow escapes. Gratitude to God for their many marvelous deliverances was the uppermost feeling in their hearts. Mr. Hurlburt and Mr. Ross spoke most impressively on this wonderful providential care that had been over them.

The Indians, except those whose duty it was to see to the welfare of their masters and mistresses, were all now asleep. Wrapped up each in his blanket, they lay around on the rocks in picturesque places.

During the evening all the other boats had arrived from Norway House, and so it was arranged that if the wind continued favorable they would make an early start in the morning. When Mr. Ross felt that it was time to break up the delightful circle he asked Mr. Hurlburt to take charge of the devotional service. Always hallowed and precious were these sacred hours of worship in the forest or on the shores, and this last one was not less suggestive and profitable. First from memory they all repeated the one-hundred-and-third psalm, then they sang the sweet hymn "Abide with me," and at its close Mrs. Ross's sweet voice struck up "Blest be the tie that binds." Then Mr. Hurlburt, the devoted missionary, led in prayer. Heaven seemed very near as the good man talked with God and commended Frank, Alec, and Sam to his loving, omnipotent care during the long, varied journey before them.

"Say good-bye as well as good night," said Mr. Ross; "for we may be off in the morning without disturbing those who remain behind."

So the tender farewells were uttered, and all the ladies of the party retired to the large, commodious tent that, as we have seen, had been prepared for them. Mr. Ross, Mr. Hurlburt, and the boys went to the camp beds that had been long waiting for them on the dry beach. Here the Indians quickly tucked them in, and soon they were fast asleep—so fast that Sam declared when he heard the sharp call, "Leve! leve!" in the morning that he had not had time for even one sweet dream.

Quickly were the morning preparations made. The kettles were soon boiling and a hasty breakfast prepared. When this was eaten the Christian Indians asked Mr. Hurlburt to take charge of their morning devotions. This he cheerfully did, and so, as was customary, the service was conducted in Cree and English.

Then the cry was, "All aboard!" The boys—Frank and Alec, we mean—could not help casting their eyes toward the snow-white tent in hopes of at least one more glimpse at two of its inmates. They were almost in despair, when Sam's cheery voice rang out:

"Don't lose heart, my hearties! If all the boys should go to China, the girls would surely go to Pekin. Sure they are *peekin'* now, and here they come! Hurrah, and welcome!"

Yes, here they come. Love's ears are sharp, and so Rachel and Winnie heard the call to the travelers, and up they had sprung and dressed, and now, radiant and lovely, once more they came in their sweet beauty to greet and say "Good-bye" again, and "God be with you till we meet again." For a few minutes they chatted, and then the "All aboard!" again rang out, and so they once more lovingly saluted each other and parted. Rachel and Winnie at once returned to the tent. Frank and Alec were soon in their places in the boat. One after another of the boats pushed off, until the whole little fleet was under way. The wind was favorable, and so it was a pretty sight to see the whole brigade speeding on over the rippling waves with the white sails filled by the northern breeze.

Spider Islands were nearly reached ere much was said by anybody but Sam. His good humor and mirth were irrepressible, and soon it became contagious. He had tried his hand at a big oar, and, "catching a crab," had tumbled back amid some boxes, much to the amusement of all.

Thus on they sped. At Montreal Point they stopped long enough to boil their kettles, and then their journey was resumed. At Poplar Point they spent a few hours and had a good sleep. Then next morning, bright and early, they were off again. At Beren's River they stopped for dinner, then on they sped. At the Narrows they saw a great black bear swimming across the channel. Poor bruin got into a tight place. Some of the boats headed him off, and when he attempted to return he found that others were between him and the shore. His perplexity was very great and his temper much ruffled. Soon the bullets began to whistle around him, and these added to his trouble. A bear swims very low in the water, and so, unless in anger he inflates his lungs and raises himself up to growl, there is very little to fire at. The result was, in this case, the flintlock guns did not seem to be able to pierce his skull.

Mr. Ross, who could not bear to see even a bear tortured, took out his rifle and, loading it, handed it to Big Tom, to kill the animal at once. Big Tom took the rifle, looked at it and then at Sam, and gravely said:

"Sam ran away from his first bear, suppose he shoots his last one."

Nothing could please the reckless Sam better, and so he quickly sprang up beside Big Tom, who at once gave him some directions about allowing for the motion of the boat.

"Now," said Big Tom, "I will swing the boat so

that his head will be right in front of you. When I call he will raise his head, and you hit him right between the eyes."

Quickly was the boat swung in the right position, and as from Tom's lips there was emitted a sound like the call of another bear, the one in the water instantly raised up his head, in a listening attitude. Instantly the report rang out, and a dead bear lay there in the water.

"Well done, Sam!" shouted Frank and Alec, while perhaps Big Tom was the proudest man in the boat.

The bear was hauled on board by the crew of one of the boats in the rear. That night the men skinned the bear, and as rapidly as possible dried the robe, which was carried home to Ireland by Sam with his other trophies.

Thus day after day passed. Sometimes there was hardly a breath of wind, and then the men rowed all day. A couple of days were lost on account of strong head winds, but, on the whole, they had a fairly good trip, for at the end of the tenth day they entered the mouth of Red River and camped on its low, marshy shores, amid its miles of reedy morass and its millions of mosquitoes. This was the boys' first experience of them for the season, but it was enough for a lifetime.

"The pious villains!" said Sam. "They sing over us and they prey upon us!"

But the longest night has an end, and next day the boats were rowed up to Lower Fort Garry. Here the boys bade good-bye to Big Tom and the other Indians, after they had taken them up into the Hudson Bay Company's store and bought for each some handsome presents. Mr. Ross found urgent letters here awaiting him, and so that afternoon horses were secured, and he and our three boys were driven along the beautiful prairie road, on the western bank of the winding Red River, twenty miles up to Fort Garry.

This was the first glance the boys had ever had of a genuine prairie. They were simply wild with delight at its vastness and inimitable beauty. Seeing it as they did, in this early summer time, with its rich grasses at the greenest and its brilliant spring flowers at the perfection of their beauty, it was no wonder that they were in such raptures of delight. Twenty miles of travel brought them to Upper Fort Garry. This old historic fort had long played a prominent part in the history of that country. Here they were hospitably entertained by the officers of the Hudson Bay Company.

A few days only were needed to make all preparations for the long trip across the prairies to St. Paul, in Minnesota. Some Red River carts, each drawn by an ox, were secured to carry the baggage and supplies. For the boys a double-seated buckboard wagon, with a canvas top, was purchased, and Baptiste, a famous half-breed French and Indian driver, was hired to manage the rather uncertain horses that in relays were to drag the affair along. Saddles were also taken along for them to travel on horseback when they so desired.

As there were all sorts of rumors and stories of troubles among the hostile Sioux and Chippewa Indians along the route, it was decided that the party should join a large brigade of carts that, loaded principally with buffalo robes and furs, was just starting for St. Paul. These brigades carried the trading flag of the Hudson Bay Company. Its motto was, "Pro pella cutem" ("Skin for skin"). It is a remarkable fact that for generations, even among the most hostile tribes of Indians, this flag was respected, and those carrying it were never robbed or in any way interfered with.

With sincere regret and sorrow the parting between Mr. Ross and the boys took place. However, they were delighted at his promise that, if all went well, he would see them a couple of years hence in their own homes in the old land.

Just as they were leaving in the early morning the bells of St. Boniface rang out their silvery notes. These are the bells, the first out there on the lonely prairies, that Whittier has made famous by his beautiful poem:

"The voyageur smiles as he listens
    To the sound that grows apace;
Well he knows the vesper ringing
    Of the bells of St. Boniface—

"The bells of the Roman Mission
    That call from their turrets twain
To the boatmen on the river,
    To the hunter on the plain!

"Even so in our mortal journey
    The bitter north winds blow,
And thus upon life's Red River
    Our hearts as oarsmen row."

As some officials of the Hudson Bay Company went along with the large brigade, our young folks had some capital company. After a few days the trip lost much of its excitement and interest. The prairies, beautiful as they at first looked, became somewhat monotonous. Every little lake—and they passed many—was greeted with pleasure. As the horses could travel faster than the oxen, sometimes Baptiste would hurry on ahead to some well-known lake full of wild ducks, and here the boys and their friends would have some capital shooting, which largely and agreeably added to the food supply.

When out about a week they were told by some of the outriders, who came galloping up from the front, that a herd of buffalo was not far distant, and that some Sioux Indians were preparing to run them. Saddles were at once put on some of the relay horses, and Frank, Alec, and Sam, and some of their comrades, at once set off to the front to see the exciting sport. They fortunately reached a high swell in the prairie just in time to have a splendid view of the whole affair. The buffaloes numbered about six or eight hundred. Attacking them were perhaps fifty or sixty of the finest horsemen in the world. Their horses were trained buffalo runners, and entered into the mad, wild sport with all the enthusiasm of the riders. All the saddle these riders had was a small piece of buffalo robe so securely fastened on that it could not slip. There was neither halter nor bridle on their horses' heads. One end of a long lariat was fastened loosely around their necks, while the rest of it dragged along the ground.

The Indians availed themselves of a great swell in the prairies, and so were able to get quite close to the herd ere they were discovered. Very few of these warriors had guns, but they were well armed with their famous bows and arrows. About two miles away from our party they began the attack on the opposite side of the herd. The result was that as the frightened animals came thundering on before their dreaded foes the boys had a splendid view of the whole scene. For a time it looked as though they might be involved in the mass of terrified animals, as the slope up toward them was very gradual and they were in the direct line of the rush. However, Baptiste and others, who well knew how to meet such an emergency, quickly bunched the party together, and had all the guns fired off in quick succession. This speedily parted the oncoming herd, and so they in two divisions thundered by on the right and left, with their merciless pursuers on their flanks and in the rear, rapidly thinning their numbers.

It was a most exciting scene, and one to a genuine sportsman that was worth many a day's travel to see. The boys were wild to plunge into the fray, especially when the great buffaloes went galloping by not two hundred yards on each side of them; but their horses, although excited, were untrained for such sport, and in all probability if started off at full speed would soon have stumbled into some badger's hole or prairie dog's nest, and thus send their riders over their heads. So Baptiste wisely restrained their ardor. The next day our party visited the village of these noted warriors of the plains.

St. Paul at length was reached. Here passage was secured in a flat-bottomed steamer, with its great wheel at the stern. Down to St. Croix, on the Mississippi, in this they voyaged. Then across the State of Wisconsin to Milwaukee they traveled by railroad. At this city they secured passage in a steam propeller to Montreal. The trip through Lakes Michigan, Huron, St. Clair, and Erie was very delightful. In the Welland Canal the boys were much interested as they entered into the series of locks by which great vessels go up and down the great hillside. On they steamed through the beautiful Lake Ontario. Then out into the great St. Lawrence River they glided. The Thousand Islands seemed like fairyland. The rapids, down which they plunged with the speed of an express train, very much excited and delighted them. Toward the evening of the fifth day from Milwaukee the towers and steeples of Montreal became visible, with its splendid mountain in the rear. Soon they were alongside of one of the wharves of that great, busy shipping port, and this part of the journey was ended. By telegraph their berths had already been secured for them, and so all our travelers had to do was to oversee the transshipment of their boxes and bales from the lake propeller to the ocean steamship.

As a day or two would intervene ere the voyage would begin, they had an opportunity for a drive or two around the glorious mountain which gives the city its name. They also visited the quaint old cathedral and other places of historic interest in that famous city.

In due time the ocean voyage was begun. The great St. Lawrence is a magnificent and picturesque river. Quebec, in its stern grandeur, very much charmed the boys, and they gazed with interest as some well-read travelers pointed out Wolfe's Cove and the place up which Wolfe's gallant men clambered in the night, to fight the next day, on the Plains of Abraham, that fierce battle that caused half of the continent to change from French to English masters. Then on again they steamed. Soon they were out on the stormy Atlantic. The voyage was uneventful, and in ten days or so they sighted the coast of Ireland. On and on they pushed, until the Mersey was reached. The tide was favorable, and so there was no delay.

Here they were at length, after all their wanderings, in dear old England. Very green and beautiful did the country look, after their long voyage on the stormy ocean. Yonder, in the distance, is Liverpool, that mighty city where at its marvelous stone docks are seen the ships of every sea. The boys are excited now. They are nearing home. The coming of the ship has been reported hours before, and now, as she gallantly feels her way among the many vessels passing out, the boys, with staring eyes, are at the front, gazing for the sight of loved ones that they are sure will be there to meet them.

"Hurrah!" they shout; for there, with waving handkerchiefs and excited gestures, are representatives from three families to welcome home our Frank, Alec, and Sam. Delightful is the home-coming; joyous are the welcomes.

Here we leave them. We have had a very happy time together. We are loath to separate from them. Whether we shall see them again and take them back to those interesting regions to meet and wed their sweethearts, left in that far-away country, will much depend upon events which are beyond our ken at present. Suffice to say that the year spent in the Great Lone Land proved to have been one of the most profitable of their lives. They had returned in the most perfect health. Their readings had not been neglected, and then they had in addition the rich stores of knowledge and information that a year so full of varied adventure could not fail to bestow.

They had also returned with something like correct views of the red Indians of North America. Instead of war whoops and scalping scenes, they had seen how the genuine Indian, when honorably dealt with, is a peaceful person, and can under decent treatment become the most loyal of friends. They delighted also to speak most emphatically and encouragingly of the work accomplished by the self-denying missionaries among them, who had been instrumental in winning thousands of them from a degrading paganism to Christianity, and successfully introducing among them the best phases of a genuine and abiding civilization.

RMER & HARLEY, LTD.,
PRINTERS,
OWPER STREET, FINSBU

www.ingramcontent.com/pod-product-compliance
Lightning Source LLC
Chambersburg PA
CBHW032016220426
43664CB00006B/267